PETER OWEN

NOT a Nice Jewish Boy

PETER OWEN

NOT a Nice Jewish Boy

Memoirs of a Maverick Publisher

PETER OWEN
AND
JAMES NYE

www.fonthillmedia.com
office@fonthillmedia.com

First published in the United Kingdom
and the United States of America 2021

British Library Cataloguing in Publication Data:
A catalogue record for this book is available from the British Library

ISBN 978-1-78155-848-5

Typeset in 10pt on 13pt Sabon
Printed and bound in England

Acknowledgements

There are many I would like to thank for their invaluable support, in particular my husband Yoh Nye Sakurai and my friends Tania Woodford, Fran Heath, Alison Whitewood, Vidya Wolton and Simon Nye. I am greatly indebted to Peter Owen's eldest daughter Antonia Owen, editorial director of Peter Owen Publishers, and managing director Nick Kent. I also thank my agent Guy Rose, publisher Alan Sutton, and those who generously spared time to help with queries and interviews: Jenny Botsford; Brian Braithwaite; Doris Campbell and Groucho Owen; Kanad Upanishad Chakrabarti; Reid Echols at the Harry Ransom Center, University of Texas; Peter Ellson; Filomena Estomago; Gloria Ferris; Duggie Fields; Fenella Fielding and Simon McKay; Dan Franklin; Van Gessel; Tim Hatton; Roberto de Hollanda; Masako 'Mako' Kawashima; Rose Knox-Peebles and Fleur Smithwick; Michael Levien; Lene Lovich; Tony Lunn; Kirsten Morrison; Robert Offenstadt; Ben Owen; Susan and John Paine; Pociao; Jeremy Reed; Patricia Hope Scanlan; Richard Shillitoe; Simon Smith; Tom Sroczynski; Stephen Stuart-Smith; Michael Sullivan; Georgina, Bill and Louis Trythall; Victoria Walker and the Anna Kavan Society; Kate Wightman.

James Nye, Literary Assistant to Peter Owen

Contents

'England has always been disinclined to accept human nature.'
— E. M. Forster, *Maurice* (1971)

The verb to naturalise clearly proves what the British think of you. Before you are admitted to British citizenship you are not even considered a natural human being ... You must pretend that you are everything you are not and you must look down upon everything you are.
— George Mikes, *How To Be an Alien* (1946)

1

Rickets, Semolina and Other Nuremberg Trials

The first of Shakespeare's Seven Ages of Man is famously the infant 'mewling and puking in the nurse's arms'. I can't honestly say I remember much mewling, but one of my earliest, most abiding memories is of a significant amount of puking. Food went everywhere. As soon as my nanny spooned the nasty mixture into my mouth I would regurgitate: over the bed, over the curtains, all over the room. They were feeding me spinach—lots of spinach!—mashed carrots and semolina gruel, horrible messes they sometimes fortified with cocoa or sweetened with raspberry syrup. Once, when visiting from London, my maternal grandmother Sophie came to the nursery at feeding time but declined to repeat the experience, saying she could never again sit through anything quite so disgusting.

I was born into a German-Jewish family as Peter Lothar Offenstadt in Nuremberg, Bavaria, on 24 February 1927. Winnie, my mother, experienced her first birth pangs while dancing at a party and was whisked back home where a nurse had been installed in anticipation of my arrival. The birth, I gather, was relatively easy. Winnie, however, was totally unprepared for motherhood. She was vain with a tendency to run to fat so starved herself while pregnant. She managed to keep her figure, but I was born knock-kneed, pigeon-toed and blighted by rickets. Her refusal to breastfeed once I was born compounded matters. At that time rickets was an illness common to children malnourished as a result of poverty. In my case there was no excuse—my family was quite affluent but sadly lacking in child-rearing nous.

In those days it was common to leave the messy bits of bringing up children to employees. Children were 'seen and not heard'—in my case not seen very much either. Most of the women my parents employed to attend to my care were not especially keen on me, and I wasn't too upset when they disappeared in quick succession. Margareta was different though. Wearing a uniform and low heels, her hair scraped back tightly, she was unusually cultured and had a warm disposition. Though coolly efficient and superficially dowdy-looking, I knew she liked me and was very fond of her. The closeness of that relationship somewhat tempered the effects my parents' emotional neglect might otherwise have wrought.

We referred to Margareta as *Schwester* ('sister'). She was a Fröbel-trained nanny paid for by my mother's parents. Friedrich Fröbel (1782–1852) was a surprisingly forward-looking German pedagogical theorist. The *Kindergarten* was his concept, the word his invention, and he hugely influenced the development of modern education. Where tradition had tended to favour rote learning, rigid conformity and systematic beatings to ensure good behaviour and educational success, Fröbel insisted otherwise. Perhaps my elders harboured some good and progressive intentions in spite of their apparent indifference.

At home in Nuremberg Schwester Margareta, confident in her skills, firmly took charge despite my care being her first job. My doctor directed that my chronic tonsillitis, rickets and general sickliness be treated with that unappetizing nutritional mixture, one so revolting that, despite her generally kind disposition, I had to be force-fed. The consequent expectorations were surely inevitable. An only child, I lacked emotional contact from the family and in particular from my parents who were often away from home and not demonstratively loving. Perhaps not surprisingly I was devoted to Margareta.

Margareta quickly realised that my mother was frivolous, pliable and unused to handling babies. She also made it plain to Betty, my domineering paternal grandmother, that she would brook no interference. Margareta got on with the job briskly while Grandma Betty fumed impotently on the sidelines, furious not to be in charge but thankful to be spared the likelihood of being showered with semolina and spinach.

My parents didn't favour taking servants on holiday, nor me for that matter, but once took Margareta and me on a holiday to Austria. I remember the trip mostly for pigs being slaughtered in the hotel grounds, the sound of which put us off our sausages. The holiday also sticks in my mind as the only occasion my father slapped me. The cause was undoubtedly trivial—perhaps I had merely been insufficiently deferential. I was unbruised but shocked and frightened at such a sudden outburst of unjust violence. Margareta came to my defence. 'Herr Offenstadt,' she admonished him, 'one does not hit children!' He regularly shouted at and bullied me in subsequent years but never again hit me.

In 1930, when I was three, Margareta left for the United States. Probably my grandparents could no longer afford her. I was heartbroken. Those first three years were the only time in my life I felt really secure. Some years later, when Margareta visited us in London, my mother and I failed to recognise the sophisticated lady who greeted us at Victoria Station as the dowdy young nanny she had once employed.

Dr Frankenau, who had presided over my birth, would frequently attend me in Nuremberg to dispense medicine. He was a kindly man, and it cheered me to hear him, stethoscope and paraphernalia at the ready, climbing the stairs to the nursery. He often brought me sweets made of quince which I adored. Contemporary medical advice suggested a supposed cure for my rickets: every morning I was to lie on my bed for hours with sandbags on my legs, pinned down by their weight. I don't think it did anything to improve my condition, but it certainly kept me out of my parents' way. Daily the *Kinderfräuleins*—the governesses-cum-nannies who succeeded Margareta—would immobilise me with the bags before feeding me the vile breakfast, which I then spat back at them.

Those Kinderfräuleins merge in distant memory with the animals I saw during daily visits to Nuremberg Zoo. I remember this as a leafy green paradise, beautifully landscaped and featuring a lake. This famous *Tiergarten*, where I spent many innocent hours as a toddler, was moved after the Nazis came to power. It gave way to Albert Speer's grandiose *Reichsparteitagsgelände* (Reich Party Congress Grounds). There the Nazis enacted the hideous pomp of the Nuremberg rallies so chillingly documented in Leni Riefenstahl's propaganda films. There, too, were passed the Nuremberg Laws which further disenfranchised Jewish citizens, paving the way for the Holocaust.

Of Margareta's successors, only the last of my governesses, Fräulein Liesl, who joined us in London after I moved there in 1933, made an impact. Liesl and I were very fond of each other. She was a very kind young woman, and I was devoted to her. Her loss upset me so greatly I never forgave my mother for dismissing her. It aroused such fury I tried not to think about it. The events unfolded like this: while my mother was in Paris for the Exposition of 1937 my father made a pass at Liesl. Greatly perturbed, she informed my mother on her return. They sacked her, seeing her as a liability and were, I believe, quite unpleasant. I found out the true story many years later. At the time Mother told me she was worried Liesl might kidnap me and take me back to Germany. Codswallop, of course.

I was ten years old at the time of Liesl's dismissal. After that my daily life went downhill. The family couldn't really be bothered with me. Neither my mother nor her sister Gladys had been taught anything useful in terms of managing a house, cooking or child-rearing. They expected to have servants to take care of all that and were given instead lessons in singing, dancing, deportment and elocution—things for which they probably had no talent. When I became a father in the 1950s Winnie and Gladys took turns looking after my daughter when my wife was out. Neither of them could change a nappy, and my daughter by then somehow managed to tie them herself.

In Liesl's absence my parents recruited no replacement, and my mother continued with her social engagements, going out every afternoon. She was unprepared to bring up a child and admitted years later that she'd neglected me. On the subject of parents, I agree with Philip Larkin: they certainly mess you up, unintentionally or otherwise. Larkin ended his most famous poem with the warning not to have any kids. I don't think my parents should have, and sometimes wonder whether I was wise to have had any children myself. As it happens, all three of mine turned out fine, but I wasn't a good father, and, with such rotten genes in the family, it could have been disastrous.

2

Mother

Winifred Friedmann, my mother, was born in London of thoroughly anglicised, non-observant German-Jewish parents. Jacob, her father, had left the family farm in Kronach, Bavaria, and emigrated to England, leaving behind his widowed mother Rosa. Unusually for a Jewish family of the time, the Friedmanns were well-connected gentlemen farmers—one of Jacob's cousins was solicitor-general of Bavaria. Jacob and his siblings saw little future on the farm and most of them emigrated. His elder brother made his fortune in Russia, while their sister, having married, prospered in the United States.

Grandpa Jacob met Sophie Pretzfelder, my grandmother, in the mid-1890s when he was in his thirties. They were distantly related, and Jacob was rather taken by the photograph he saw of her while visiting a mutual relative. She was seventeen, beautiful, and one of many siblings. Only one other of her sisters was attractive, and the two of them were married off to wealthy suitors whose lives they proceeded to make utterly miserable. Sophie's wealthy bachelor uncle then undertook the arduous task of marrying off their numerous plain but much nicer sisters. They preferred not to marry into East European Jewry so were stuck with a small pool of westernised Jews in Germany and London, many of them vaguely inter-related. Surprisingly, Sophie's uncle disposed of them all. I suspect money, as dowries, contributed to his success.

Jacob spent his working life in London as a glass buyer at Falk Stadelmann & Co., a well-known business specializing in lighting and electrical goods. The company was started by Salomon Falk in 1881, and Jacob, I think, must have been a friend of the founders. He eventually became a director of the company and was prosperous by the time of his marriage. Extremely well connected—he knew the Rothschilds, for example—he preferred not to socialise widely and was happiest alone in his study tending his stamp collection.

My father's mother, Betty née Wassermann, was a cousin of writer Jakob Wassermann, author of *The World's Illusion*. She was a bony, diminutive widow whose husband Louis Offenstadt had died in 1911 of peritonitis when my father was just ten years old. Photographs show Grandpa Louis looking well-dressed, portly, bewhiskered and thoroughly bad-tempered. I was fortunate to have been spared knowing him. Grandma Betty wore mourning clothes for the rest of her life and pronounced regularly on her late husband's outstanding qualities. Grandma Sophie bitchily countered that Louis was hardly a saint—Betty and Louis, she claimed, had always fought like cat and dog.

In family lore the Offenstadts were originally Offenbachs, related to the German-born French composer Jacques Offenbach. My Offenbach ancestors supposedly regarded their name as *déclassé* and, repelled by association with 'itinerant musicians', changed it to Offenstadt. It's more likely that they merely wanted to differentiate themselves from the ubiquitous Offenbachs. Either that or it's a complete myth.

Much of Grandma Betty Offenstadt's income had evaporated during the First World War through inflation and the dishonest machinations of Eugen Wassermann, the youngest of her three brothers. Tuberculosis eventually killed off all three. By the time my parents met in the mid-1920s Betty was living in some style on the charity of her relations. She must have been aware that marriage to Winnie was an ideal alliance for my father—he would be well off for life. No one had foreseen that the families would grow to detest one another.

Vivacious, spoilt and precociously flirtatious as a teenager, my mother was once caught sitting on a boy's lap and promptly dispatched from her home in London to a finishing-school in Wiesbaden. Born in London in 1903, Winnie was very pretty with thick dark hair and unusually beautiful blue-brown eyes. She was always somewhat vain and wore a lot of make-up—lipstick and mascara, powder and rouge—and plucked out her eyebrows only to spend a considerable amount of time pencilling in arched substitutes. It was shortly before attending finishing-school that she met my father, Arthur Offenstadt, during one of her family's annual sorties to visit my great-grandmother in Nuremberg. Arthur, who had been born in Fürth, Bavaria, in 1901, was distantly related to Winnie. His Uncle Eugen was married to Netta, one of her cousins.

It seems strange to say my parents loved one another. I mostly remember them arguing fiercely throughout their marriage. Neither Jacob nor Sophie wanted their favourite daughter to marry in Germany and tried to dissuade her, but Winnie and Arthur remained determined. Grandpa Jacob employed a private investigator who pronounced the Offenstadts sufficiently respectable and adequately solvent. A dearth of suitable matches in England meant that Jacob and Sophie relented and the wedding took place in 1925. It was a huge financial coup for the relatively impoverished Offenstadts who became the talk of the town. Winnie's dowry was about £5,000 which equates to something close to £300,000 today. It was mostly invested in the Wassermann family's leather-goods factory into which my father was promoted as junior partner alongside his Uncle Eugen.

The Nuremberg factory was a substantial enterprise—there was even a chauffeur-driven Mercedes-Benz for deliveries. My father once took us for a day out on the chauffeur's day off. He was a terrible driver and managed to smash it up quite badly. Years later, after his emigration to London, he was once driving so badly the police stopped and breathalysed him. Convinced he must be drunk, instead they pronounced him stone-cold sober. He would dither and dawdle along causing frustration and alarm. When I started driving myself I was disappointed to discover I had inherited his poor coordination and feeble sense of direction. Neither of us ever felt at ease behind the wheel and wisely retired from driving before any serious accident transpired.

Money can't have been quite such an issue in the 1920s as it became in the 1930s. The Wassermanns and Offenstadts eventually lost money on the sale of their factory, but it went bust largely due to their own incompetence. Stupidly, Jacob Friedmann's Russia-based brother had left quite a bit of money invested in Germany which was eaten up by hyperinflation in the 1920s. The US dollar, worth forty-eight marks at the end of 1919, bought over four trillion marks by November 1923. In the same period a loaf of bread went from costing a quarter of a mark to eighty billion. Actual wheelbarrows full of cash were need for basic commodities. You could order a coffee only to find it had doubled in price by the time it was served. I assume Jacob still had substantial savings in England because, though usually parsimonious, he paid for my parents' lavish wedding festivities in Nuremberg, to which all the English relatives were invited. Everything was beautifully decorated with white roses, but sadly there are no pictures. No one had thought to hire a photographer.

After a honeymoon in Venice my parents returned to live in the modern architect-built house in Nuremberg that Jacob had bought for them. It was beautifully furnished with art-deco furniture and a grand piano that remained unplayed. Two years later I was born.

3

Kin Hell

After their daily trips to Nuremberg Zoo, the Kinderfräuleins who cared for me were under strict orders to take me to see Grandma Betty, the black widow. They rarely did. Betty was a fearsome little woman who treated her servants badly. The Kinderfräuleins and I were afraid of her despite the fact she was less than five feet tall and, apart from her bosom, hardly physically imposing. Once widowed, Betty wore black for the rest of her life and eschewed all jewellery apart from diamond stud earrings. She wore no make-up save a coating of face powder applied with a puff from a compact my father had imported for the family business. The top of one of her fingers was missing, which I found sinister. It had been caused by blood poisoning years earlier. Without antibiotics, the only medical option had been to chop it off. She attempted to disguise this by curling her fingers into her palm.

Betty's iron-grey hair was worn in a tight bun, and she dressed in a neat old-fashioned way, all in black, including her stockings, and with stiletto heels to gain more height. Slim but large-busted, she swished around the house in black satin petticoats before getting properly dressed in the morning, as did her younger sister Getta when she came to stay. I liked Getta. Though plainer than Betty, who had been regarded as unusually good-looking in her youth, Getta had a sense of fun. Betty ruled the entire family and was strict, intolerant and domineering. Louis, her late husband, had been notoriously bad-tempered, and Betty had the knack of turning my father, too, into a screaming, shouting, raging neurotic. My mother, like many of Betty's own relatives, hated her.

Rather than risk a visit to Betty, after a morning at the zoo my Kinderfräulein would usually return me to the house, take me upstairs to the nursery for another disgusting meal, then put me to bed for an afternoon nap. If my parents were at home I might see them later, but Mother often went to her tea parties, and Father was usually out attending to the family business. He had extramarital affairs that kept him busy, too, so I didn't see much of either parent. At six o'clock another round of appalling food would precede bedtime.

In 1932, by the time I was five, the family was beset with financial problems. My mother's generous marriage settlement had been invested in my great-grandfather Heinrich Wassermann's leather-goods factory. It had been a successful, reputable business, but my father's uncle, Eugen Wassermann, the senior partner who inherited it, drained it of funds. Rumours from well-wishers and local gossips reached my mother that it wasn't being run properly. Neither Eugen nor my father knew enough about business, and, in the beginning there was so much money around that they simply didn't care. Instead of working, my father and Eugen were spending most of their time at the Grand Hotel boozing lavishly and chasing after women. As well as their incompetence and malfeasance there was an international recession to contend with. Germany was paying the price for losing the First World War with the punitive reparation payments the victors had imposed. Economic strife was inevitable, and multiple bankruptcies followed. In Nuremberg—a city that had become increasingly hostile to Jews—our house was shut up, and I was sent to stay with Grandma Betty in her apartment.

I had mixed feelings about staying with Betty. Her flat was modern and comfortable, but I was somewhat fearful and in awe of my grandmother. She had strange ideas about child-rearing. I once had intestinal worms and was given laxatives disguised as chocolates. I had never before been offered anything so delicious, so scoffed the lot. By rights I should have been dreadfully ill but was strangely untouched. The following night Betty placed a tempting box of chocolates on my bedside table. 'You won't eat any of them, will you?' she said. Of course I didn't and indeed couldn't—I was far too frightened of her to touch them.

My spell with Betty suited neither of us. My daily trips to the zoo ended, and I was mostly kept indoors, left with a maid, while Betty was out all day visiting friends. Each successive maid was a country girl terrified of Betty. Life must have been as lonely for them as it was for me, and none stayed long. While Betty was out we would sit and chat, but as soon as we heard the click-clack of her heels on the pavement outside we would scuttle back to our respective rooms and wait in dread for the old witch's return. The food at least was slightly better, and central heating was a welcome novelty. Visits from my parents were rare.

While I remained with Betty in Nuremberg, Winnie and Arthur moved to Munich to run a shop. My parents thought Munich less hostile to Jews and were able to sell off what remained of the leather goods. My father had relatives in Munich called the Auerbachs—a cousin and his wife, who had no children of their own, and an elderly aunt. They were very kind and offered to look after me during the war. My father declined the invitation—a pity as I would have liked to have gone with them when they emigrated to California.

In 1933, after I had spent nine months with Grandma Betty, my mother took me to London to stay with her family, the Friedmanns, to learn English. The journey was a nightmare of shouting porters and Mother being seasick, but we made it to my grandparents' house in Brondesbury Park where she left me and returned to Munich. I didn't mind too much. By now I was used to being dumped with relatives, and things were somewhat better in England. I was, for example, given much more suitable clothes. Betty, who was deft with knitting needles, had always kitted me out in ludicrous hand-knitted ensembles in hues of raspberry and lavender. My mother, in turn, had made me wear flamboyant velvet suits, one red and another in maroon, so I looked like Little Lord Fauntleroy. I was quite proud of these but, as soon as she saw them, Grandma Sophie marched me down to Kilburn High Road where I was bought decent shirts, a tie and some smart flannel trousers. At a photography studio, portraits of me in the new outfit were taken to send to my parents. Unfortunately I was still pigeon-toed, so the effect was rather spoilt by custom-made and rather ugly orthopaedic shoes, an inconvenience I endured until my thirties when I realised I could wear ordinary ones.

Everyone spoke English in the Brondesbury Park house, even though German was the mother tongue of my grandparents and their maid Teresa. A native 'miss' was appointed whose efforts to instruct me in the English language were hampered by Grandma Sophie's somewhat guttural rendition. For reasons unclear, Sophie decided I needed to learn the expression 'It doesn't matter', but, an anxious child, it took me ages to master the phrase let alone the sentiment behind it. Perhaps I never have.

4

A Couple of Old Cows

My grandmother Sophie Pretzfelder had arrived in England at the age of seventeen. Hoping to maker her more marriageable, her parents had her taught gourmet cooking at a top hotel in Regenberg where the staff soon dubbed her 'the beautiful Fräulein'. Slim, auburn-haired and of medium height, she was, like her daughter Winnie, somewhat vain. As an older woman she put on weight but continued to dye her hair auburn and wear expensive fashionable clothes, jewellery and make-up. One of her favoured pastimes was haranguing my mother about her poor choice of husband. She was tactless, hurtful, insensitive and frequently vicious in her written correspondence and verbal exchanges. Bossy and interfering, like many bullies, she would, when challenged, swiftly become upset and burst into tears.

My grandfather Jacob was considerably older than Sophie. Sadly, I remember little of him, other than that he was a kindly gentleman who stoically endured her bossiness and allowed her to treat him very badly. Sophie had once been delighted by a beautiful necklace of valuable natural pearls Jacob gave her, but she was otherwise very hard to please. She had been more in love with Jacob's brother than him, so took it out on poor Jacob throughout the marriage. His heart weakened by the drugs for chronic asthma that he inhaled through a machine, Jacob died in 1936 when I was about nine. After his death the maid said Sophie had fits of crying. 'It's not grief,' my mother pronounced, 'it's guilt!'

Frankly, my grandmothers were a couple of old cows. Betty was simply old-fashioned, a small woman who liked to rule the roost and aroused intense dislike. On visits to Bavaria I was taken around the few relatives with whom she was still on speaking terms, mostly her sisters—she never went near the great-uncle she had offended who lived in Fürth. Many people loathed Betty, but I don't think she was as intrinsically unpleasant as Sophie, who, by the time I reached my teens, had become a really nasty woman. She despised my father and his mother's family, the Wassermanns. At first I got on with her well enough. Having quickly grasped that she disliked Betty, I would tell her how horrible she had been to me in Germany. Sophie would feign sympathy and avow disapproval but was storing up my tales of woe as fuel for later family feuds.

Sophie could be extraordinarily cruel. At the start of the war her sister came over from Nuremberg for an extended stay. Poor Frieda was almost penniless and had trouble walking, but unlike Sophie was extremely nice. Sadly, Sophie encouraged me to tease her and even to trip her over. Later I felt great shame over this. Sophie would also delight in reminding Frieda that the Nazis had invaded Denmark and would doubtlessly subject her daughter to imprisonment, or worse.

In 1934, things were beginning to get as bad for my parents in Munich as the had they had been in Nuremberg. One day the hotel receptionist, apologetic and embarrassed, asked them to leave. The Nazis had ordained that no hotel could take in Jews. For my mother this was the final straw. With dual British-German nationality, she had been travelling to and from London a great deal, attempting to help relatives escape the Nazis and extracting as much of her dwindling fortune as she could. So now she announced that she was returning home to London permanently—with or without my father. He had little alternative but to cut his losses and follow, leaving Betty behind. The Wassermann family business had disintegrated by this time, and my much of my mother's fortune slid with it, apparently into the pockets of my Great-Uncle Eugen who continued to live well in an elegant villa before tuberculosis finished him off.

The house in Brondesbury Park, where the Friedmann family lived in some style, was filled with heavy old-fashioned oak and mahogany furniture but large enough for all of us. My parents' arrival didn't really make much difference to me. My father was out all day. From an office he had been given through Jacob Friedmann's connections with Falk Stadelmann in Holborn, he sold imported German and Japanese imitation jewellery, paper fans, artificial flowers and other rubbish. Mother mostly left me to my own devices while she shopped or visited friends. At least by then I had something of a life outside the home.

By the time my parents settled in London I had become fluent in English through my governess's elocution lessons and was then sent to a nursery school. This brought welcome contact with other children for the first time. There were further compensations too. In Britain the food was much better, and Sophie's maid Teresa was an excellent cook. She was also a thief and used to help herself to any money or valuables she found lying around. Later we found out she had a duplicate set of keys to every lock in the house. She was devious, steaming open letters, reading them and sealing them up again. The family had their suspicions but, because they so enjoyed her cooking, put up with her dodgy activities for years.

After Grandpa Jacob's death in 1936 a second maid joined us to assist with the tea parties which Sophie, his newly liberated widow, held more frequently. Mrs Griffiths, the new maid and cook, was a pleasant, ruddy-faced woman who endured employment with the Friedmanns for over thirty years despite a great deal of bossing about by Sophie. A decent woman and a true cockney, she came and went from service as serial pregnancies and hospital admissions permitted. This eventually exasperated Sophie so much that she rudely suggested that Mrs Griffiths might want to stop sleeping with the undeserving husband who regularly beat her. Mrs Griffiths could probably only dream of such independence. As our maid she had her idiosyncrasies, referring to mashed potato as 'smashed potatoes' and enlivening my mother's dinner parties by breaking her best china and crystal glasses while washing up. As with Teresa, this never seemed to lead to her dismissal. Perhaps my grandmother feared that any replacement would be worse. Indeed, 'better the devil you know' is a maxim I seem to have lived by, too, often to my cost.

When my father joined us in London there had been some suggestion that, as a German national, he might be sent to an internment camp. This was the fate of many German refugees, including Jews, but the authorities quickly realised that he was harmless, and his tribunal spared him imprisonment. They did restrict his movements though, and for years he was forbidden to travel more than twenty-five miles from London, not that he ever really wanted to. After a year or so of staying with the Friedmanns my parents found the three of us an apartment in Wembley Park.

Winnie never did much, though at one point, thanks to my grandfather Jacob, she had spent a few months demonstrating ornamental Falk Stadelmann paraffin heaters in Harrods. She was paid commission, and her sales technique impressed them enough that she was offered a permanent job. Unfortunately the fumes and heat made her unwell. Any money she made was spent on medical bills which cancelled out her earnings, so she packed it in and went back to being a lady of leisure. Owing to our reduced economic circumstances my parents wouldn't employ a live-in nanny. I was either left on my own or they asked Mrs Edgson, the kindly old lady in the flat upstairs, to keep an eye on me. On other occasions I was sent to Sophie's to be supervised by her maid. In some ways I felt more at home there than in my parents' house in Wembley. Our place was mostly just for show, with two living-rooms, one of which we didn't use, kept purely for guests. Fairly large, it was still quite a contrast to my home in Germany which, with its three living-rooms, seemed comparatively enormous. Once more I was quite lonely. Despite nursery school I didn't have many companions, and I was shy. I didn't make friends especially easily.

British-born and thoroughly anglicised, Mother's experiences of Nazi Germany encouraged her patriotism and desire to help the British war effort. At the outbreak of hostilities she loaned her German passport and a pair of field glasses to the British government so that they might be used for spying purposes. I don't know whether there were any British agents in Nazi Germany masquerading as my mother—the government probably used passports as models to forge new documents—but both the passport and the field glasses came back intact after the war.

By this time I had been in England six years, was twelve years old and felt myself very English. In London, despite my origins in Germany, I was home and living a more settled life.

5

Wonderland?

For some time I knew something of what was happening in Nazi Germany, though not the details. Even after settling in London in 1933, in the pre-war years in several occasions I was sent back with Sophie's German maid to visit Grandma Betty for a couple of weeks at a time. While Sophie's maid visited her own family, Betty would drag me round to see the few relatives she hadn't totally alienated. I shared with most of them only a mutual lack of interest, though they were often very kind to me. I would play with Betty's Great-Nephew Edmund who was slightly younger than me. Edmund's father loathed Betty and her sister, his mother-in-law. They once infuriated him so much he kicked them both out of the house and changed the locks. While he cooled off they stayed overnight in a nearby hotel.

In about 1935 I stayed with Edmund's family in Würzburg. It was a smallish town where his father was the leading optician. Everyone must have known the family was Jewish. I remember boys on bicycles shouted 'Dirty Jews!' at us when Edmund and I were walking back from the shops once. By that time Jews were already prohibited from going into restaurants and some shops had signs up saying 'Jews Not Welcome'. There was no way I could not notice increasingly open antisemitism. I saw all the uniforms, heard all the shouting. I also remember a teenage relative who told me that she saw Hitler one day in a parade. 'Of course people thought I shouldn't have watched and said I should have scarpered,' she told me. 'But it was part of history, and I wanted to see it.'

I never saw Hitler myself, nor anyone else senior in the Nazi regime. I did, however, see the Hindenburg airship on one of my holidays in Nuremberg. This vast zeppelin had first toured Germany dropping propaganda leaflets and blasting out Nazi speeches and music before making crossings to New York. The Hindenburg's last transatlantic *Amerikafahrt* took place in May 1937 and ended in spectacular catastrophe. I may well have seen it departing towards its doom.

I hadn't particularly liked living in Germany—my life there had been lonely and rather loveless. My prospects were better in England, though there had been an initial language barrier to overcome as German was my first language. For a while before the war my father bullied me every Sunday into writing a letter in German to his mother. I was no good at it and it bored the pants off me. I was quite glad to put it behind me when he gave up bothering. Though Sophie's German accent was still noticeable, my mother Winnie, her elder sister Gladys and their much younger brother Rudolph were all born in London, so English was their mother tongue. The little German they knew was spoken with distinct English accents. I would probably still be speaking with a slight German accent myself, rather than my impeccable English, had Sophie not had the foresight to bring in a governess to teach me English elocution and help me with my reading.

It must have been a very boring job for that governess. I was quite precocious, and every afternoon the poor woman had to listen to my indignant ravings about my wicked Grandma Betty in Germany. Once I'd let off steam she would instruct me to read aloud from *Alice's Adventures in Wonderland*. I began to realise she wasn't really listening or had nodded off, so I just made it up as I went along. After a while my embroidered version had become so fantastic, so implausible even for Lewis Carroll, that she jolted awake. 'That isn't in the book!' she snapped. By the time I graduated from nursery school my English was perfect. At my first proper school, a teacher proclaimed, 'There's only one boy who speaks English properly in this school, and he wasn't even born here!'

Brondesbury College, where I was sent in 1935 at the age of eight, was a small, badly run, slightly dotty private preparatory school in an old house near Queen's Park Station in north-west London. There were about sixty pupils in all. Dr Price, the headmaster, was an eccentric, fat little man who wore pince-nez glasses and stained suits. His wife, a bit of a harridan, supervised cleaning and cooking at the school. The pair had terrible public rows, and Dr Price enjoyed a double life with a mistress on the side. Knowing Mrs Price, this didn't much surprise us boys. In private the Prices' hobby was beating each other up. When Dr Price had a stroke the school was sold off.

The food and teaching were awful at school, but compared to the lonely life I'd had before I was relatively happy and certainly not one of Shakespeare's 'whining schoolboys ... creeping like a snail unwillingly to school'. I could enjoy there a more carefree life, mess about and make friends. Nevertheless, I don't remember inviting children home, and I often envied them. They all seemed to have much more ordinary, pleasant home lives. Because of the Bavarian influence, everything about my home and family life was different—the culture and atmosphere, the furnishings, the antiques. All quite alien.

At school Brian Braithwaite soon became my best friend—the first I'd ever had. We lost touch after our school days, and I didn't see him for another forty-seven years. By then he was one of the directors of the Condé Nast magazine empire. Brian remembers our headmaster Dr Price as 'a benevolent old buffer who did not much like teaching, a task he entrusted to a small band of underpaid teachers'. The worst of them, he said, 'were swift to mete out violent punishments for even the most minor infractions'. But, like me, Brian was not unhappy there. Perhaps we were both incorrigibly well behaved. He recalls sports being played in Gladstone Park and the pair of us enjoying school outings to London Zoo and the Aldershot Tattoo.

My father expected me to be top of the class of course, or at least in the top three, but the school was fairly easy-going with little emphasis on academic work—an ideal atmosphere for a lazy child like me. I'm ashamed to admit that a friend and I bullied a wretched boy who used to cry at the drop of a hat. It wasn't terribly serious—we made him miss his bus and minor things like that. The poor boy turned up at my next school, and I assured him when he arrived there that I'd grown up a bit and wouldn't give him further trouble.

I never liked my father particularly. He shouted a lot—usually at my mother, sometimes at me and often at both of us. Perhaps inspired by his own mother, he was a bully. Having been brought up in an environment that was not particularly friendly to children, he didn't know what to do when he become a parent himself. My mother told me that my father was sometimes jealous of the attention she gave me as a child. He would occasionally take me to his office where I would play with his imported samples. But there was no real warmth. If I had done well at something at school he might deign to reward me with a penny, otherwise he provided little or no pocket money—certainly not as much as other boys received—which is why I took to shoplifting for a while. It wasn't on any grand scale, but when I was eight or nine I stole sweets or stamps for my collection. I wasn't exactly a Dickensian street urchin, and there was no Fagin behind the scenes pulling my strings—it was sheer opportunism. Many children go through such phases. Once I swiped a bar of chocolate from a shop at a railway station and the ticket collector saw me and gave chase. I got away, but it frightened me enough to prompt a long-overdue fit of conscience. I regretted and agonised over my crime for months and never did it again.

Though not as severe as in Germany, antisemitism was rife in England in those days and no one bothered to conceal it. I was still Peter Offenstadt from Germany, and although there were other Jewish boys at the school they were English Jews, so I sometimes felt very much an outsider. A lot of the antisemitism was more to do with class snobbery and a lack of cultural assimilation. It sounds awful now, but many European immigrants, especially European Jews, were seen as lower class, foreign and alien. I learnt to take little or no notice at some of the more casual antisemitic remarks. For instance, one of my closest friends told me he stopped fancying Betty Grable once he heard a rumour that she was Jewish (although, actually, she wasn't). I usually didn't comment on that sort of thing but did once end up in a street fight. Something very minor probably triggered it, but I lost my temper and gave one of my friends a terrific black eye. He forgave me, but his father was apoplectic with rage and threatened to call the police. I was almost expelled, but my Uncle Rudi drafted a letter to the headmaster and I was put on probation. Years later, at that same friend's wedding, he warned me to avoid going to the corner of the church hall as his father was there and still hadn't forgiven me.

The school had a handful of other German boys, though often not the sort I could befriend. I particularly remember Gabby Schweitzer, the son of a Nazi sympathiser whose pernicious views he had absorbed. I always suspected that his father was a German spy. Gabby was fifteen while I was just nine, so he was quite intimidating. Often on the way to school he would pull me to one side and threaten me. He'd hiss, 'You stinking Jew!' and curse me in German, or detain me in the playground after school for more abuse. My mother had a word with Dr Price, who caned the boy. Like other German pupils at the school he disappeared at the outbreak of war. He was either interned or deported back to his homeland to face whatever came his way—something unpleasant, I rather hoped.

6

Bugger Bognor

It was war that put an end to my time at Brondesbury College. We ended up evacuating to Middleton-on-Sea, east of Bognor, as Sophie had often holidayed there. We lived in a flat for a while, then she managed to find somewhere worse—a bungalow something like a wooden chalet. Intended as a summer house, in winter it was bloody freezing.

I went to the local school, which was dreadful. It was the only time I experienced state education. The teaching was poor, and the local children had no intention of making friends with me. They just wanted to beat me up. I had a posh London accent, and my German surname didn't exactly help me blend in. Boys, quite tough lads, used to follow me when I went to catch the bus. On one occasion I remember hiding from a gang of thuggish pupils behind a hedge only for the owner of the garden to come out and box my ears for trespassing. He threw me out on the street where the boys attacked me.

Bognor wasn't all bad though. I learnt to ride a bicycle, something I'd always wanted to do, and got a paper round. It was the first money I ever earned, but in the end neither the freedom it gave me nor the cash I was paid compensated for just how early I had to get up. After three months none of the family could stand our Sussex exile a moment longer. Sophie, in particular, missed her London life. Since there had been no sign of the anticipated air raids we decided to return and take our chances with the Luftwaffe. Of course as soon as we got back to London the bombing started.

The chilly Bognor bungalow can't have done me much good. In those days few houses had central heating, and I got chilblains every winter. My health had hardly been robust from the start, and I don't suppose food rationing helped. It seems incredible now, but rationing dragged on for fourteen years. Even items that weren't rationed were in short supply. Back in London I got severe measles followed by glandular tuberculosis with, for about six weeks, a really high temperature. My doctor would have recommended recovery in a sanatorium in Switzerland had it not been for the war. Instead I had to make do with a spell in Torquay where I was minded by an intimidating matron. It was quiet—there were few tourists because of the war—and the climate was good. I've no idea how—they were as rare as hen's teeth at the time—but my mother managed to get me oranges from a local greengrocer as I needed the vitamin C. Later, in my days as a prominent publisher, Mother was always embarrassed if my tuberculosis was mentioned in interviews. She thought, like rickets, it was a disease of poverty. Laid up in bed for a couple of months, I missed school for a further nine. Grandma Sophie, showing her talent for cruelty, reminded me that my father's uncles had all died of tuberculosis. 'Your father will probably die of TB as well,' she said, 'and so will you!'

When I was confined to bed to keep warm and aid recovery, the air raids finally arrived. Even now I remember the time a land mine exploded so close that the flash lit up my bedroom through the blackout curtains. I leapt about a foot in the air from fright. Where we lived, in the Wembley area, dozens of bombs were dropped between October 1940 and June 1941. Unexploded bombs still turn up occasionally today. In the early 1940s we didn't have a shelter to go to. If things got really hairy we would huddle in the hallway with our fingers crossed. Towards the end of the war, and by the time it was far too late to be of any use, we bought a Morrison shelter—a sort of indoor metal cage. Apart from the odd close call we grew strangely used to the bombing.

Once a week, when I was well enough, I went fire-spotting. They'd give you a stirrup pump and a sand bucket and tell you to stand lookout, though I can't remember ever spotting anything. Most people did at least something for the war effort. My father was in the Home Guard and Mother was in the Women's Voluntary Services for a short while. She found it boring and soon threw in the towel saying she had to look after her son, which was hardly the truth—she was never at home! Every day she'd be out having tea with her lady friends. Usually she sent me to a Lyons Corner House to do my homework and then dropped by to pick me up on the way home. I think perhaps once a term I'd get tea at our flat. With our cleaner pretending to be a waitress, Mother would put on a tea party for all these old hags. At a certain point they'd call for my entrance. I'd go in to be shown off and there'd be a bit of cooing, the odd gushing remark and a bit of forced small talk. But really they didn't want to see me and I didn't want to see them. It was all so silly.

I was thirteen in 1940 and should in theory have been bar-mitzvahed. In preparation I was sent for Hebrew lessons with my Uncle Bobby's father, a very nasty old man. He usually charged five shillings a week, but, because of the family connection, my father managed to negotiate a charge of half a crown—just two shillings and sixpence. It was still too much. The lessons took place in a dank basement in Kilburn that smelt musty as the windows were never opened. I loathed going there and played truant most of the time.

When I did turn up I was punched black and blue. Eventually my mother saw the bruises on my arm and asked how I got them. 'It's Mr Abelson,' I said. 'He keeps punching me!' After that, my parents decided I needn't attend any more classes. I was relieved when they gave up on the idea. It wasn't as if we attended synagogue regularly, and Hebrew was incomprehensible as far as I was concerned. Neither parent was fervent when it came to Judaism, and consequently I have never felt particularly Jewish myself. If there hadn't been a war perhaps my bar mitzvah might have happened. In the end, Father didn't fancy shelling out for a party, and Mother certainly couldn't be bothered to host one either.

My mother's family had strayed fairly far from their Jewish background. Betty, my father's mother, had moved to London in 1939, just before war broke out, and settled in West Hampstead. She'd given up her Nuremberg flat and had exhausted the patience of her three sisters. She had been foisting herself on them in succession. London life was quite an adjustment for her. She was appalled to discover that the Friedmanns celebrated a traditional English Christmas and decried them all as disgraceful heathens. She only ever invoked Judaism when it suited her, though, and never attended synagogue in London as it failed to provide the social contact she had enjoyed in Germany. She also managed to reconcile scoffing her favourite smoked ham and beloved sausages with a verbal abnegation of pork. My father was also very fond of ham sandwiches, a fact he concealed from more orthodox friends.

After Brondesbury College my parents intended that I should go to the ancient and prestigious Merchant Taylors' School in Hertfordshire. Brian Braithwaite had been sent off to Mercers', a similarly distinguished school in Holborn. But my long educational hiatus meant that I was behind in my schooling and would not have passed the entrance examination. Having been off school for nearly a year with tuberculosis I was especially poor at maths. My mother took me instead to view a couple of private church schools in Harrow, both run by clergymen. The first was a rather scruffy place, as was the clergyman in charge. The second we inspected, Kings School in St John's Road, was very clean. Kings was a High Church school run on private-school lines under the auspices of the Church of England. The Bishop of London was one of the governors. It had been set up and was run by Father Waterton, a former African missionary. To my relief no entry examination was required. 'I go by character rather than academic qualifications,' Father Waterton told us. I probably seemed like quite a nice Jewish boy at the time, so was welcomed in.

There were two other Jewish boys at Kings School, one who was a German refugee, the other a boy I never really got to know and didn't like the look of very much. Both asked to be excused chapel, whereas I saw no reason not to go. Betty would have had ten fits if she had known, so we never told her. She remained blissfully ignorant of the fact that I went to a Christian chapel service every morning for four years and came to know more about the New Testament than the Old—unusual for someone born Jewish. The school didn't ever press me to believe in anything, but I liked singing the hymns and, in the school certificate, ended up with a distinction in religious studies.

Even though it was much more strict that my previous school and required that I work hard, I really enjoyed Kings School. I was fairly good academically, and it was properly run. The teaching was pretty good, too. Most of the men available were broken-down wrecks who were utterly useless, so, unusually for the time, we had a lot of women teachers. I regret never having gone back to tell Father Waterton how grateful I was for what was really a very good education. All in all I couldn't have gone to a better school. Had I hated it I would have cracked up completely. As it was, I did have a mercifully short-lived breakdown in 1942 when I was fifteen.

7

Breakdown

I was an insecure adolescent, but the extent of my loneliness dawned on me gradually. I was fairly well behaved at school but a little neurotic. Most of the time I had supposed my life was like everyone else's. Coming into close contact with other children made me realise just how different it had been. I became very angry and resentful and one day broke down. Fortunately my uncle, Bobby Abelson, was a GP and psychiatrist and helped me to cope. Bobby's family had been relatively poor, so, upon his marriage to my mother's sister Gladys, his surgery was set up with financial assistance from my grandfather Jacob with the proviso that he only practice psychiatry in his spare time as Grandpa 'didn't want to subsidise that sort of thing'.

My anger terrified me. Anxious and obsessive, I was so mad with rage I became frightened I might actually kill someone, in particular my parents or grandmothers. Through Bobby's analysis we discovered that the rage, mostly in reaction to my grandmothers' cruelties, had built up over time. It mixed with resentment at my father's bullying and my parents' emotional neglect. Bobby wondered if religion might be a help. I wasn't naturally religious and told him I couldn't involve myself. My governess had brought me up to say a prayer when I was younger, and I had swallowed this for a bit. I never really believed in it though. Father Waterton was extremely intelligent, but I had found his sermons unpersuasive and knew I had no faith. Bobby admitted that as a scientist he didn't believe any religious codswallop either. We agreed to drop the idea. I'm still puzzled as to how anyone intelligent manages to sustain religious beliefs.

I was only off school for a few days but had psychoanalysis with Uncle Bobby for some time. A lovely man with kindly eyes and a gentle nature, he was one of the first to recognise the condition of shell-shock in his fellow soldiers during the First World War. I had known Bobby since early childhood and had much more confidence in him than I would any other psychiatrist.

I also had a much better relationship with him than my own father. He may have been exaggerating, but Bobby once said that the emotional neglect I had suffered had been some of the worst he had encountered. Going to school was a boon though. I was happier there than at home, and it was a useful distraction that helped me, in psychiatric terms, to sublimate my anger.

When I was ill and off school with tuberculosis I had read voraciously. In Germany, as a young child, I had read traditional stories like the Grimm Brothers' fairy-tales and the extraordinary *Struwwelpeter* (Shockheaded Peter). I found terrifying its cautionary tales of the perils of inattention to personal grooming, its child immolation and scissoring of thumbs. I also read more comforting fare—the *Just William* books and *Emil and the Detectives*. By the time I was laid up with tuberculosis in London, reading was already a treasured hobby and a useful way of fending off loneliness and boredom. I remember reading, perhaps rather precociously, works by Tolstoy and the Claudius novels of Robert Graves. I was impressed by Wilkie Collins's *The Woman in White*. I had no idea Collins was famous. It was all fairly random—I just picked what I liked.

Grandma Sophie was less aggressive back then, so I could visit the flat she shared with my Uncle Rudi, her youngest child, and freely borrow his books. From Rudi's library I read the collected stories of D. H. Lawrence as well as classics by Dickens and Thackeray. Some of his books were way beyond me, especially those on psychiatry, psychoanalysis and philosophy. As a sensitive boy in my early teens they were troubling. I think this was part of what led to my breakdown. It was too much information, too early, of a disturbing and discouraging kind. I wonder now whether Freud's ideas ever really helped anyone overcome anything.

Radio was another welcome distraction. Wireless sets were part of the furnishings in those days and were housed in large, attractive cabinets. My parents took me with them when they chose ours from the showroom at Falk Stadelmann where my grandfather worked. Radio was pretty much the only entertainment we had, especially during the Blitz when theatres and cinemas were closed. My mother would often have dance-band music playing, but more to my taste were the comedies. Bebe Daniels and Ben Lyon in *Hi Gang!* and *Life with the Lyons* I found particularly entertaining.

At the time of my breakdown rumours of the horrors of the Holocaust had started to spread within the Jewish diaspora. Betty had copies of a German-language newspaper called *Aufbau*. Founded in New York in 1934, it published information and advice for German-speaking Jewish refugees. There were articles by prominent Jews such as Albert Einstein and Thomas Mann, and after 1939 it became a leading anti-Nazi paper that also circulated in London. There were nasty glimmers of what was going on, but I suppose I really became aware of it in on a visit to Germany just before the war when one of Betty's nieces was crying because her mother and aunt had been sent to Theresienstadt. I knew they were imprisoning and maltreating people there, or else deporting them. By 1942 we knew that one of my father's cousins had been in a concentration camp and had become mentally deranged. Most of my great-aunts were nice old ladies—I knew all of them. After the war we discovered that they and many of our Offenstadt and Wassermann relatives had died in concentration camps. Berta Offenstadt, my great-aunt, died at Treblinka. Great-Uncles Leo and Julius, and Great-Aunts Sabine, Agnes and Johanna Offenstadt all perished at Theresienstadt, while Nathan Offenstadt died at Drancy. There were many more, of course, including relatives on my mother's side, the Friedmanns and Pretzfelders.

So my formative years had this background of dread—the growing awareness of what was going on in Germany, the land of my birth, and general worldwide hostility to Jews. There was xenophobia and antisemitism to contend with in England, too. It wasn't virulent or systematic in the way it was in Nazi Germany, but it was there. One of the things I hated was having a German name which, alongside my Jewish origins, made me a target. People pounced on the name Offenstadt which was doubly unfortunate because it was, to native English speakers, unpronounceable. There was no easy way to anglicise it, and I found it an embarrassment. Asked to give your name, there was no point in saying it; you had to spell it. To avoid this, my mother used my father's first name and called herself Mrs Arthur in shops or at the hairdresser's. My father and I weren't allowed to naturalise and change our surnames until after the war in 1946. When he did, my father, for reasons unknown, chose to name himself after Nesbitt Owen, a colleague he admired. It could have been worse. The relief of losing the surname Offenstadt certainly made up for any awkwardness associated with people forever assuming my background was Welsh.

8

Brief Encounter

I suppose all Jewish families have the expectation that their sons will turn into nice Jewish boys, become successful in business and marry a Jewish girl. However, I've never felt particularly Jewish and had no interest in Judaism. My Christian education meant that I had more in common with gentiles than Jews. If I'd married a Jewish girl it would have had to have been a rebellious one. Though nothing much came of it, one of my most pleasant teenage memories is a dalliance with Fenella Fielding who later became a famous actress. Her parents were both East European Jews, and like me she became something of a rebel. We met by chance in Torquay in 1944 when our families happened to be staying at the same hotel. She seemed very beautiful and sophisticated. We were born in the same year, but she was sixteen and I was seventeen at the time, and it was all very innocent and naive. At the time I was Peter Offenstadt and she was Fenella Feldman. Her brother Basil was there, too. He eventually became a plastic-toy magnate who manufactured yo-yos and Sindy dolls and who made his way up to the Lords as Baron Feldman of Frognal, his elevation sponsored by Margaret Thatcher.

When we met in 1944 Fenella had a protective dragon of a mother there who fortunately realised I was relatively safe. Fenella and I went for walks in Torquay and on a couple of dates when we returned to London. We didn't have that much in common though, and at seventeen I was really only out for one thing. It became clear I wasn't going to get it, so the relationship fizzled out. But Fenella was charming and fun and provided my first introduction to the dives of Soho. She told me about Quentin Crisp who was largely unknown at the time. I was intrigued and once spotted him walking down the street in South Kensington and knew immediately who he was from her vivid description.

Years later, in the 1960s, I saw Fenella at a party but don't think she remembered me. It wouldn't have been diplomatic to attempt to jog her memory, especially as I had been the one to break off our relationship all those years ago. I admired her though. She was the only person I knew in those days who said what she was going to do and actually did it. At sixteen she had said, 'I'm going to be an actress!' I thought she had as much chance of doing that as flying to the moon. I was terribly impressed years later when she starred in the 1958 musical *Valmouth* and, the following year, *Pieces of Eight*, a revue show with Kenneth Williams. I thought her a phenomenal actress but had no idea about the *Carry On* film aspect of her oeuvre. The series was never really my cup of tea.

I can recall exactly when that holiday in Torquay took place because news of the Hitler assassination attempt came on the radio: 20 July 1944. Though they failed to kill him, the conspirators gave him a hell of a fright and blew his trousers to shreds. Typically, Hitler cheered himself up by watching films of the perpetrators being strangled repeatedly and hanged from piano wires.

It took another ten months or so before the war ended in Europe. On V. E. day, 8 May 1945, I didn't go out—I had no money to celebrate, didn't drink much in those days and, unlike Princess Elizabeth, didn't join the throng in Trafalgar Square. But I remember it was exciting. The end of the blackout was very cheering and the neon lights went on in Piccadilly and all over the West End for the first time in years.

The relief and excitement at the end of the war was tempered by the amount of destruction we had witnessed and the revelations about those who had been incarcerated in the concentration camps. I remember the reports, how some journalists were so appalled they were physically sick and had mental breakdowns. No one could have prepared them for what they saw. The first Nazi concentration camp at Dachau had been constructed in 1933 shortly after Hitler became Chancellor, so the idea that the camps were any kind of secret is ludicrous. The Holocaust caught up with everyone and respected no distinctions. Even some of the Rothschilds perished in the camps.

I don't understand why the Germans and Japanese were forgiven so quickly for what they had done and weren't subject to more punishment. At the same time, I wish people were more aware of the people who resisted—the White Rose group, for example, or the Kreisau Circle. There were many tales of heroism and decency, and we need them in these frightening times. In later years I published several books which examine these themes. *Survival in the Shadows* (2002) by Barbara Lovenheim, an American writer and journalist, describes people who housed Jews in Hitler's Berlin and moved them from one safe house to another. *Hitler's Loss* by Tom Ambrose (2001) catalogues the enormous gains in science and art Britain and the United States made through European exiles who fled Nazi Germany. Perhaps the best of these books is *Legacy* (2007), a novel by Iván Sándor based on the deportation of Jews from Hungary. It describes how Carl Lutz, a Swiss diplomat, managed to save over 62,000 Jews from the death camps. Yad Vashem, the official Israeli Holocaust memorial, declared Lutz Righteous Among the Nations alongside other rescuers and resisters like the more famous Oskar Schindler. I wish Carl Lutz were better known and more people would read Sándor's book.

9

The Publisher's Apprentice

I became a publisher more by accident than design. I was seventeen and a half when I left Kings School in 1944, and naturally my parents asked me what I wanted to do. They had no ambitions for me to get a degree—neither of them had gone into further education—so I needed a job. There was nothing that really appealed, but I had an idea that I wanted to be a journalist. I'd read *The Street of Adventure*, Philip Gibbs's bestselling novel of 1919, which made Fleet Street seem fantastically glamorous. I managed to persuade my father to let me do a Pitman's shorthand and typing course for a year in preparation for what I imagined would be a dazzling career in journalism. The senior typing instructor was a fierce eccentric who scolded me for having a touch like an elephant. But learning to type proved extremely useful—perhaps the most useful thing I ever learnt. My shorthand was pretty useless though—if I managed to write anything down I couldn't read it back.

Journalism turned out to be a childish fantasy. I'd had no idea how tough the industry was and how hard it would be to get a job. After I'd finished at Pitman's I half-heartedly tried to get work on a local paper as a cub reporter. It was nigh on impossible though—Fleet Street was overstaffed as so many experienced people were coming back from the army. I was pretty hopeless at getting work. Beginning to despair, my family persuaded me that publishing was a back door into journalism. So began the first of a number of short-lived experiences in the publishing industry.

I was a bit vague about what a publisher did back then, but my father cajoled his brother-in-law, my Uncle Rudi, into using his contacts in the book trade to get me something relevant. He thought he'd never be rid of me otherwise. Rudi persuaded Stanley Unwin to grant me an interview with his manager at The Bodley Head who took me on very cheaply as a favour, rightly assuming that I'd be fairly useless. I suppose Unwin thought he had nothing to lose by taking me on and might have hoped he would get a few more orders from Zwemmer's, the large bookshop that Rudi managed in Charing Cross Road. The job was as office boy, a general dogsbody, and the wage was thirty shillings a week—even then a paltry sum.

Stanley Unwin—not to be confused with the comedian and inventor of Unwinese gobbledygook who shared the same name—was a distinguished publisher who had founded Allen & Unwin in 1914. The publisher of books by Bertrand Russell, Mahatma Gandhi and others, Unwin was also responsible for commissioning Tolkien's *The Hobbit* and *The Lord of the Rings*, both recommended via reader's reports by his discerning young son.

The jobs I did for 'Stanley' were menial. I had to paste press reviews into a scrap book, duplicate memos and make coffee for the staff, a task I performed so badly they soon volunteered to make their own. In the afternoons I was supposed to sort the mail in a more secluded area, but there wasn't much to do, so I hid and read a few of the firm's more interesting books. I learnt very little, but, although bored much of the time, I did get a taste for publishing and wrote around for another job.

Sometimes I learnt more from the bad publishers than the good ones—their mistakes were instructive. As it happens, my next job was with one of the worst publishers I ever encountered, so I learnt a great deal. The Alliance Press was run by a rather nutty egomaniac journalist called Philip Paneth who had married into a lot of money. He was a terrible hack. His father-in-law had set him up in business and was willing to pour in cash to try to create a respectable, legitimate publishing house. Paneth wasn't having any of it—he just wanted to publish his own crappy books of cheap journalism, so it became more of a vanity press with him as the sole client. His father-in-law brought in plenty of respectable, experienced people to help, but Paneth just ignored their advice, convinced that his own rubbish was great publishing.

By a stroke of luck one of the people appointed to help was Rudolf Ullstein, the acclaimed German publisher. Ullstein had been interned on arrival in England, but various publishers, Stanley Unwin included, campaigned for his release. Ullstein Verlag, his family business and one of the biggest publishers in Germany, had been forcibly taken over by the Nazis whom he detested. At Alliance Press Ullstein was production manager and was meant to be helping professionalise the business and turn it into a proper concern. I was employed as Ullstein's assistant, and since he had little to do—because Paneth wasn't taking the business seriously—he gave me a course in book production. I was very lucky, because at Ullstein Verlag he had been in charge of printing and really knew his stuff.

I got on very well with Ullstein who was a lovely old-world German-Jewish gentleman. He was in his early seventies by then, and I felt very sorry for him. Ullstein Verlag had been started by his father in 1877, and, since 1899 when their father died, Rudolf had been running it with his four brothers. It was an enormous company mainly publishing magazines. The Nazis took it over in 1934, forced out anyone they regarded as non-Aryan and by 1937 had renamed it Deutscher Verlag. Rudolf fled to England and, once he'd been freed from internment, ended up engaged in fairly lowly publishing jobs. He had a strong German accent but spoke English fluently—just as well as my German was pretty rusty by then. He could have done a great job at Alliance but didn't get the chance and left after a few months—so I went, too.

When Ullstein returned to Berlin in 1949 he planned to retire. His brothers were all dead by then, but he fought for full restitution. I was glad to hear that after three years of legal wrangling the company was restored to him with some ceremony. Having not expected to survive long enough to see that day, Ullstein wept. He was old and quite unwell but managed to run the company until 1960 when it was sold on to various global publishing concerns.

The knowledge and experience Ullstein gave me were invaluable and his name still had a certain cachet in the business—which was fortunate as my father was appalled that I'd fled from yet another job. Ullstein's teachings also meant that when I started my own company, at a time when it would have been very difficult to afford outside freelance help, I knew just enough to do the production myself for the first couple of years.

My next job was with C. & J. Temple, a new firm where the staff were pleasant but fairly amateur. They had a bit of money behind them but lasted only until 1952 when they were liquidated. During the war many classics had gone out of print as paper had been in such short supply. Shops desperately needed stock, so these set-ups did work temporarily—anyone could make a bit of money publishing old classics in those days. The production manager and art director at C. & J. Temple was a Hungarian author and prolific illustrator called Val Biro who counted Arthur 'Raggybag' Wragg as a major influence. Biro later went on to work for John Lehmann, but while he was at C. & J. Temple he asked Wragg to illustrate many of their classics, such as *Moll Flanders* and the works of Elizabeth Gaskell.

While I was with C. & J. Temple I also did some sales-rep work for Sydney Fowler Wright, a prolific old author who had written crime mysteries, science fiction and screenplays. He was a conservative and anti-modernist. While he warned of the dangers of Nazism and eugenics, he was also profoundly sceptical of other innovations, such as birth control and the motor car. Sydney was a bit of a rogue, too—a wholesaler who never paid anyone properly. I was to meet many more of these.

Another short-lived appointment was with poet and translator John Rodker who ran Pushkin Press and Imago. I found him very unpleasant. Like me the son of Jewish immigrants, Rodker had worked in Paris on the second edition of Joyce's *Ulysses* in the 1920s. He set up Imago in 1938 and worked with Anna Freud to produce a complete edition of her father Sigmund's works.

Freud had just arrived in London, and the original German edition of his work had been destroyed by the Nazis. Rodker also published Gertrude Stein and Blaise Cendrars, both of whom I published myself later. Though I thought Cendrars a very funny writer I didn't get a chance to look at his books at the time—I was too busy packing them. Most of my work was dispatching Rodker's expensive German editions of Freud all over the world.

Rodker was actually a very good publisher, but I really didn't like him. He was terribly pedantic and carefully taught me to pack and do slipknots as this was to be my main task. I wanted to learn to do editorial work and hated such menial jobs. When Rodker went off on a foreign trip I knew I'd had enough, but his secretary persuaded me to stay until his return. Some people might have just downed tools and left, but I decided to do the decent thing. As sole packer I had to keep a post book accounting for everything. My figures at best aren't very good though, and I have always loathed bureaucracy. It involved pre-decimal calculations, too, so was quite tricky. When Rodker returned he found the post book didn't tally and insinuated that I'd pocketed some money—about thirty shillings. It was simply an error—I'd forgotten to write things down or bungled the addition. I should have stood my ground because I was innocent, if a bit lackadaisical, and he was terribly insulting. It was the end of that job, but this was no disappointment as I'd been planning to leave anyway.

10

A Rajah in Beggar's Rags

It must sound as if I had plenty of work after I left school, but all these lowly jobs were very short-lived. I was mostly unemployed, so lounged around local libraries reading voraciously. My mother, who was all for keeping up appearances, made me leave home every morning at the same time to fool the neighbours into believing I still had a job.

One other job I did get was with Tambimuttu. Known to most people as Tambi, Meary James Thurairajah Tambimuttu came to London from Sri Lanka (then Ceylon) in 1938 and published his *Poetry London* magazine from early 1939. He was just twenty-two, a graduate of Colombo University, and had already published three volumes of his own poetry. He was confident, charismatic and handsome but could be childishly temperamental and was capable of flying into rages. Having established the magazine, in 1943 Tambi managed to persuade Nicholson & Watson to back Editions Poetry London, a new book publishing venture, even though it was predicted to make a loss. He told them his books would 'add lustre' to their reputation. They sacked him for bad behaviour in 1949, and he returned home to Ceylon. In the 1960s he spent time in the United States enjoying the decadent countercultural scene before returning to London in 1972 to start publishing again. In 1983 Tambi, possibly after some of over-enthusiastic boozing, fell down stairs at the October Gallery where he'd taken up rent-free residence, and died not long after from a heart attack.

There are many legends about Tambimuttu, and sometimes it's difficult to disentangle fact from fiction. T. S. Eliot admired him, as did George Orwell. He was obviously clever at spotting literary potential and was a fearless editor and a successful hustler when it came to getting financial backing. Personally I thought him dreadfully unscrupulous and unsavoury. Anaïs Nin, a writer I later published myself, writes of meeting Tambimuttu. In a journal entry for summer 1956 she mentions a sadly typical encounter: 'Unlike most Hindu poets he likes Western drinks too much, and so his white costume is soiled and his dark-blue jacket stained.' In his book *London Calling: A Countercultural History of London Since 1945,* author and cultural historian Barry Miles, whose book on the Beatles' spoken word record label, *The Zapple Diaries*, we published in 2015, recalls that Tambimuttu 'wore the same clothes until his staff could no longer stand the smell and would insist on him taking a bath', a duty his secretary was forced to undertake. She even had to scrub his back.

For a while Tambi lodged with the Shaw-Lawrences, some dotty friends of mine. I was told that old man Lawrie was a cousin of Lawrence of Arabia, though others said this was nonsense. I found Lawrie a very pleasant man and a brave one, too. Apparently he was a fighter pilot in the First World War. Attacked by the Germans with machine guns, all he had to defend himself was a revolver. During the Second World War his extremely pretty wife Paula became distraught having discovered Lawrie up to mischief with their maid. It sent their marriage haywire. Paula was an eccentric and kind-hearted character who loved hosting and attending parties. They had known Tambimuttu for a long time and rented a room to him in their flat above Kensington High Street. He, in turn, regarded them as his English family. One day Paula Shaw-Lawrence had a few friends round for a boozy evening with her daughter Bettina, a talented painter. Miscalculating the extent of their thirst, they ran out of drink. A moment of inspiration hit them: they knew that Tambi always kept a bottle of cider stashed under his bed. The cry went up to 'fetch the silver goblets', which they filled to the brim, knocking back the contents which turned out to be rather flat and nasty. It was only afterwards they discovered that Tambimuttu would relieve himself into the bottle at night when he was too drunk to make it to the lavatory.

In the late 1940s there was a thirst for books, as so many had gone out of print during the war. The scarcity of paper also meant that little new work had been published. It was said that you could sell almost anything, and I ended up having to prove it. I had gone to Tambi hoping for editorial work. Instead he asked me to try to sell his books in the suburbs. It was an almost impossible task, but I did manage to gain a few orders, something no one had managed before. Tambi was delighted, but, as with Fowler Wright, not so delighted that he actually paid me, nor anyone else if he could help it. At the time it was awful. I had no money to live on or even to pay bus fares, so left Tambi's employ, sold some of his books and pocketed the cash in lieu of commission. I wish I'd kept them now as they're worth a small fortune. It was my first encounter with the books of writers he published, authors of the calibre of Elizabeth Smart, David Gascoyne, Dylan Thomas, Kathleen Raine, Lawrence Durrell and many others, some of whom I later got to know or published myself. He was also the first to introduce to Britain the writing of Henry Miller, Vladimir Nabokov and Anaïs Nin. But as far as I'm concerned he was a dishonest drunk who would use his female admirers disgracefully and take all their money. Tambi spent his nights carousing on epic pub crawls around Fitzrovia—or Soho if he could stagger that far. To say that he was an important literary figure is, in my view, to give him too much credit. He was fortunate to be the right person, in the right place at the right time to give a chance to a lot of under-appreciated writers. He had many admirers, though, and, despite my personal misgivings, I later published a collection of tributes to him with samples of his own work in a limited edition book called *Tambimuttu: Bridge Between Two Worlds* (1989) for which Kathleen Raine acted as consultant editor.

Some will think me harsh but I really thought Tambimuttu a charlatan. In her autobiography Kathleen Raine describes him as 'a rajah in beggar's rags' and 'a most beautiful human being' for whom 'poetry was the end to which mere wealth, worldly position or power were at best a means'. She says of his publisher's eye that he somehow 'among all the dross ... picked out the gold of pure imagination'—including of course her own work. She admits of his bohemianism that it was 'extreme, and alarming in excesses to English eyes unused to so truly Oriental a contempt for even minimal securities'. Clearly she revered him, but perhaps her generous view of Tambi would have been different had he treated her to the performance he gave one American heiress, a potential financial backer. As told to me by the horrified public relations man who was present at the time, this grand lady (who had already fished out her chequebook and was prepared to give him a substantial amount of money) returned to her drawing-room from an urgent phone call to find that Tambimuttu, the 'avatar of dancing Shiva'—as Kathleen Raine called him—having drained a bottle of whisky, had decided to expose himself to her. 'I thought you might like to see my little man!' said Tambi. He was wrong about that. The chequebook was smartly put away and the butler summoned to escort him from the mansion.

A few years after my encounters as a sales rep I met Tambi again on a trip to New York. At that time he had plenty of financial backing for *Poetry London-New York*, his latest magazine venture, and was relatively well-off, his office run by enthusiastic volunteers. We all drank at the White Horse Tavern in Greenwich Village, one of Dylan Thomas's favourite pubs, and this was my first introduction to New York literary bohemians. We had round after round of drinks and all put down ten-dollar bills. I was just starting out and still terribly poor, whereas Tambi was flush with cash, so I was furious when he blithely scooped up all the change and pocketed it for himself.

After Tambi and all the other early jobs in publishing, my last in that line was one my father's secretary got me. However, working in the magazine advertising department at Hutchinson was something I hated, so I was almost glad when fate intervened. In May 1946 my father and I had became naturalised British citizens, swearing an oath of allegiance to 'His Majesty King George the Sixth, His Heirs and Successors'. As a reward I got called up for National Service.

11

The Reluctant Plonk

I arrived to enrol at RAF Padgate on 10 December 1946. With my rickety legs and other problems the RAF had seemed the safest bet. I never flew a plane—it was just a training camp outside Warrington in Cheshire. I probably had to march about a bit or something—I really can't recall—but I never achieved anything higher than AC2, the lowest rank of Aircraftman Second Class, referred to in RAF slang as a 'plonk'. It wasn't the worst experience of my life but was very far from the best. I didn't like sleeping in a dormitory and the meals were horrible, but I knew I'd have to put up with it. At least I had a two-ounce weekly sweet ration to spend in the NAAFI canteen, and I did meet a few nice people there. One of them had worked in publishing in the Australian office of Collins, but I lost track of people after I left. Someone once told me that many famous people passed through RAF Padgate in those days, including Bob Monkhouse and Bruce Forsyth—though of course to be honest I wouldn't have known them from Adam at the time.

Military discipline didn't come naturally to me. At one point I was caught on leave in uniform without my cap on. I was rude to the officer who spotted me who promptly put me on a charge. I really was totally ill-suited to military life and eventually became quite ill. My neurosis and anxiety had given me something tantamount to a stomach ulcer. The place was very damp, too—it was pretty much built on a swamp—and it was a particularly cold winter. As a result I got severe sinusitis, though my experiments in pipe-smoking can't have helped much. The military doctor warned me that my sinus trouble could turn into meningitis, but foolishly that night I kept an appointment I'd made—an assignation at the nearby rubbish dump. It was freezing cold and very unromantic, but there was little alternative for conscripts and their girlfriends. My health deteriorated, and I was invalided out in July 1947. I wasn't much good to them anyway. The war was long over, so it had all seemed a little pointless.

My mistake after Padgate was to return home to my parents. I should have stayed away but had almost no money. It would have been impossible to live elsewhere unless I'd managed to get a decent job. I had enjoyed working at C. & J. Temple—a job I'd managed to obtain myself—and would have liked to have gone back but couldn't. The turnover of jobs I had was so quick it was bound to be off-putting to potential employers, so my father was furious when I turned down a genuine offer from Hodder & Stoughton. It was in their advertising department, and after the experience at Hutchinson I thought I'd be bored stiff. I was silly to have told him, as it inevitably resulted in a prolonged bout of shouting at me. Until I could find a way out, I reluctantly agreed to work for my father who had started a business with his brother-in-law, my Uncle Rudi.

When my father arrived in England as Arthur Offenstadt he was pretty well stuck for a job. He was clearly no great business impresario as the fiasco at the leather factory in Nuremberg had shown, but my grandfather Jacob Friedmann had managed to get him office space at Falk Stadelmann in London. There Arthur worked as an import agent for German and Japanese goods—a fairly dicey occupation when you consider the international politics at the time. When war broke out, importing from the Axis powers was finished and he lost his income. He was lucky my mother's family had some money to cushion the impact. He then picked up with other agencies selling novelty and fancy goods, most of it junk.

After the war, when paper became more available, Arthur and Rudi set up the publishing firm they called Vision Press. It was all Uncle Rudi's idea—he had an extraordinary knowledge of literature and as manager at Zwemmer's Bookshop knew there was demand for certain titles. There was no John Webster material in print, so *The Duchess of Malfi* and two other plays were their first publications. With what I'd learnt from Rudolf Ullstein I had enough experience to help out and was co-opted to do a little freelance book production. The books I designed for them were, admittedly, grotty-looking, as I didn't have the skills I acquired later. After a while their production demands got too sophisticated—compiling plate sections and so on was way beyond me. Besides, I knew I had to get out from under my father's shadow and strike out on my own.

12

Peter Nevill

Although my father and I had become naturalised British subjects in 1946, we didn't officially relinquish our Offenstadt surname until May 1948. When I started my first publishing venture that year, I was able to do so under my new name. I first ran a business in partnership with Neville Armstrong (1914–2008). Born in Sri Lanka, Neville was an enthusiastic individual who had trained as an actor before joining the army and serving mostly in India. After demob he was briefly a theatre impresario, then worked in music magazines before starting a long career in book publishing. After all my work experiences I knew there was no future in slogging away for someone else but was aware that, at least to begin with, I'd need a business partner. Neville was one of several who answered an advertisement I placed in the *Daily Telegraph* for someone with capital to join me in a new publishing venture. After meeting in a Regent Street café, we teamed up and named our new venture Peter Nevill.

Because paper was strictly rationed, I'd had the foresight to chat up a girl at the Board of Trade while still in RAF uniform. She had taken pity on me and allotted me a quota of six tons—enough to publish twelve books. So with that and £20 demob pay (worth about £700 today) Neville and I set up shop. As well as his own useful experience, Neville brought with him his own valuable paper quota. At just twenty-one I was probably the youngest publisher in Britain.

Neville and I rented a tiny first-floor office on the Old Brompton Road in South Kensington which provided a couple of rooms. Following Uncle Rudi's advice, our first publication was a book by the essayist William Hazlitt, then as now sadly unfashionable. We also published a book of the *Poems of John Keats* edited by John Middleton Murry with illustrations we commissioned from Michael Ayrton, some of which I still have. Despite being a beautifully produced book, sales were disappointing, and Neville decided to treat Rudi's advice with some scepticism. In his memoir *Catching Up with the Future* he describes Rudi—whom he liked to call 'Uncle Trudi' behind his back—as 'a large man with a feather duster' which he used to flick dust from what he called his 'lovely books'. Rudi's sexuality was complicated, but unlike Neville I never thought he was gay or, as Neville put it, 'queer', though it had crossed my mind.

It was Neville's idea to publish an edition of the Restoration dramatist Sir John Vanbrugh's comedy *The Relapse or Virtue in Danger* with photographs of the cast from a popular production he had just seen. The photos included a snap of an actress displaying an ample cleavage which no doubt helped to make the book a modest hit. Neville's next idea was that we sign up Algernon Blackwood. Steeped in occultism and mysteries, Blackwood, though he looked very conventional and was by that time eighty, still had an enormous following owing to his popular radio shows and ghost stories. In 1949 he agreed to write for us *Tales of the Uncanny and Supernatural* which became a book-club choice and our first bestseller. In 1950 we also republished his 1923 memoir *Episodes Before Thirty* for which he was very grateful. It was not to last. Blackwood, our elderly star author, died the following year.

Another of our early successes was *Intimacy*, a translated collection of Jean-Paul Sartre's short stories known in France as *Le Mur*. These 1939 stories were only mildly erotic but still caused us problems. The first three printers we approached refused point-blank to take on the book on the grounds that it was 'obscene'—a fourth would only do it after a solicitor's letter absolved them of all responsibility. It was ridiculous really, but when we published the book in 1949, eleven years before Penguin won the *Lady Chatterley's Lover* obscenity trial, the censorship laws were harsh and often vigorously enforced. A sample of the text gives a flavour of the work. At one point Sartre refers to a character as 'feeling herself alert next to this soft, captive flesh', while of another he writes, 'if he wanted someone educated all he had to do was marry Jeanne Beder, she's got breasts like hunting horns but she knows five languages'. Comic and tame enough by today's standards, though disconcertingly surreal, it would have seemed strikingly informal at the time and somewhat titillating. Once in print we had no legal problems, and the book went through six impressions within three years. Neville took the rights to *Intimacy* with him when he formed his own solo company and continued to sell huge amounts throughout the 1950s and 1960s. When I published a selection of Sartre's *Essays in Aesthetics* at Peter Owen Ltd in 1964 it proved not to have quite the same commercial allure.

Probably at Rudi's suggestion we also published *The Earth Is Our Heritage* (1950) by the German author Ernst Wiechert. A prominent humanist and anti-Nazi, Wiechert had been arrested and interned in Buchenwald concentration camp after condemning the arrest of the anti-Nazi cleric Martin Niemöller. He fortunately survived, but sadly we couldn't replicate the popularity his work had gained in Germany. We also published Edgar Mittelholzer, an interesting Guyanese writer who was one of the first professional English-speaking novelists to emerge from the Caribbean. Unfortunately sales were pretty poor for anything other than the Sartre and Blackwood books.

Although I was probably being stupidly pretentious I began to feel uncomfortable about the way the list was going. I might not turn my nose up at many of the books now, but at the time I felt we weren't aiming high enough and were taking unnecessary risks. Things really fell apart in 1951 after Neville bought a best-selling novel from the United States called *A Diary of Love* by Maude Hutchins. It was a fairly literary book but, as with all her novels, was basically about sex. Printing costs were cheaper in Holland, and while we were awaiting notice of delivery in Harwich we discovered that Her Majesty's Customs and Excise had impounded the entire shipment as they considered the book obscene. We ended up in court arguing for the book's literary merits with witnesses including John Middleton Murry and the translator and author Margaret Crosland. Customs were concerned about references in the book to what they considered 'phallic objects', so Middleton Murry countered that they 'might as well claim that a cucumber is obscene'. Alas, the court was unpersuaded and the magistrate ordered the entire stock destroyed. Maude Hutchins was terribly upset, Neville was furious, and I got cold feet about the partnership.

By that time we had attracted the former actor Malcolm Kirk as a third partner. We often couldn't afford staff, so all three of us, as co-directors, did nearly everything—bookkeeping, typing, packing and delivery. Malcolm had invested a significant and welcome dose of extra cash into the partnership, but after the Maude Hutchins debacle he bought us out and decided to carry on the business on his own. Neville described Malcolm as a bore and a failed writer—I thought him actually a perfectly nice man but slightly mundane. The books he wanted to publish were unremittingly dreary. Neville had an interest in the burgeoning occult scene and was more of a populist than me. I realised that I'd have to set up on my own if I was to publish what I wanted and avoid too much compromise. Essentially all three of us at Peter Nevill had wanted different things, and dissolving the partnership in 1951 left Neville free to set up Neville Spearman and collaborate with John Calder as Spearman & Calder, while I went off to set up my own eponymous publishing house.

For a while, I ran Peter Owen Ltd from independent offices close to those of Peter Nevill at 50 Old Brompton Road. Perhaps, inevitably, under Malcolm's sole directorship the firm Peter Nevill went bankrupt. He was ordered to quit his offices in 1954 and we lost track of him. On his own, Neville Armstrong developed an eclectic and idiosyncratic list with a heavy sprinkling of books about Nostradamus, vampires and occultism. Erotic and sometimes sleazy fiction remained popular, despite strong censorship, so he once teamed up with a mail-order vendor and distributor of that genre and published titles such as *My Sister, My Bride* and *Stranger on Lesbos*. At the same time he published literary work by Simone de Beauvoir, Henry Miller and Anaïs Nin but was fairly peeved to miss out on Nin's diaries which I ended up publishing myself. Neville and I had got on fairly well to begin with—we once holidayed together on the Côte d'Azur—but I found him somewhat erratic and was only too glad to go solo.

13

In For a Penny

When I started Peter Owen Ltd in 1951, people in the trade told me I would need between £10,000 and £50,000 to start a company, depending on the sort of list I wanted to publish. I was aiming at the literary rather than the commercial end of the market and would have been better off with the higher figure. Instead, combining the sum from the sale of my share of Peter Nevill and a small overdraft guaranteed by my mother, I had about £1,000 all told (worth about £30,000 today)—ten times less than the lowest figure I had been advised I would need. Not surprisingly, my mother's bank was so chary of the enterprise they demanded some of her share certificates as security. I was prepared to work extremely hard and did so, initially on my own, but I wouldn't have got very far in those early years without the help and advice of family and friends. Chief among them was Uncle Rudi, who had an extensive knowledge of contemporary literature as well as psychology and philosophy and some useful contacts in publishing and bookselling, mainly through his work as Zwemmer's senior manager. One of the most important of his contacts for me was the American publisher James Laughlin who became a supportive friend.

James's family had made a fortune in a steel company his grandfather had founded. One of his school teachers was a translator who gave him introductions to Ezra Pound and Gertrude Stein because he was interested in literature. When they met in Italy, Pound told James he was a rubbish poet and should do something more useful. So, using the family cash, he founded New Directions in 1936. Initially a hobby business, it became one of the very best publishing firms in the States. James's first publications were anthologies that included work by Henry Miller, e e cummings, Wallace Stevens and other modernists. Luckily there was sufficient family money to keep New Directions going, even though it didn't turn a profit for a decade or so.

Thanks to James, I launched Peter Owen Ltd in 1951 with Julien Gracq's *A Dark Stranger* as my first publication. Gracq, a significant author in France, was close to the surrealist movement and André Breton in particular. When he refused the Prix Goncourt it did wonders for his sales in France but, sadly, not over here. James tipped me off that *A Dark Stranger* had been printed but not published and was available for sixpence a copy from the liquidator. I had it bound with my imprint on the spine and the book gained a few good reviews despite the fact it had been badly proofread and was liberally sprinkled with errors.

James also influenced me in the importance he placed on design. Just as he had hired Alvin Lustig to establish a style for New Directions, I was lucky enough to employ Keith Cunningham for Peter Owen Publishers. We had very little money but, from 1963 onwards, Keith managed to produce some striking and elegant graphic designs for us, often using just two colours, and he contributed greatly to our success.

Another legacy of James Laughlin's influence was my becoming Ezra Pound's British publisher, starting with his translation of the *Confucian Analects* (1951), his monumental *Guide to Kulchur* (1952) and several more books throughout the 1950s and 1960s. Pound was undoubtedly a major international literary figure who supported and encouraged many young modernists in the first three decades of the twentieth century. He had ended up imprisoned, and naturally James involved me in his tenacious campaign to secure Pound's freedom after the war.

Pound had moved to Italy in 1924 and by the 1930s had embraced fascism. He started writing antisemitic tracts for Italian newspapers in 1939 and publicised his views in hundreds of letters and articles blaming 'the Jews' and an international banking conspiracy for the outbreak of both world wars. It was his rambling talks on Italian radio that sealed his fate though—the Americans regarded them as treasonous. He was apprehended at the end of the war, and, after cracking up during a gruelling, debasing confinement in an American army base near Pisa, he was transferred to St Elizabeth's, a psychiatric hospital in Washington, to await trial. His lawyer viewed incarceration on the grounds of insanity as a better deal than life imprisonment for treason, the other option Pound was facing.

I received a few letters from Pound. They weren't completely nuts. They were in his idiosyncratic spelling, but he wasn't mad—certainly no madder than most writers I know. They detained him at St Elizabeth's to avoid an embarrassing show trial. His radio broadcasts had been ridiculous, a result of his egomania and messianic fervour rather than anything genuinely treacherous. There are certain things you shouldn't do, especially in wartime, but I don't think his talks would have convinced anyone. They were less like the broadcasts of Lord Haw-Haw and more like those P. G. Wodehouse made to the people of Berlin—foolish rather than truly malevolent, I thought. Anyway, James galvanised international support from T. S. Eliot (who had had his own poetic dalliance with antisemitism early in his career), W. H. Auden, Kathleen Raine and others. Eventually Ernest Hemingway, despite suspecting that Pound would never abjure his beliefs, joined the campaign. Encouraged by James, I joined an early wave of supporters and wrote a letter that was published in *Time & Tide* in 1952—not that it did much good. Reading it all these years later it doesn't sound much like me. I suspect Rudi or James helped me to write it. In the letter I pointed out that Pound, 'whose eccentricity can be excused because of his genius, remains incarcerated whilst dubious Nazi leaders and men like Krupp whose guilt was real are released'. I'm not sure now that genius excuses antisemitism, but the point about Alfred Krupp and others remains true.

Krupp was an industrialist who had collaborated with the SS during the war using slave workers from concentration camps, including children, in many of his factories. He was tried at Nuremberg in 1948 and found guilty of crimes against humanity. His sentence was twelve years' imprisonment, but, at the behest of the American High Commissioner for Germany, he was released after less than three and all his forfeited property was returned to him. Other prominent industrialists were released at the same time. It was pure expedience—the Americans claimed they needed industrial expertise to rebuild the German economy and strengthen it against Russia during the Cold War. So Krupp served less than three years while Pound was incarcerated for over twelve. He had already been confined for seven years when I wrote my letter. It was manifestly unjust, and this must have been in my mind when I wrote it.

Pound's unrepentant association with neo-fascists undoubtedly delayed his release. However, after a legal challenge, the hospital psychiatrists affirmed that as he was, in their view, incurably insane, his confinement served no therapeutic purpose. He was released in 1958 to a life of slow but relentless decline. It took him until the end of his life, a few years before his death in 1972, to recognise his mistaken prejudices and regret the damage they had done. He said that he had been 'not a lunatic but a moron'. Which is fair enough.

14

Wendy

While working hard establishing Peter Owen Publishers I hadn't been totally neglecting my social life. I was twenty-five when I met my future wife at an English Speaking Union snowball dance. Still going strong today, the Union was established as a charity to encourage cultural exchange. It was also renowned as a place one could pick up someone fairly classy—or be picked up by one.

The idea of a snowball dance is simple, which is just as well. Having had rickets and being a perennial sufferer from poor coordination, dancing is not my forte. A large outer ring of people watches a few dancers in the middle. When the band shouts 'Snowball!' the central dancers grab a partner from the outer ring and the process repeats until everyone is dancing. It was Wendy who made the first move. She was quite proud that she picked me up rather than the other way round. A few days later I invited her for tea, then we went on a date in Soho. In a contemporary letter, written to a friend in November 1952, Wendy described how we explored 'the dives in Soho'—the ones Fenella had told me about years earlier. Wendy wrote that they were 'colourful, to put it mildly!' adding that we met 'various arty characters, poets, writers, painters, etc.' She even describes an encounter with a spiritualist whose clairvoyance impressed her at the time.

Wendy had spent a few terms in New York as an art student—the family were briefly living on Long Island—but her father had insisted that she trained as a nurse in London instead. He had thought initially that Wendy was studying something practical and vocational at the Arts Students League—graphic design rather than fine art—and came from the sort of family that didn't mind paying for expensive private education for boys but begrudged forking out for the girls. Wendy's sister Aileen had wanted to train as a doctor, but their father refused to underwrite the expense and made her go into nursing, too. By the time we met, Wendy was training as a nurse at Putney Hospital and had to request all-night passes to go on dates. Her parents had paid her membership of the English Speaking Union so that she could meet what they thought would be 'nice, genteel people'. It just happened that I was on the rebound from a rather intense love affair, and so we met at just the right time. Wendy was pretty, talented, very funny and vivacious. She enjoyed the arts—particularly fine art, opera and classical music—and came from a well-off family with some French Huguenot ancestry on her English-born father's side. We got on well and eventually became engaged.

Before I met her, I had somewhat sadistically kept Grandma Betty informed of the few liaisons I had with non-Jewish girlfriends. She was gratifyingly horrified, and my father told me it would kill her if I announced my engagement to Wendy. He was sadly mistaken. Far from keeling over, Betty quietly accepted it, knowing I was no longer in any way malleable. To please my family I had gone to a Jewish club for a while, but not for long—it just wasn't my scene. I did make one Jewish friend in Pearl, who lived near me. She, too, was in revolt against parental narrow-mindedness, so we had got on very well and we kept in touch for decades. Shocking Betty with some of the things Pearl said had been a pleasant bonus. Whatever Betty had in mind for me probably never existed in reality. I knew I could never please her and quickly gave up trying.

Wendy's background was even more complex than mine. Her father Henry Demoulins had been born in London to upper-class parents. They'd married at St George's in Hanover Square, so it must have been quite a match, but the supposedly ultra-respectable Henry often gave the wrong date of birth in an attempt to disguise the fact that he'd been born illegitimately the year before.

Wendy and Aileen's mother was Henry's second wife. After they divorced she took the girls to live in London but developed an alcohol problem and lost custody. The girls were returned to Henry and his third wife Becky at their home in Fawley, Hampshire where he was senior manager of a brand-new oil refinery. A chemist by training, he worked for Anglo-American Oil, the UK distributor for John D. Rockefeller's Standard Oil, which later became the Esso Petroleum Co., Ltd. There was a main office in Whitehall, but Henry, who was appointed a director of the company in 1947, lived in Fawley, near Southampton, until he retired to Jamaica. Henry and Becky ended up returning to Britain and moving to Budleigh Salterton in the early 1960s, so we saw a rather more of them them, unfortunately.

Having worked in the oil industry for over thirty-one years, Henry had amassed a considerable fortune and also inherited money from his stepfather, a distinguished lawyer. But Henry wasn't given to acts of generosity. When Wendy wrote to him telling him of our plans to marry, a letter came back making it clear, before any word of congratulation, that we shouldn't expect any money as there was none! He must have known that I was aware he was living in a mansion in Jamaica with servants—and you can't do that without wealth. It was insulting of him to assume I was after their money.

I can't really complain about the way Henry and Becky treated me. In the end they realised that my family weren't exactly East European barrow boys, but I do feel very strongly about the way they treated Wendy's elder sister Aileen. Henry, or Pops as he was known by his relatives, was very tight with his money and almost nothing got passed on to his descendants after he and his third wife died. Henry hadn't even bothered to attend his daughters' weddings or check out his potential sons-in-law, let alone offer to pay for the celebrations. He really was a crashing old bore too. If one asked him a question he would go into a long spiel, wittering on and meandering all over the place, and end up by saying 'Well, that's it in a nutshell!', by which time his audience had nodded off. He was also convinced he deserved an OBE for the creation of the oil refinery at Fawley, but his successor got the award instead. He would have been furious to know I had ended up with one myself.

Families are difficult, and the more I hear of them, the more disgusted I am. Henry made himself out to be a paragon of virtue, but, once his daughters were no longer children, he treated Wendy unsympathetically, and Aileen, who was more independent-spirited, appallingly. Their stepmother Becky, formerly a hospital matron in Australia, behaved no better. After a troubled teenage life, Aileen had married well into a respectable and moneyed Catholic family. But Henry was not only antisemitic, he and Becky were anti-Catholic, too. About a year after Wendy and I married, Becky wrote her a letter saying of their sons-in-law, 'a Catholic and a Jew—what a bitter pill to swallow!' It's hard to imagine anyone being stupid enough to write that kind of letter. It was grotesque. And hypocritical, too. I later found out that Becky had had an affair with a Jew when travelling alone on a liner from New York to Southampton.

Wendy and I married on 10 July 1953 at Kensington Register Office with my parents as witnesses. There are some quite good photographs. I had put out a press release saying someone famous might being getting married there—consequently a handful of press photographers had turned up. Afterwards we held a cheap reception at home, as Wendy's father wouldn't contribute anything towards the event. My father took us to lunch afterwards to celebrate at Csarda, a favourite Hungarian restaurant in Dean Street, Soho, which sadly no longer exists, then sent us off on a honeymoon in Château-Thierry in northern France.

Ours was a typical 1950s marriage. I was the breadwinner, and, prompted by my parents, I suggested Wendy give up her nursing training. By then I was making just about enough money to support us as long as we lived frugally. Wendy did all the cooking and housework, as well as assisting in the business by stuffing catalogues into envelopes, hosting dinner parties and organising book launches. In the early years Wendy did some design work and illustrations for me, including the original dust-jackets for Hermann Hesse's *Siddhartha* (1954) and *The Prodigy* (1957). She was always interested in literature and often came up with ideas for commissions or acted as a reader of manuscripts for me, recommending novelists she admired. Rather than her art, to my surprise it emerged later that her real talent was for writing, and she became a successful novelist.

15

Prince of Zwemmer's

I've already mentioned Uncle Rudi, my mother's younger brother, a brilliantly intelligent intellectual in a family of philistines, and his importance in helping my career. Unlike many members of my family, he and I got on well. Even though he was terribly spoilt and often completely nuts he was still a very nice man. I was always very fond of him.

Born in 1914, he was much younger than his sisters Gladys and Winnie. Sophie, their mother, adored her 'little prince', and he was coddled from the beginning, becoming her proxy husband after Jacob's death. A bout of German measles while Sophie was pregnant may have contributed to Rudi's many problems, and part of her protectiveness was based on guilt. Rudi spent his entire life living with his mother, but achieved some satisfaction in life through his extraordinary writings, his impressive publishing and editorial work at Vision Press and most of all as senior manager at Zwemmer's bookshop in Charing Cross Road.

I first met Rudi in 1931 when I was four years old and living in Nuremberg. Just seventeen, he had suffered a breakdown and was diagnosed as having schizophrenia. Uncle Bobby, Rudi's brother-in-law, had suggested that he explore a new therapy in Germany: insulin shock treatment. For weeks on end patients were given daily insulin injections until they went into a coma. After an hour or so they were brought back to consciousness with intravenous glucose. Some patients had convulsions, and eventually the treatment was abandoned by sceptical clinicians when alternatives became available. In Rudi's case it is clear that the family thought he had benefited. He bonded well with his German psychiatrist, too. Rudi eventually helped him to migrate to London.

After Rudi's insulin treatment he came to stay with us in Nuremberg for a while. His father had enrolled him as an apprentice in a factory there, but Rudi, who was going through an adolescent communist phase, took it upon himself to lecture his fellow workers on their rights and attempted to convert them to the revolutionary cause. His employers telegrammed his father in London, and Rudi was summoned home after just a week.

He was closer to me in age than the rest of my relatives, and, in a family where I was often lonely and seen as an encumbrance, he took an interest and brought some much needed cheer to the house. In 1933, dumped by my mother in London, I was glad to catch up with him again. He made me laugh—a boon for a lonely little boy in a strange country. All the same, it was clear there was still something wrong with him. He would behave strangely now and then and was subject to sudden fits of rage. Even as a child his closeness to his mother seemed odd to me—I could see it was far too intense.

Whereas my education was done on the cheap, Rudi had been sent to an expensive private day school in Finchley Road. A voracious reader, in the school holidays he had loved spending his pocket money at Zwemmer's Bookshop. All he ever wanted to do was to work there. After the fiasco in Germany, and having exhausted every other option, his father put in a word and got him a job there as an apprentice. Rudi proved so good at the job he was eventually promoted to manager and pretty much became the shop—an entertaining and hugely knowledgeable character who drew in authors and other intellectuals.

The bookshop had been founded by Dutch-born Anton Zwemmer who settled in London in 1914, having already worked in the book trade in the Netherlands. By 1922 he had gained a reputation for selling art books, and bought the shop at 78 Charing Cross Road that became an internationally famous cultural hub. He expanded the business again by adding an art gallery round the corner in Litchfield Street from where he sold modern artists whose work he imported from the European capitals. Eventually he purchased 76 Charing Cross Road, too—a premises that specialised in modern literature and psychology under Rudi's enthusiastic and erudite management. Exempted from military service on account poor health, Rudi continued to work there even during the war.

By contrast with today, Charing Cross Road had a seedy reputation in the 1930s. In 'Road of Books and Vices', an article in the *Independent* magazine, Stephen Spender recalls that it 'flowed south from Tottenham Court Road like some fertilising fog-yellow river swamp bearing its cargoes of highbrow culture and lowbrow sex. Here were the wonderful bookshops displaying in their windows recent publications and clasping in their innards second-hand classics.' He characterises some of the famous shops: 'Foyles for everything, Collet's with left-wing books sharp as sickles, Zwemmer's for wonders of modern art (and a very amusing, highly updated, opinionated shop assistant called Rudolph Friedmann).' He says a visit might even afford 'a glimpse of grandiose Mr Zwemmer himself in canary-coloured waistcoat, looking fresh from some deal in Paris with Picasso.' Rudi once bought a Picasso painting from Anton Zwemmer, but was forced to sell it back at cost, even though it had probably appreciated in value a hundredfold. Meanly, Zwemmer so nagged Rudi he finally gave in. I imagine it was even better than Rudi's rare Picasso print that I have on my wall—one Rudi also bought from Zwemmer but refused to sell back.

In those days Rudi was tall, strong and good-looking, though his confidence must have been challenged when he lost his hair, and by the port-wine-stain birthmarks on his body, especially where visible on his hands. He dressed in a neat, conventional way—I don't think I ever saw him out of a suit and tie. He was very conservative as an adult once he'd got over his youthful communist phase, though he retained a streak of intellectual libertarianism. Though at school I had been complimented as the only boy who spoke proper English, I got slightly sloppier with age and remember Rudi reprimanding me: 'Mind the way you talk. Remember—you're upper middle class!' It seems utterly ridiculous now, but I suppose in those days there was a meaningful distinction—at least for Rudi. He once gave my daughters a penny each. Antonia, the older one, thanked him politely while a dismayed Georgina, thinking of visiting a sweet shop, declared, 'You can't buy nuffink wiv a penny!' From then on, as far as Rudi was concerned, Antonia was an aristocrat while Georgie was a 'chocolate-eating peasant'. Perhaps Rudi and his eldest sister Gladys were competitively frugal. Antonia remembers years later planning to visit her Great-Aunt Gladys in Eastbourne where she'd retired. On hearing this, Winnie told her to make sure she paid for their lunch. 'When she opens her purse the moths fly out!'

I admired Rudi. He was a brilliant man but was damaged by the way his mother had simultaneously coddled and undermined him. He could be verbally unpleasant, too. I remember him saying of his sisters, 'Look at them! Those girls had everything—piano lessons, singing, dancing, deportment, elocution—but they're so dim!' Early on he had scared me with a fit of anger all the more frightening for its rare vehemence. He had a sense of superiority and was a cultural snob so didn't form relationships or close friendships easily, but he did have a strange attraction to older, slightly matronly women. He was clearly very touchy about it. Stupidly, my mother once made some teasing remark about 'Rudi's old women'. Infuriated, he swept the crockery off the dresser smashing the lot. I was about eight at the time and very shocked, so said nothing and carried on picking at my serving of warmed-up leftovers as innocuously as possible. Rudi suddenly knocked my plate to the floor as well, saying, 'One more little Jewish appetite gone!' He calmed down eventually and exited the room leaving us all stunned.

A writer quoted in Nigel Vaux Halliday's study *More Than a Bookshop: Zwemmer's and Art in the Twentieth Century* describes Rudi as 'elaborately impolite' and 'a rather sinister figure, tall wavy-haired, undulating, and with very red raw-looking hands'. In his book *Inside the Forties: Literary Memoirs, 1937–57*, Derek Stanford, Muriel Spark's early boyfriend and collaborator, described Rudi as 'a tall dandified figure in a blue striped suit' who was 'a culture snob of the deepest water'. He goes on to quote an admirer describing Rudi as 'meditating, handling the books carefully, lovingly, a man of books who hates the vandal, the goth, the destroyer of delicate book jackets'. Stanford also quotes a famous Rudi anecdote: a mother came and asked for a book on trains for her son. '"Books about trains?" intoned the princely Friedmann. "Books about psych-Ology, phil-Osophy, the-Ology; but books about trains for children, no, madam. Over the road to Foyles!"'

16

Oh, Rudi!

I had met Muriel Spark during my Peter Nevill years. Her excellent debut novel *The Comforters* (1957), a metafictional story of a writer going mad and hearing voices, includes the character Baron Willi Stock, loosely based on Rudi, complete with the 'ology' anecdote Stanford mentions in his book. Muriel describes the Baron as 'knowledgeable, loquacious and apparently sympathetic, popular but with few intimate friends'. She adds that he has 'a dark side to his character, private, nocturnal, interested in satanism and actively involved in criminality'. I saw no evidence that Rudi was a satanist, but he did have dark secrets and an embarrassing brush with the law.

During the post-war crackdown on street crime, Rudi was arrested in the West End for approaching a female officer who was posing as a prostitute. The end of the blackout made the extent of prostitution glaringly obvious, so the Labour government had initiated stern measures. Sophie sent me to the prison where Rudi had been remanded to hand over a small suitcase of books and other essentials. After a week or so he was fined in court and released. Sophie paid the fine and somehow managed to stifle any publicity. One of Rudi's notebooks shows the experience continued to haunt him. He expresses fear that, unless he can overcome his psycho-sexual Oedipal problems, he would 'return to prostitutes', something he had got used to doing for the thrill. Publicly he turned his anxieties into defiant pieces of writing.

Rudi's modest literary career included contributing some of his more outlandish essays to *Neurotica*, a magazine founded by Jay Landesman in the United States in 1948. The blurb to an anthology of all nine issues describes *Neurotica* as presenting 'some of the best and most original minds of the time—the minds that historians would later call the Beat Generation'. Uncle Rudi was no English Jack Kerouac though, and the blurb goes on to say that the magazine 'was much more than just the Bible of the Beats', and that it 'brought together an unholy alliance of existentialists, surrealists, radical sociologists, psychoanalysts, playwrights and musicians to create the first underground critique of American life.'

The inaugural issue of *Neurotica* features Rudi's surreal 'The End of Feeling' as its first item. Funny and dark by turns, it is permeated by Rudi's favourite themes—Oedipal longings and the schizoid personality. A husband chases his wife around their bed 'until the incestuous struggle of the dead mother's desire for life and reality within the body of her son rises up in the man's face so that he burns with the strength of pure guilt'. The second issue of 1948 contains his essay 'The Attack Upon Prostitution as an Attack Upon Culture'. An unconvincing libertarian defence of prostitution, the piece is preceded by an author biography, presumably written by Rudi, which describes him as 'a Conservative democrat' who seeks to draw attention to 'the puritanical repression of the libido' and 'the total withering away of the sources of feeling (creative affect—life) in a social democracy'. The essay itself describes the arrest of a man for soliciting a prostitute. 'I'm really quite harmless,' the man protests. 'I handed my genitals over to my headmaster before leaving school and I never asked for them back.' The officer says that his task is to enforce the oppressive 'rules and regulations of the Labour Party' which intend that 'the West End must be turned into a vacant suburban cemetery' because 'honest working-class girls' should not be tempted to 'earn money in a pleasurable way' through 'not working'! Still smarting from the subterfuge involved in his own arrest and prosecution, Rudi concludes that 'a city without prostitution is a city without culture ... the use of the police spy terror is a direct and most dangerous attack on the freedom of the individual.' Comically paranoiac, he concludes, 'If we look too intelligent and original we will be followed and in due course arrested.' In Rudi's third contribution to *Neurotica*, *Struwwelpeter*, the shocking children's story I had been read as a child in Nuremberg, is subjected to Freudian psychoanalysis as a fable of castration anxiety.

Aside from *Neurotica*, the main publisher of Rudi's work was *Horizon*, one of the great literary magazines of the time. Published from 1940 to 1949, its founding editor Cyril Connolly was keen on Rudi's work, as was his assistant Sonia Brownell who, I suspect, did most of the hard work. Sonia married George Orwell, whom Connolly had known at Eton, in October 1949 after a lightning three months' courtship. Orwell, who also contributed to *Horizon*, died in January 1950 a few months after the wedding. Rudi was quite smitten with Sonia in the 1950s. I got to know her a little in the 1960s by the time I was reasonably successful. She came to a few dinner parties Wendy and I hosted, and she struck me as a fairly tough woman who cared deeply about books and literature. Though she was perfectly friendly, Sonia could be snooty. She remembered Rudi—her circle was his kind of scene: glamorous and intellectual—but I made a terrible *faux pas* when I said to her, 'You've done an awfully good job publicizing George Orwell.' 'Well,' she replied coldly, 'George *was* a major writer.'

Horizon, which published some experimental work, though nothing as extreme as *Neurotica*, was financed by margarine heir, art collector and philanthropist Peter Watson, who also financed the Institute of Contemporary Arts. *Queer Saint*, a biography of Watson by Adrian Clark and Jeremy Dronfield, describes how Watson once whimsically signed himself 'Peter Pumpkin Pants' and had nicknames for his friends, too. Cecil Beaton, Lucian Freud and Cyril Connolly were Cellyboy, Lucio and Squiggles, for example. Stinking rich and madly keen on the arts, Watson showered his money all over the place—Tambimuttu was another grateful recipient. *Horizon* was a triumph though—a brilliant magazine. I once had a full set, over a hundred issues, but in the 1950s times were tough and I sold everything I could to keep going.

It was in the pages of *Horizon* that James Laughlin first spotted Rudi's work. James wrote to me while I was still at Peter Nevill and said he regarded Rudi as the most interesting writer to come out of England since the war. He admired Rudi's 1943 *Horizon* piece on Kierkegaard (in which Rudi identifies what he saw as Kierkegaard's 'schizoid' characteristics) and encouraged me to publish it as a small book. I brought out *Kierkegaard: The Analysis of the Psychological Personality* at Peter Nevill in 1949 and produced an edition for New Directions, too. Rudi never pushed his work, so this came about through James's interest—a remarkable piece of luck for us all.

17

The Men of Vision

Aside from making a living importing all sorts of inconsequential fancy goods of dubious quality, my father made money by setting up the publishing firm Vision Press with his brother-in-law Uncle Rudi. Father wasn't literary and had no knowledge of publishing—he was just interested in making money—but Rudi made sure that Vision had a very classy and imaginative literary list, even though he could only work at it part time owing to his job at Zwemmer's. Rudi was a brilliant editor and, with his bookseller's experience, was ahead of the curve in everything, pioneering translations of the psychoanalytical maverick Wilhelm Reich and the philosopher Martin Heidegger, for instance. Rudi could read German and worked closely with the translator to edit Heidegger, which was quite a specialist task. As an editor he was entirely self-taught and could have been a great one had he not been so timid. Of course Rudi's job at Zwemmer's helped Vision Press sales considerably. He was able to promote their books there, though old man Zwemmer eventually became suspicious of the huge orders Rudi was putting through.

The founding of Vision Press was announced in a November 1946 issue of *The Bookmart*. Rudi is quoted as saying the firm was to publish 'works of high intellectual merit'. The list eventually included a 1954 edition of Céline's *Journey to the End of the Night*. In 1948 he'd brought out *The Secret Life of Salvador Dalí* (which went into several more editions over the years) followed by *Dalí on Modern Art* in 1958. They also published Herbert Read, Stephen Spender and the pioneering psychologist Georg Groddeck who was becoming fashionable at the time. Groddeck, who also wrote psychological novels, was a younger contemporary of Freud and was credited with naming the Id. Lawrence Durrell had written a piece about Groddeck for *Horizon* in 1948, and Vision Press published Groddeck's *The Book of the It* and *Exploring the Unconscious* in 1950.

Rudi bought the Groddeck books from publisher C. W. Daniel (1871–1955), a vegetarian pacifist and philosophical anarchist who was into alternative medicine. Daniel had published Tolstoy and Kierkegaard and other radical thinkers but was prosecuted twice, first in 1916 for his own pamphlet exposing the horrors of war and again in 1918 for publishing Rose Allatini's novel *Despised and Rejected*. Daniel had published it for its pacifism and was mortified to be prosecuted for its gay themes which he claimed not to have noticed. One journalist described it as 'a thoroughly poisonous book, every copy of which ought to be put on the fire forthwith ... pestiferous filth ... literary fungus'. Of course most of Rudi's list, including Groddeck, has fallen out of fashion now. For all his adventurousness, he was slightly chary of some titles, too. He wouldn't touch Sartre's *Intimacy* which we published so successfully at Peter Nevill. He didn't have the confidence and thought the contents too sexually explicit. Now it's nothing!

Publishing must have been in my family's blood. I recently discovered I am related to a French publishing dynasty Éditions Offenstadt Frères, the Parisian publishing house founded in 1899 by four Jewish brothers. Their father had emigrated to France from Bavaria, where my family came from. They published a variety of popular weekly magazines including what were considered scandalously saucy stories illustrated with titillating drawings of scantily clad young women, often with a breast or two strategically exposed. The magazines were also bundled as albums, one of which, *Pantalons Blancs et Culottes Rouges*, is mentioned in James Joyce's *Ulysses*. Frequently censured and censored, the Offenstadt brothers were often victims of antisemitism, especially during the Nazi Occupation when they were stripped of ownership. I like to think that some of my own publications would have given the brothers' sauciest output a run for their money.

In the early days of my own company I travelled to the United States quite a lot, often to liaise with James Laughlin. There I picked up the rights to a few reference books that helped eke out our early lists. I was able to take small quantities, and, for a small finder's fee, I passed on to Rudi those I thought good enough to publish but didn't fancy bringing out myself. James also helped me out at Peter Owen with the UK rights to three significant New Directions titles. The first of these was Ezra Pound's *Confucian Analects* (1951), which we followed with Henry Miller's *The Books in My Life* (1952) and finally *New Russian Stories* (1953), which included short fiction by Tolstoy, Pasternak and several others less well known today. However, by far the most important book was *Siddhartha*, Hermann Hesse's 1922 novel on Buddhist themes. New Directions published the book in 1951, and when I read Hilda Rosner's translation I realised that it was outstanding and wanted to publish it myself in Britain. I was much less experienced as a publisher then and never imagined it would sell so well or that it would have such wide appeal. I was very lucky indeed.

I went on to publish several Hesse novels, but when I first published him he wasn't widely known outside Germany despite having won the Nobel Prize for Literature in 1946. I'd read good reviews of the 1949 translation of *The Glass Bead Game*, which had been published as *Magister Ludi*, so thought introducing translations more widely wouldn't be a bad idea. James told me that the UK and British Commonwealth rights to *Siddhartha* and other novels were available and gave me Hesse's address in Switzerland. Frau Ninon Hesse responded to my letter saying that her husband would not deal with an unknown publisher, especially one that didn't even have its own headed notepaper. As a compromise I ended up publishing the book in 1954 jointly with Vision Press, which was already well established, initially using a dust-jacket designed by my wife Wendy.

Of the several books I published jointly with Vision, the Hesse books were by far the most important, and it was *Siddhartha* that really launched Peter Owen as a publishing house. The rights cost me a paltry £25 advance (worth around £770 today), but the book received enthusiastic reviews everywhere and, with the quest for enlightenment as its theme, struck a chord with the Beat generation who were into Indian spirituality and marijuana. Of course I didn't know much about either—I wasn't into religion or drugs—but I did recognise a good book when I read one. Apparently Hesse didn't care for the association with the Beat writers, drugs, or the way their hippy heirs appropriated his work. Though rebellious himself, he was from a deeply religious family and had been schooled for a time at a theological seminary in the 1890s—an experience that inspired his novel *The Prodigy* which I published in 1957. He saw himself as a serious, philosophical, cosmopolitan man who had gone on an independent spiritual journey—one very different from the contemporary countercultural scene. But the sales of his books increased enormously, and eventually they were published all over Europe as well as in the United States. He had been controversial in Germany, and his popularity had waned over time. But the Hesse renaissance of the 1950s and 1960s must have been an enormous help to him financially.

We published Hesse's brilliant novel *Demian* in 1958. Until then it hadn't been available in an English translation. Interest in Hesse was phenomenal in the United States especially. All the important bookstores, especially the 8th Street Bookshop in New York, wanted as many copies as they could get. They would have ordered a hundred at a time, but the German publisher Suhrkamp, who managed the rights, told us we could export only twelve hardbacks a week. I think they were hoping that rationing it would help sell the rights to an American publisher.

Siddhartha kept on requiring reprints—we were churning the books out like sausages—so all the paperback publishers in Britain were after the rights. For years, while demand for the hardbacks was still high, I refused their offers. Pan came on the scene, and, despite my repeatedly turning down a sale, kept expressing their keen interest by taking me out to expensive lunches. I could have dined like a king every day on publishers clamouring for the rights! Many lavish lunches later, and as hardback sales flattened, I finally conceded that there would have to be a mass-market paperback of *Siddhartha* and that the auction rights were pretty valuable. By then I had bought out the remaining rights from Vision Press. Arthur and Rudi weren't stupid—they knew they were worth quite a lot—so I paid almost as much to acquire their share of the rights as I would have if I'd bought the entire company! I could afford it only because the Hesse hardbacks had been so lucrative.

Before auctioning the paperback rights to *Siddhartha* my father gave me some advice which this time I followed. It was a time of massive inflation, and he said, 'Whatever you do, whatever price you name, it has to guaranteed in Swiss francs!' At the end of yet another lunch, Simon Master, the managing director of Pan Books, asked me what I really wanted. The advance I asked for was modest. I have never believed in big advances, either paying or receiving them. Unless you need the money up front, it's much better to get royalties coming in steadily. So I made a quite outrageous demand for the time: I insisted they buy paperback rights to six of my other titles as part of the deal. Though known for publishing thrillers like the James Bond series, Pan had Picador as a literary imprint, so one of Simon's senior editors chose six of the best titles on my list. Her choices included fiction by Anna Kavan, who was still pretty unknown, *The Book of Grass*, a Monique Wittig novel and a work by Blaise Cendrars.

Other key aspects of the deal included a separate contract for the translation and an exceptional sliding royalty agreement. Usually they start at 7.5 per cent but with *Siddhartha*, we started at 12.5 per cent reaching a top rate of 17.5 per cent after sales of 250,000—which was extraordinary in those days. Neither Simon nor I expected it, but sales surpassed that fairly quickly in five or six years, often reprinting twice a year or more. Pan's editors were very good while they had *Siddhartha*, keeping it in print and making it a huge bestseller.

We've been getting a huge royalty on *Siddhartha* ever since. After the contractual term expired with Pan, Penguin wanted a deal. Again, I told them they'd have to buy six of our other titles, and they did. We struck a similar deal on royalties, and once again got way beyond the 250,000. So you could say that much of Peter Owen Publishers' success and staying power was down to the genius of Hermann Hesse and a pinch of my own chutzpah.

18

Courteous Maniacs

While Muriel Spark was still establishing herself as a writer and relatively impecunious she did a little work in publishing. In December 1949 she began working for us at Peter Nevill as an editorial assistant and secretary for three days a week and continued there on and off until the company went bust under Malcolm Kirk's sole directorship in 1954. Muriel had been renting a room in a flat at 65 Old Brompton Road, Kensington, so the Peter Nevill offices at number 50 were close by. Malcolm also rented her a work space for a while. I continued to see Muriel often as, when I launched Peter Owen Ltd in 1951, I did so from independent office space in the same building. She came to work for me as assistant editor while waiting for her first novel to be published.

Muriel's first books were mostly written with her boyfriend Derek Stanford. Peter Nevill published a couple of them, while for Peter Owen I commissioned *Emily Brontë: Her Life and Work* (1953) and a selection of the *Letters of John Henry Newman* (1957). We also included some of Muriel's poems in our *Springtime Two* anthology in 1963. Thirty years later, when I agreed to buy up the rights to her Brontë material and reconfigure the original book as *The Essence of the Brontës: A Compilation with Essays* (1993), Muriel insisted that we cut Derek's contribution completely. She had her reasons for turning on Derek. Perhaps in revenge for her ingratitude and for dumping him as a lover, he had gone on to sell behind her back scores of personal letters she had written to him and even sold off some of her early manuscripts. He also wrote an unauthorised biography of Muriel in 1963 and a memoir in 1977 that were hugely inaccurate and at times pure fantasy. The inaccuracies were down to sloppiness rather than malice, but it made Muriel furious. However, the way she treated him was pretty disgraceful. He was generally regarded as a kind and gentle man, if a little affected, and they had once been a very loving couple and had even considered marriage.

Though Derek was a perfectly nice man, he was, to be honest, a mediocre writer and a worse researcher. Muriel always regarded writing as a business so, ultimately, wouldn't put up with his amateurishness any more than his betrayal. She devotes pages of her slender autobiography *Curriculum Vitae* (1992) to cataloguing some of his inaccuracies. Ironically, in 1993, when it came to re-editing *The Essence of the Brontës*, which drew on a number of sources, she struggled to make it uniform, and her initial editing was very sloppy. After reading the proofs she wanted to rewrite sections; this was impossible in those days because it would have meant re-typesetting the entire book. Today it would be a relatively easy matter to correct on a computer, but at the time we would have had to pay a fortune in type compositor's fees to have the book and index reset from scratch. Muriel had become grandiose and difficult by then, so we told her, in so many words, to get lost.

During the period I first knew Muriel she was undergoing a religious transformation. She got herself baptised as an Anglican in 1952, then confirmed in 1953, but, having decided the Church of England was 'too modern', was received into the Catholic Church in 1954. She even contemplated becoming a nun. She dumped Derek, having started to see their relationship as sinful, though their increasingly shaky friendship continued for a while. During this time of renewed religiosity, and perhaps not coincidentally, she had begun taking amphetamine tablets. In those days you could still buy Dexedrine at the chemist as a diet pill, and, besides helping her economise on food and lose weight, it kept her alert through nights of fervent research and writing. But the combination of overwork, malnutrition and Dexedrine sent her quite potty.

Throughout 1953 Muriel had became obsessed with the writings of T. S. Eliot and insisted that he was sending her prolific threatening messages through complicated cryptographic anagrams embedded in his work. At one point she even claimed Eliot had been eavesdropping on her friends by posing as a window cleaner. Discontinuing the amphetamines and taking a prescribed antipsychotic put an end to her paranoid delusions, some of which had included antisemitic abuse, perhaps because her father was Jewish. Muriel had help from her new circle of Catholic friends, but it was Derek who provided the crucial support by soliciting funds from her admirers. I don't know what she'd have done without him. Her supporters included David Astor, Graham Greene and Evelyn Waugh; the last of these fictionalised his own drug-induced madness in his 1957 novel *The Ordeal of Gilbert Pinfold*.

At the end of 1954 Muriel retreated to lodgings in the Carmelite priory at Aylesford in Kent. While there she asked Derek to clear out her room in Kensington, which was presumably when he purloined some of her papers to sell off later. Though her beloved poetry had failed to get her noticed, she was well-enough established as a critic, essayist and prize-winning short-story writer for Macmillan to express interest in a novel. By the time she was well enough to return to London in mid-1955 she had written the first chapters of her debut novel *The Comforters*, which cleverly transformed her experiences of madness into what is still a striking and readable book. Macmillan prevaricated so long over the contract that Muriel came to work for me at £5 a week salary for three days' work. At 50 Old Brompton Road conditions were fairly spartan, but we got on well and she seemed generally thorough and efficient, despite staying up all night working on *Robinson*, her second novel.

In all her writings I never knew Muriel say anything disparaging about me and, even after she left my employ, she would often attend our parties, write to me inquiring about the family or send us holiday postcards. I often gave her books I thought she'd like, including Anna Kavan stories ('I think them most unusually good'), Cesare Pavese's final book *The Comrade* and Anaïs Nin's *Children of the Albatross*, partly in the hope that she would review them. In return she gave me signed copies of her novels. One of Muriel's letters, from July 1960, thanks me for recommending her to Penguin who made her an offer for the paperback rights to her first two novels.

When I first started out I had attempted to do pretty much everything myself, so it was a boon to have someone as efficient and reliable as Muriel working with me. She would proofread and help with publicity, editorial and secretarial work—she could even take shorthand. A biography of Muriel says that she guided me towards foreign literature such as Hesse, Cocteau and Pavese, but that is erroneous. Though she certainly approved of them and liked working on the manuscripts, I had already discovered these authors through other connections and influences. In her memoir she says she enjoyed the atmosphere working with me and her colleagues, Mrs Bool, the office manager and secretary, and Erna Horn, our bookkeeper.

Known to the family as 'Horn', Erna was an unmarried Austrian-Jewish refugee of uncertain years whose eyes bulged through thick-lensed spectacles on account of a thyroid condition. She was somewhat demanding and difficult, and lived with Grandma Betty in West Hampstead as a retainer and carer. Betty can't have known, but Horn had swung both ways sexually and had dabbled in drugs in decadent pre-war Vienna. She cheerily confessed this to her gossipy optician in later life. At work we eventually built a cubicle around Miss Horn to isolate her. She had been given to moaning at everyone about her lot, bothering us incessantly in loud, strongly Viennese-inflected English. Hiving her off seemed the kindest solution.

Of working in our small premises, Muriel writes that 'we were very attached to each other' and describes working 'with one light bulb, bare boards on the floor, a long table which was the packing department, and Peter always retreating to his own tiny office to take phone calls from his uncles'—meaning Rudi and Bobby. Like all of literary London, she knew Rudi from shopping at

Zwemmer's, and he must have known he was the basis for the Baron in *The Comforters*. He never commented on this, and, knowing his temper, I didn't think it politic to bring it up. Rudi had a sort of act he performed at the shop, and would pontificate if people asked him for reading suggestions. He got to know a great number of authors and literary figures who doubtless found his advice useful and were amused by his foibles. Muriel was adept at using elements of real life in her fiction. As with Rudi and the Baron, Caroline, the main character in *The Comforters*, is partly Muriel yet not wholly her. I also recognise many of Muriel's early experiences in publishing in her 1988 novel, *A Far Cry From Kensington*, though I do not believe the character of the book publisher is based on me.

Muriel worked with me until her success was sufficiently assured for her to work full-time as a writer. Derek Stanford was so upset by her acclaim that he had a breakdown. She was relieved when he put himself in the hands of a psychiatrist and wrote to her saying he'd been advised not to see her—it made him ill, he said.

As well as correcting the record in her memoir, Muriel exacted revenge on Derek in her fiction, mercilessly lampooning him as the '*pisseur de copie*' Hector Bartlett in *A Far Cry From Kensington*. Derek, who died in 2008, must have been aware of this. She could be pretty ruthless, and also put it about that Derek was gay. I don't know whether he was or whether she was just being vindictive. I remember in *The Comforters* Caroline tells the Baron that her typewriter is writing the novel of her life. 'Is the world a lunatic asylum then?' she asks. 'Are we all courteous maniacs discreetly making allowances for everyone else's derangement?' The Baron thinks she's 'largely' right and warns her that she may be mad. Caroline replies: 'The intelligentsia are all a little mad ... that's what makes us so nice. The sane are not worth noticing.'

Fame didn't make Muriel any nicer. Many of her friends, who, like Derek, had helped out in the early days when she was poor and unwell, also found themselves dumped. She became increasingly glamorous and grand, cultivating high-society friendships to match. Her appointment as a Dame in 1993 seemed to exacerbate matters. She became quarrelsome and litigious. Bruce Hunter, her agent, used to be terrified when she came to town. Her public relations manager at Constable was similarly intimidated but once told me of his relief when he heard Muriel had abandoned an intended visit because, on the way from her home in Italy, she'd 'had a quarrel with her girlfriend'. Penelope Jardine, her long-time companion, always denied that she and Muriel were lovers, but everyone I knew assumed they were—which was somewhat ironic considering the rumours Muriel put about regarding Derek. My friend the literary agent Gloria Ferris once said to me, 'I don't particularly like Muriel, but then my friends aren't particularly nice. I don't particularly like nice people.'

Muriel had a very unpleasant quarrel with her son Robin, too, who must have felt terribly neglected. He had a tough life from the start. In early 1944, when he was five, she abandoned him to some nuns in Rhodesia while she fled from her mad husband. Arriving in England, she briefly joined the intelligence services. When she finally got Robin back in autumn 1945 she dumped him with her parents in Edinburgh while she pursued her career in London. I suppose that was the only way she could pursue a career. I remember Muriel coming to a dinner party in the early 1960s after the triumph of *The Prime of Miss Jean Brodie*. 'Look what Robin made for me!' Muriel said proudly, showing off the rings he used to make from semiprecious stones. They were still on good terms, but things soured terribly as Robin continued to pursue his Jewish heritage in his life and in his paintings. She notes in her memoir that her parents, who did all the hard work of bringing him up, were pleased when Robin 'decided to be a Jew'. She paid for his bar mitzvah party, despite the implication that she wasn't impressed herself. I suspect that this was Christian disappointment rather than outright antisemitism, but she was furious when he later claimed that, as well as her father, his grandmother was Jewish. It was, she thought, wishful thinking and simply untrue. Ruthlessly she cut him out of her will. In *Curriculum Vitae* one can't avoid noticing that she's much more effusively loving about her cat Bluebell than her son.

When Martin Stannard interviewed me for his authorised biography of Muriel I told him to expect endless bother. He was sure I was wrong—Muriel had given him *carte blanche*, he said, all the contacts he needed, and access to her letters and vast archive. I was right though. When he submitted the manuscript she blocked it completely. It wasn't published until several years after her death, and then only after Penelope Jardine had raked over it and removed anything she disliked.

If I had first met Muriel in her Italian years—from the late 1960s onward—I don't think I'd have liked her much at all. She was never deliberately nasty to me, though I felt snubbed when she refused an autograph slip for *The Essence of the Brontës* (1993). Miss Jardine wrote to me saying 'Dame Muriel is unwell and cannot meet your request,' even though you would have to be practically dead not to be able to comply with such a trifling request.

Our last encounter was in 1996, ten years before her death, when Muriel was receiving the highest French literary award, becoming Commandeur de l'Ordre des Arts et des Lettres, at the French Embassy. I went up to her after a while to say hello. 'Oh! It's been a long time!' she said, neither unfriendly nor particularly warm.

After Muriel left my employ she recommended one of her friends who lasted about a month before I kicked him out. The author Elizabeth Berridge became my next editor after I met her at a party. She lasted four years, often filling in later when other editors came and went. Like Muriel, Elizabeth enjoyed the work and was very good. She found it a change from writing and said that it taught her a lot about book publishing useful for writers who tend to assume that the industry just means some big fat cat siphoning off their money. When they see how it works and how hard it actually is, it's quite a revelation. Both Muriel and Elizabeth, after working as editors, saw publishing through completely different eyes.

A display at the National Book League celebrating the company's twentieth anniversary in 1971 included my old letter appointing Muriel. Her weekly pay of £5 for three days' work, the figure she'd asked for herself, was much commented upon in the press, but Muriel was kind enough to write from Rome to the *Times Literary Supplement* in my defence, saying she didn't feel underpaid and had often worked for less. Though it sounds a tiny sum it would be worth about £120 today. 'The main point is that Peter was a jolly nice person to work for,' she wrote. 'I know he was struggling against great commercial odds, as was I in my literary work (which I practised on the other four days). The do-it-yourself quality of his office … appealed to me very much and left me with very happy memories. Money isn't everything.' Elizabeth Berridge felt the same, and when John Calder's sister worked as my secretary, any money I paid her she surreptitiously returned to petty cash, so worked for me for nothing. Those were the days!

19

Caligula's Horse and Other Tales

In my early days as a publisher I often took reference and non-fiction titles from the United States. Despite often being badly edited, they were useful in building up our backlist and sold well in emerging economies like Egypt and India. This success brought its own difficulties, and we weren't alone in frequently encountering rights infringements. We discovered alarming numbers of pirated and unlicensed editions, especially in India. I would try to get redress, but it was often hopeless—the sleazier publishers would just deny it. Eventually we asked for an official audit from one particularly piratical outfit and they had to pay us significant damages for the books they stole.

Our *Springtime* anthologies brought us a little more prestige and were partly inspired by *New Directions in Prose and Poetry*, the long inaugural series James Laughlin began in 1936. With only three volumes, my series was rather short-lived, mostly because finding enough good-quality writing proved endless bother. This difficulty in finding good English language writing is also one of the reasons I published so much literature in translation.

The first volume of *Springtime: An Anthology of Young Poets and Writers*, published in 1953 and edited by G. S. Fraser and Iain Fletcher, contained work by several writers who became much admired. As well as the work of Philip Larkin, Thom Gunn and Elizabeth Jennings, it included a couple of poems by Kingsley Amis who shot to fame the following year with the publication of his first novel, *Lucky Jim*.

Manya Harari, the Russian-born daughter of a financier, instigated and subsidised the first volume of *Springtime*. Her husband was also a man of means, but their son Michael, who wrote poetry, was very unwell. Publishers weren't very interested in his work, so, very discreetly, she asked if I would publish an anthology and include him.

A very nice woman of Jewish decent, I have fond memories of Manya Harari. Motivated largely by the love of good literature, she set up Harvill

Press with another rich entrepreneur, her friend Marjorie Villiers, 'Harvill' being a combination of the first syllables of their surnames. They brought out many good books, and, coincidentally, Mrs Villiers became a neighbour of mine.

Manya once did me a very lucrative favour. Like her son, she translated from Russian; among the many books she worked on she co-translated Pasternak's *Doctor Zhivago*. Pasternak had been tipped for the Nobel Prize for some time before it was awarded to him in 1958, so it was lucky that I'd bought the anthology *New Russian Stories* from Noonday Press in the United States and published it in 1953. It included a Pasternak novella called *The Last Summer* which I republished on its own in 1961 to capitalise on his newly widespread fame. Billy Collins, an old rogue who still ran bits of William Collins & Sons, owned the UK rights to *Doctor Zhivago*. When the book was given another boost by the multiple-Oscar-winning 1965 film, old man Collins was after the rights to my Pasternak novella, too, and anything else he could get his hands on. He called me to a meeting to negotiate. Manya Harari, as co-translator and expert in Russian literature, sat beside him and generously signalled, through discreet nodding and shaking of her head, that under no circumstances should I let it go. I didn't, and we went on to sell so many that we had to reprint. These days I sometimes wonder whether Pasternak would have done quite so well if it were more widely known that his surname translates as 'parsnip'.

Wendy and I decided to edit *Springtime Two: An Anthology of Modern Prose and Poetry* and we published it in 1958. We asked far and wide for contributions, but most submissions were appalling—some were even illiterate. The more egotistical of the poets, often the least talented, were so offended by rejection that we received a fair number of abusive letters and phone calls. Many of the best submissions were from American writers, but the book also included work by Muriel Spark, Bernard Kops and Kenneth Allsop.

In 1968 Kenneth also wrote for us *The Angry Decade*, a survey of the cultural revolt of the 1950s. As a small independent publisher we were often overlooked by literary agents so had to be resourceful and, in lieu of interesting submissions, think up serviceable ideas ourselves before commissioning them. Allsop was a good writer and took apart the whole 'Angry Young Men' scene, making most of them look silly, which they were! It was a seminal book and was quite a success, going into two or three printings.

'Autumn Relationships', a piece in *Springtime Two*, was actually written by Uncle Rudi, though, at his request, we attributed it to Incitatus, Emperor Caligula's favourite horse, the one he was supposed to have promoted to the rank of consul. Perhaps Rudi thought it might attract more attention under a pseudonym. A stream of consciousness that begins, 'Two streets touch without kissing', it's typical of Rudi's work in that sadly, though he had visual and descriptive imagination and great turns of phrase, in the end Rudi couldn't write fiction convincingly—not even surrealist fiction. He was too remote from ordinary life and unable to render dialogue well.

Michael Levien and I edited *Springtime Three*, which we published in 1961. Most of the writers we included were already established as we couldn't find many worthy unknowns. Prose selections included extracts by Anna Kavan and Violette Leduc and a striking piece by the painter F. N. Souza. Poetry included work by R. S. Thomas, Elizabeth Berridge, Muriel Spark, Ithell Colquhoun and lesser-known poets from Romania and India. More significantly there were poems by Laurie Lee, who I knew from the Queen's Elm, the literary pub in Chelsea, and Mervyn Peake, whose work I continued to promote, with a biography and collections of his writing and illustrations, often assisted by his son Sebastian.

Springtime Three proved to be the last of the series. I'm glad we did them, but it was a time-consuming endeavour and sales weren't exactly stellar. Though I published some poetry in subsequent years, I tended to firmly avoid it after that. Aside from the abuse rejected poets tend to hurl at you, poetry is notoriously difficult to profit from financially. There are many more specialist publishers better equipped to tackle it.

20

The Beast-Men of Varang-Varang

During the UFO boom of the 1950s I issued a couple of science-fiction novels by William Dexter in attempt to capitalise on the trend. They contrast rather embarrassingly with Henry Miller, Julien Gracq and the more literary fare I was publishing. *World in Eclipse* (1954) describes how a small group of humans, held captive by the 'terrible sentient quasi-vegetable creatures' of the planet Vulcan, are returned in flying discs to reclaim a scorched, post-apocalyptic Earth. Dexter's sequel, *Children of the Void* (1955), is set in the far-off 1980s when the hapless survivors of his last book must again set off in flying discs, this time accompanied by bronzed Virians and frog-like Nagani, to do battle with the Beast-men of Varang-Varang. Equally implausible was *Flying Saucers on the Moon* (1954) by Harold T. Wilkins, which purported to be non-fiction. Wilkins was a journalist who wrote all sorts of nonsense about lost civilisations, pirate treasure and mysteries that included the *Mary Celeste* and a talking mongoose. Wilkins's UFO book was complete rubbish but did rather well. The launch party was memorable only because there Wendy and I first met John and Susan Paine. Once home I found my jacket pockets stuffed full of John's visiting cards advertising his architectural and building services. The Paines became great friends to Wendy and me, accompanying us on holidays now and then and coming to all our parties. John, who was a renowned Lothario, had been married to Susan since 1951. After working in Bodkins, a friend's bookshop in Kensington, Susan eventually became a loyal secretary to my company for many years and was Wendy's closest friend. Like Wendy and me, Susan had an interest in art—in later life she became an accomplished painter. John loved the Soho scene and often took me to his favourite boozy clubs and dives. Francis Bacon, who lived opposite my second business premises in Kendrick Mews, South Kensington, was particularly fond of him.

Amid those tales of extraterrestrials Wendy and I welcomed an arrival of a terrestrial kind, but I was visited by inner-space horrors I thought I'd left behind me. Antonia, my first daughter, was born in April 1955. The marriage had been fine until then, but Wendy and I knew nothing of what to expect when becoming parents for the first time. Wendy was highly strung and Antonia's birth triggered a severe post-natal depression, a condition not well recognised at the time. While she was in hospital the epilepsy that had led to her expulsion from school at fourteen made an unwelcome comeback. Referred by Uncle Bobby, Wendy saw the best neurologist in the country who prescribed tablets that brought her epilepsy under control. To make matters worse, shortly after Antonia's birth I experienced a second really catastrophic breakdown. Every night I hoped I wouldn't wake up in the morning, though I don't think I would have committed suicide—I had to think of Wendy and Antonia.

I wasn't jealous of my daughter, but all the same, I hadn't expected Wendy to be so infatuated with our baby. Having experienced so much loneliness and insecurity as a child, it seemed the emotional security I had secured in marriage was evaporating. It's probably absurd to assume one ever has complete security; all relationships are complicated. People were not particularly clued up about childcare in the 1950s. The NHS, founded in 1948, was still in its infancy, and I don't think there was quite the support—health visitors, antenatal and postnatal care—that came later. Wendy and I did not anticipate the hormonal and emotional changes that occur after one gives birth to a child. Like my mother before us, we were not primed properly. We thought we had fallen out of love with one another and never quite retrieved the closeness that we'd had in the first years of our marriage.

My depression went on for a very long time. I don't know how I managed to keep working. That year, thinking I could cope, I went by sea to New York. The itinerary was planned and everything was arranged—I'd even had a course of hypnotism to try to prepare me. Unfortunately I experienced claustrophobia on the boat which became even worse in New York with all the skyscrapers looming over me. I'd gone to meet James Laughlin and other contacts. While James was very helpful, I knew I couldn't stay there on my own; I was simply too ill. I set off for home after three days. I was very apprehensive about returning to New York the next year, but fortunately that trip went well.

Having been through something similar herself, Muriel Spark was sympathetic to my breakdown. Elizabeth Berridge, Muriel's editorial successor, was also supportive. Wendy, still dealing with her own problems and the novelty of motherhood, could support me little. In fact she was rather unsympathetic at the time, which made it much more difficult for me to cope. She had never seen me as I really was—vulnerable and prone to anxiety—and was disappointed when I cracked up and shattered her illusions. She seems to have expected me to be some kind of superman and never fully recovered from the realisation that I wasn't—far from it. Eventually Wendy came to terms with my fragility, but things never properly recovered between us however much we tried.

Muriel suggested that I might go to Aylesford Priory in Kent to recuperate, just as she had, and through her Wendy and I got to know the Catholic convert Father Brocard Sewell. As well as taking charge of the Priory, Sewell was a printer, publisher, commentator and supporter of various authors. He had become a somewhat progressive Carmelite friar by 1952, entered the priesthood in 1954, and was editor of a controversial literary review from 1955 to 1968. He wrote on forgotten decadent authors and artists of the 1890s, the Pre-Raphaelites, Arthur Machen, Montague Summers and others. He was broad-minded and forgiving, saying, 'Perhaps most of us have, at least potentially, something of the decadent in us.' Muriel understandably deplored Sewell's early flirtation with Mosley and the British Union of Fascists, but he was a very literate man who had helped her through her breakdown and religious conversion while she was at Aylesford.

Wendy and I took up Muriel's suggestion and spent a weekend at the Priory with John and Susan Paine. It was a pleasant, peaceful place but hardly our scene, though a quiet break might have helped had I stayed there longer on my own. With the business to run it was impossible just then. John remembered the place as being very atmospheric with lovely wooden beams everywhere—quite idyllic until cockroaches started dropping from the timbers. He also recalled that I had become peckish and attempted to break into the kitchen for a midnight sandwich only to find it impenetrably bolted.

It always puzzled me why so many literary folk like Muriel and Edith Sitwell converted to Catholicism around that time. Whether they did this from faith or because it was fashionable I never had the guts to ask. I always felt that intruding on someone who demonstrated a religious conviction was a rotten thing to do. It's better just to leave them to it.

Back in London I had to force myself to keep going with the business, but every moment of the day I was battling my neuroses and intrusive thoughts. I would wash my hands obsessively and was remained terribly claustrophobic. The whole experience was utterly hellish, and I only got through it again with the support of Uncle Bobby and his wife Gladys, my mother's elder sister.

21

The Comforters

Bobby and Gladys Abelson were two of the nicest members of my family. Sophie and Jacob, my mother's parents, didn't really want Gladys, their eldest child, to marry Bobby. Having sent Winnie off to a finishing school Wiesbaden to keep her out of mischief—she had, to their alarm, been caught sitting on a young man's lap—they set about finding her sister a suitable match. They knew marrying off Winnie wouldn't be a problem. Both girls had unusually pretty blue-brown eyes, but whereas my mother was slim and attractive, Gladys was a bit of a frump. When my aunt expressed an interest in Bobby, Sophie made Jacob visit his family to vet them only for him to declare, 'No daughter of mine is going to marry into that family!' Snobbishly they regarded the Abelsons as far beneath them. The Friedmanns thought of themselves as educated, posh Jews completely distinct from East European Jews who spoke Yiddish, ate different food and were working or mercantile class. It was an unspoken rule that one didn't generally mix or intermarry—it just wasn't done. But, as well as being a kind and thoughtful man, Bobby, a trained psychiatrist and general practitioner, could hardly be considered beneath them. My grandparents ultimately relented and condoned the match. When it came to Gladys, Bobby was the only taker.

Bobby's social circle and patients were mostly drawn from his own community. Gladys was was very shy and hardly ever socialised, but, if pushed, occasionally went along with him on visits. She didn't have a great sense of humour, but I remember one time a friend of Bobby's had said how bad business was. Gladys asked what they did, and, misunderstanding their accent, thought they said they made guns. She couldn't see how business could be bad in wartime. 'No!' they said. 'Not guns, gowns!'

Gladys had been a very naughty child, and I know her parents had beaten her. Luckily governesses intervened to discourage too much corporal punishment. Sophie said that Gladys, as a toddler, had shoved buttons up baby Winnie's nose when she was in her pram. I imagine that she was jealous at her younger sister getting all the attention. One of her German grandmothers so took against her that she exclaimed, 'Never bring that child again. She's far too wicked!'

Gladys liked to play practical jokes as an older child. One victim was an old man, a friend of her father, who visited him every Sunday. Once, not long after his arrival, her governess took her out for a walk but noticed her charge giggling to herself as they got farther from the house. Gladys wouldn't tell her why, but she'd secretly locked the old man in a room and taken the key with her. At home they were going berserk trying to get him out! He was so outraged that, once released, he never returned. They punished her of course, and after a number of these beatings she withdrew into sullen submission. Sophie took against her and treated her most unfairly, even leaving her much less than my mother in her will. Of her children, Rudi was the favourite, followed by Winnie, with Gladys trailing far behind in third place.

Whatever their shortcomings, my mother's family was unused to the idea of adultery so there was surprise and disbelief when Gladys, who had been such a frump in her youth, got herself a boyfriend behind Uncle Bobby's back. At that point she had slimmed down a bit and dressed fashionably, but my mother still wouldn't believe it even after she caught Gladys kissing her beau. The man in question was Rabbi Goldberg, a lawyer from Grantham. He and his family were patients of Bobby's, and we knew them reasonably well. I was quite friendly with his daughter, and my mother once consulted Goldberg about divorcing my father. Ironically, this was at the same time as the rabbi was conducting an adulterous affair with her sister! If Bobby ever knew about his wife's Goldberg variations he must have forgiven her.

Gladys and Bobby's only child Ivor, my cousin, caused no end of trouble. Bobby had put war bonds in Ivor's name to avoid tax only to find that Ivor had cashed them in. Bobby also messed up his chances of compensation for his GP business when it was nationalised at the creation of the NHS. He'd had some very lucrative private patients, so lost all that revenue, too. He and the family were so impoverished by this bungling that they ended up living in a high-rise council flat in Roehampton. Though fond of his parents, none of my family really got on with Ivor. The final straw was when he tried to empty Gladys's Coutts bank account after she had a heart attack in the early 1980s. The bank tipped off Winnie, and she and Gladys were able to stop the transaction, much to Ivor's fury. She was to die in 1986, and from then on none of my family had anything more to do with him.

Just as with the first breakdown I'd had in my teens, Bobby and Gladys were kind and supportive throughout my second. It really was the worst period of my life when I cracked up through overwork and the impact of parenthood. At my lowest ebb, and for quite some time, I visited Bobby daily and couldn't have coped without him. At first Wendy didn't really want me to see him as she feared I would discuss our relationship, and Bobby was family. But I was short of money and didn't really have a choice. My depression was made worse by the thought that I would never get over it and be normal again. I was so deeply depressed I began to forget how I felt before and would have taken anything to make my life more tenable. I was so desperate I would have agreed to electroshock treatment or even a lobotomy. Bobby was adamant. He thought electroshock treatment entirely wrong and would never administer it. I knew not to mention a lobotomy—he would have hit the roof! We tried various medications but most of them were fairly new and ineffective. Eventually, after many months, we found one that helped a little. I could pretend not to be so unwell, but putting up a front made me worse. It was a huge strain that made the illness drag on longer. Sometimes I walked round the block a couple of times to try to compose myself before I went back home.

My parents were no help at all. Both my father and Sophie could have afforded some financial assistance to Wendy and me which would have helped take the pressure off. As it was, I really had to force myself to work. In some ways that was good—to keep going, that is—but in others ways it was awful. In retrospect I realise that Gladys and Bobby were the only ones who ever put themselves out for me. Gladys, who was fairly lazy and didn't like to have to cater for house guests, even let me stay with them for a week. Normally all her energy went into spoiling Ivor.

Feeling better, I made a terrible mistake. I'd put on huge amounts of weight from illness and medication and went on a crash diet which led to a relapse and another year of misery. The diet consisted solely of cabbage or something, and my teeth got into a terrible state. Before the illness and the diet I had never had a filling, but now I needed a whole mouthful. Appalled, I consulted a psychic healer only to be told that she didn't do teeth. So I had to submit to the dentist's drill, and I learnt my lesson: whatever the temptation, no crash diets. By then I knew my depression wouldn't last for ever, but it was still bloody awful.

I couldn't help resenting Wendy's lack of support but she couldn't help that either, with so much on her plate, including her attacks of epilepsy. Fortunately when Georgina, our second daughter, was born in October 1960 we knew what to expect, and neither of us became ill. Even so, I couldn't wait to get her into nursery school, and poor Georgie, who went as soon as she could walk, must have been their youngest ever pupil.

During my breakdown I was undoubtedly difficult to live with. I wasn't psychotic, but it was a major depression—I was very obsessional about my illness and symptoms. Mentally I kept on going over everything to do with my business and personal life. The poet Jeremy Reed, one of my closest friends, agrees with me that being so very ill permanently scars one. The only good thing that came out of it was that, knowing the way it would go, I was able to help him when he was unwell. He thought, as I had when I was very ill with depression, that he'd never come out of it—that it would last for ever. Fortunately it rarely does.

22

The Fallen Star

Rudi carried on working at Zwemmer's for years despite old man Zwemmer's growing suspicions of the exceptionally large orders his manager was making for Vision Press titles. In the bookshop Rudi's assistants were sometimes as distinguished as their customers. At one point his deputies included the Scottish poet Ruthven Todd and the German-born Paul Hamlyn, later a successful publisher and philanthropist. At the time it was rumoured that Hamlyn was stealing books to resell privately by throwing them out the lavatory window at the back, an entirely apocryphal story I'm sure.

Eventually, under pressure from his mother Sophie, Rudi decided to give up Zwemmer's and work full time at Vision Press. He part-owned the firm and wanted a small salary for all his hard work, not just a share of the profits (which were divided between him, my father and another investor). I think the salary was more a matter of principle than necessity—Rudi still had a private income from his father's estate. Even so, my father behaved very badly. As he wasn't getting a salary from Vision himself, he didn't see why Rudi should, even though Rudi was the brains, heart and soul of the operation and did the bulk of editorial work. Had my father asked me I would have argued Rudi's case, but he didn't. Rudi decided to quit, which was a disaster for Vision Press and for my father. To make things worse, my father sent Rudi a cheque for the original £500 he had invested—and that was all. It was despicable. Without Rudi, Zwemmer's went downhill a little, too. He had loved performing his act there, knew people went in to be told what to read, and had gained much satisfaction from telling them.

Vision Press would have folded sooner without Rudi, but on my recommendation Elizabeth Berridge went to work for Arthur as an editor for a while, as she had done for me. She wanted to get back into publishing as she rather liked it. She found working for my father quite amusing—when the phone rang she never knew if it was someone inquiring about fake flowers or, more rarely, books. With Elizabeth's assistance Vision Press limped on for a while but only as a result of the strong backlist Rudi had worked so hard to develop. When my father decided to retire and sell off the business he gave me first option on it. I was an idiot not to have bought it. The other director, an accountant who owned ten per cent of the company, made sure he and my father didn't let it go for a song. As I had my own successful list by then I didn't see why I should buy it anyway. I was slightly snooty about some of the books they had bought in—things like *The Story of the Bicycle*—and didn't want them on my own list. I must have been somewhat more pretentious than I am now, but it was a big mistake. Rudi's backlist would have been brilliant had I bought the lot and integrated it into the Peter Owen list. Vision did eventually sell, and I made off with their share of its Hesse titles, which I knew to be a goldmine and worth every penny of the substantial sum my father and his accountant charged me.

Poor Rudi must have felt bereaved by the loss of Vision. It left him more time at home with his obsessive mother and his conflicted emotions. She had always over-indulged him. I still have a postcard in my collection that Sophie wrote to Rudi while she was away on holiday. 'My sweet little man,' it begins. Really ghastly stuff. All the same, it must have been a terrible blow to him when Sophie died. By that time she was being cared for in a private hospital in Marylebone and died on 9 February 1964 at the age of eighty-five.

Sophie left a letter to be opened by her beloved son after her death. It infuriated me at the time but no longer seems as distasteful. In it she begs her three 'dearly-beloved children' to be always 'united in affection and trust, to give a helping hand to each other when in need either in joy or in sickness'. She forbids money to be spent on 'husbands and sons' and especially begs that Winnie not to give in to her 'kind heart' and lend money to anyone. She doesn't name me (something that angered me greatly) but says I must go to my father if I need to borrow money. Apart from a few trifles, most of which went to her favourite daughter Winnie, the entire estate went to Rudi. As well as her goods and chattels, Sophie had posthumous plans for Rudi. She writes that she wants him to remain in the flat they shared, keeping on their two maids. 'I would very much like you to get married (the right woman after 30 years old),' she wrote, 'if you will meet somebody whom you really like.'

My father's relationship with Rudi never recovered from the Vision Press debacle. By coincidence, Rudi wrote to Arthur the day before Sophie died with a semi-apology for keeping his distance and not having attended the funeral of Betty, Arthur's mother. Betty had disliked Rudi and he her, so there's no reason he should have gone. 'I think I gave of my best to Vision Press,' Rudi adds with a touch of melancholy. Needless to say, in tit-for-tat fashion, Arthur decided not to attend Sophie's funeral.

A few months later I was on holiday in Portugal with Wendy when I received a telegram telling me that Rudi had taken his own life. Always inclined to anxiety, I worried immediately that he had used information from a dictionary of poisons I had published. It turned out that, having set the breakfast table for two, as he must have always done while his mother was still alive, Rudi had taken a carefully researched overdose of barbiturate sleeping tablets. Despite being a member of an abstemious family, Rudi had washed down the tablets with half a bottle of the best champagne.

Rudi's body was found on 21 July 1964 at the flat in Wembley Park. He was fifty years old. He had warned my mother not to go there that day as he, a cricket fan, was 'going to Lord's'. Knowing that my father always kept my mother short of cash, he had left out a little money for her to pay his outstanding bills—to the milkman, newsagent and so on—which he had carefully listed. He had been characteristically thorough and as considerate as he could be in the circumstances. 'We all know whose fault this is!' his eldest sister Gladys declared. Indeed, the date Rudi chose to commit suicide would have been his mother's eighty-sixth birthday. As punctilious as ever, Rudi had made sure to die within six months of his mother's death, knowing that duty on the estate would thus be only half. He left everything to his two sisters.

Worried about the family being disgraced in the newspapers, Winnie was sufficiently panicked that she removed the note addressed to my father that confirmed Rudi's suicidal intentions. Fortunately she and my father knew Lord Nathan, a solicitor with the top London firm Herbert Oppenheimer, Nathan and Vandyk who had been friends with my grandfather Jacob. Lord Nathan ordered Winnie to hand over the note and insisted that the sisters be represented at the inquest as they benefited from the will. He feared suspicion would be cast that they had conspired to bump off Rudi to get at the family money. Ultimately the coroner was satisfied that Rudi had taken his own life, and his death was registered that August. Wendy and I didn't return from the Algarve for Rudi's funeral as Winnie, ashamed of his suicide, wanted to keep the whole thing quiet.

Rudi put his entire estate, including what he had inherited from his mother, in trust. It wasn't what one would call an ordinary household. There was a lot of very valuable porcelain, silver and crystal—unique crystal that my grandfather Jacob had bought through Falk Stadelmann that would make my collection look like absolute rubbish. The executors sold it off on the cheap through Druce, not one of the top auction houses. I was in the United States when it happened, otherwise I'd have bought a lot of it myself. I'd already taken quite a bit home when Sophie died, but would have swiped a lot more!

Rudi's surviving writings give a good impression of his preoccupations and the occasional hint of his ultimate fate. In 'The End of Feeling', a 1948 piece in *Neurotica*, a 'slowly dying schizoid' is a 'little old dried-out child' who finds his last consolation 'treading backwards … into the ever waiting and restful arms of his mother'. In the same story, the wife commits suicide by overdosing on 'lovely rounded tablets'. When Jay Landesman and his wife moved to London the year Rudi died I lent Jay some of Rudi's unpublished writings, including the beginnings of a novel. 'My god,' he said, 'it's all about wanting to screw his mother!' Years later, in 1981, when Landesman brought out the anthology *Neurotica 1948–1951*, he presented a signed copy to my mother and inscribed it, 'For Winifred, sister of a star: Rudolph'.

23

Marion

Rudi's death wasn't the only turmoil of 1964. When my son Ben was born that year I was thrilled to have a son, but, since he was born as the result of an affair, and as my marriage to Wendy had been going reasonably well, I decided that I couldn't tell my wife and daughters. They didn't know of Ben's existence for more than a decade.

It happened like this: a friend had taken me to a semi-bohemian party where I met Marion—a very talented painter who had won a Prix de Rome scholarship but who was working part time as an art teacher to make a living. She and I had a short affair, but I was careless. I went off by boat on a business tour of the world, but when I reached Bangkok a letter was waiting for me saying that Marion was pregnant. I was frantic with worry. Knowing the morality of the time, as an unmarried teacher her situation was dire. I thought she might do something terrible and commit suicide. To make matters worse, during our affair I hadn't told Marion I was married and had a family. She was a very moral person and was horrified.

It was pretty much the beginning of the tour, and I was meant to be going on to Pakistan, Australia, New Zealand then back via the west coast of the United States, with, finally, a few days in Paris. I really didn't know what to do but reasoned that Wendy would want to know why I had cut short my trip if I rushed back to England. I decided to carry on and asked a work colleague to liaise about the issue with my Uncle Bobby. I had to be terribly careful—if Wendy had found out there would have been big trouble, I felt.

Bobby discussed the matter with Marion. She agonised briefly but decided that she wanted to keep the baby. Fortunately the headmistress at the school where she taught was very understanding and suggested that Marion change her surname to Owen during the school holidays and keep her job.

For the first six months of Ben's life Marion and I hired a nanny. She had a flat in the house of a teacher friend between Chelsea and Earl's Court, not far from where I was living with Wendy and my daughters Antonia and Georgina, then aged nine and four. Wendy, Marion and I had friends in common, such as Alan Sillitoe and his wife Ruth Fainlight, so it was very tricky trying to conduct a furtive relationship with Marion and our secret son almost under my family's noses. Somehow I got away with it for years, but around 1974, when Wendy admitted to an affair, I thought that was it—I must come clean whatever the consequences. Wendy was having a fit of guilt about the chap she'd had an affair with. Their relationship had gone on for several months. She was remorseful, but I knew there was something seriously wrong with our marriage.

I left Wendy for a short time to think about it. Around a month later, Wendy and I had been invited to visit Romania as guests of the government, so I had to decide whether I wanted to go with her or not. I'd been terribly upset when she told me about her affair, but in the end I thought it was the right time to confess and introduce my son to Wendy and his half-sisters. Ben was around ten by then; the girls were both in their teens. When I told Wendy, I expected a furore, but she was actually very good about it and marvellously sympathetic. She even prepared my parents for the news, so Ben first met Antonia and Georgie at Arthur and Winnie's. I don't think the girls were terribly pleased to begin with. Antonia got over it quickly, but Georgie was unsure about the situation for a long time. Wendy and Marion met, too, and even became friendly—it helped that they had art as a common interest. Wendy was very kind to Ben. In time they all accepted him, and he is, after all, a very nice person. These days he visits me often. Marion was certainly a wonderful mother, and I like to think he had a fairly happy childhood.

Marion was a lovely woman, but I never had any intention of divorcing Wendy and marrying her. She knew that and once said to me, 'I used to think I wanted to get married but what I really wanted was a child.' She died in January 2015, and Antonia, who was very fond of Marion and Ben, attended her Quaker funeral. I was too unwell to go. Three years before that, while I was in hospital in 2012, Marion, having visited me, wrote a touching card that shows what a kind and thoughtful woman she was. She ended by writing, 'I must thank you for giving me such a wonderful son. He has been a source of happiness and fulfilment for nearly fifty years.' It could have been all been a disaster, but in the end I think Marion was very happy with her life.

24

The End of the Affair

Antonia, my eldest daughter, was looking through my photo album recently and was struck by a photo of a very pretty young woman she didn't recognise. 'That's the girl I should have married,' I told her. I met Eleanor in the early 1950s before I married Wendy. I'd had a few flippant affairs and then this one major love that haunts me even now. Eleanor and I were very much in love—especially for the first two or three months she was in London—but she was reluctant to admit it to begin with. When I asked her about the future she was somewhat evasive. Frustrated, after a while I asked outright her intentions. She explained she was engaged to Desmond, a man back home in Stoke-on-Trent who had inherited a leather factory. She intended to marry him. 'You needn't be jealous of Des,' she assured me. 'When you see him you'll realise why!' True enough, he was, to my mind, a very unattractive, somewhat boring and provincial man. It turned out he wasn't capable of running a leather factory either, but at the time Eleanor thought it would give her financial security. Not that she needed it—her father owned a very productive Staffordshire coal mine and had invested some of his excess profits in war bonds. He bought them in her name to avoid tax—as Uncle Bobby had done with Cousin Ivor. Desmond knew about me and must have been pretty gullible not to suspect that his fiancée's relationship with this man in London wasn't sexual. Eleanor should have told him the truth so that he could make a decision on their future, but he swallowed whatever white fibs she told him. Meanwhile I was hoping to persuade her to break off her engagement and commit to me.

Eleanor had been undergoing training at one of those posh secretarial-cum-finishing-schools they had in those days. However, a sudden bout of illness meant that she had to leave London in a hurry. She returned home to Stoke-on-Trent where I visited her in hospital. She was really very unwell, and I think this prompted her to be fairly candid with her parents—so much so that they knew more than I did at the time. I was summoned to see them and prepared myself for an inquisition. In the event it was all fairly cordial and superficial. I was given a cup of tea, I think—possibly a glass of sherry—and we spent most of the time discussing Eleanor and her illness. I suppose they were sizing me up, but I'm sure they'd already made up their minds to discourage me. Once I had gone they threatened to disinherit Eleanor if she broke off her engagement with Desmond to marry me. It transpired that Eleanor had Crohn's disease—a very unpleasant illness that can be managed but not cured. They told her she would need care throughout her life and that Desmond was a more secure prospect than a feckless London publisher. At the time I had only just started out in publishing and was pretty poor. Her father, who I think may have been antisemitic, saw me as someone entirely without prospects.

At various points I thought my relationship with Eleanor was going nowhere, then there would be another love letter and it all started up again. While she was recuperating in Stoke-on-Trent I poured my heart out to her in a long letter. She never received it. Her wily father intercepted it, read it and destroyed it without telling her. She assumed from my supposed silence that I'd dumped her. Of course I had no way of getting in touch after that. All her letters were being opened, and they wouldn't put any phone calls through to her. Instead, her father wrote me a very unpleasant and threatening letter warning me to keep away. I view him very harshly—he knew this was a serious relationship, and one just doesn't interfere in something like that. So for many years that was that. I put Eleanor to the back of my mind and married Wendy.

In the late 1960s, many years later, long after I'd married Wendy and my publishing business was thriving, Eleanor wrote to me out of the blue. She said she had been completely shattered when she found out that I had married, and confessed that her marriage to Desmond had been a terrible mistake. He must have treated her well, and she had obviously liked him, but she certainly never truly loved him. She told me she had never got over our affair, whereas I'd had to forget about her—I knew I couldn't marry Wendy if I was still in love with someone else. But all those years later she wrote telling me she wanted to come and see me, to tell me the truth and find out my side of things. We agreed to meet.

She had told Desmond that she was coming to see me about a book she had written. There was no book. He must have been awfully naive! In the end I felt a bit sorry for him because she hadn't been honest. He phoned me up the morning she was due to arrive. 'She's coming to talk about a book,' he said, adding 'Be gentle with her!' He was talking about my judgement on her writing, but I rather took it as a kind of encouragement. As for Wendy, I had to be cautious. Had she found out that Eleanor had come down she would have gone berserk. She knew it was serious, that I'd been madly in love with Eleanor, as once, in a drunken jag before we were married, I had told her.

Eleanor booked into the Rembrandt Hotel in Knightsbridge—luckily not a place anyone I knew frequented. She made it quite clear in her letter that she was coming to seduce me, so I set off for our brief encounter with a bottle of wine in my briefcase. We couldn't spend the whole night together. I knew if I went home later than midnight Wendy would be suspicious, so I had to watch the time.

Eleanor was still in love with me, but by that time I was no longer in love with her. I thought I always would be but I just wasn't any more. By then I was a quite confident man—I'd got over the mental breakdown, and things were going quite well. When we were first in love in the 1950s there had been that constant tension about where the relationship was going. This time there was a sense of calm. Both of us knew that this was the end, a final fling. We both knew we really couldn't meet again. I couldn't have gone to Stoke—it was too small a town and people would have gossiped. She couldn't have come to London again because even Desmond would have smelt a very large rat! Besides, had we continued the affair it would have meant two divorces. In those days divorce was still pretty scandalous. At that time, neither of us was prepared to break up our marriage and both had children to consider. However, it was clear that for Eleanor things had not been going too well. The leather factory had done very badly, and she was having to stump up from her own funds to pay Desmond's bills. 'All my money's evaporating,' she said, and showed me an enormous diamond ring saying, 'I bought this so that if there's no cash left I've still got something.' She knew that she had made a mistake in marrying Desmond. 'I made a very bad decision,' she told me.

It was a long time ago, so it's difficult to remember one's feelings, but I think she understood me instinctively. We had an immediate rapport. I don't known how you define it—it just happens when you meet someone sometimes. For instance, when I met Elizabeth Berridge I liked her enormously and always got on very well with her. We were very alike in some ways. There was nothing sexual or romantic with Elizabeth—she was just a very nice woman with a good sense of humour. When I met Wendy it took much longer to fall in love with her. With Eleanor it was almost immediate, and it was the first time I had ever properly been in love. I'd been around the block, so to speak, but hadn't had any particularly deep feelings of love for anyone. With Eleanor it was different. It went beyond sex. Even after I had seduced her I just wanted to be with her. You're lucky if you have one relationship like that in your entire life. But if it happens, I think you're meant to be together permanently.

It's difficult to define these things, but up to a point I think it's true that we were what are known as soulmates. There was no strain between us—we even thought the same way. We really were deeply in love—whatever 'in love' means, as Prince Charles once said before his own first marriage. Had we wed, I think Eleanor and I might have lasted without ending in divorce.

In recent months the memories of Eleanor have come flooding back. When one gets old one looks back on one's life, and it seems to me now that Eleanor was, aside from Wendy, the major love of my life. I can't help wondering how things might have turned out had Eleanor and I married. Had we had more time to talk in the 1950s we could have worked things out. At the time it was difficult—I was sharing a flat, so she couldn't come back to mine, and her father made sure she was somewhere where no visitors were permitted. I could have reassured her that, as a doctor, Uncle Bobby could have taken care of her. As for the leather factory, I could have explained from my own family experience that it wasn't as secure as she thought. As it was, she said she knew she was going to be ill again and was frightened of leaving home.

After our brief encounter at the Rembrandt I never heard from Eleanor again and don't know what happened to her. I'd met Wendy a couple of months after I'd first given up on Eleanor and my involvement with Wendy, our subsequent marriage and children, followed. During my breakdown in the mid-1950s I sometimes wondered whether Eleanor would have coped better and been more supportive than Wendy. The relationship with Eleanor was much deeper—we might have made it for good. On the other hand, whether I could have coped with the unpleasantness of her Crohn's disease is something I'll never know.

25

A Duke, Some Snobs and *La Bâtarde*

Despite all my personal ups and downs, by the mid-1960s the company had become internationally known and all my hard work paid off. We even had a couple of bestsellers. I was determined that alongside our literary endeavours we should publish contemporary books that chimed with the spirit of the times. One of these was the American comedian Lenny Bruce's *How to Talk Dirty and Influence People* (1966). I never met Bruce—the book was bought in via an agent—but we had a foreword by Kenneth Tynan who had shocked television audiences by using the word 'fuck' during a censorship debate in 1965. This was thought at the time to be the first instance of the word on British television. Bruce had suffered problems with censors in the United States throughout his career for similar language and themes. In public and in Parliament there was a huge furore regarding Tynan's swearing. Puritanical critic Mary Whitehouse suggested that Tynan should have his bottom spanked—something that, as an enthusiast of sexual sadomasochism, he would doubtless have enjoyed.

The Bruce book did well, but it was another humorous effort, *The Duke of Bedford's Book of Snobs* (1965), that made the bestseller lists. Inspired by Thackeray's 1848 original, John Ian Russell, the thirteenth Duke of Bedford, had originated some useful material, but the book needed a ghostwriter. First we approached Lucian Freud's brother Clement, then a radio personality, later an MP and, I thought, a thoroughly nasty man. Luckily that fell through, so I approached the Hungarian émigré George Mikes (pronounced 'mee-kesh') and his illustrator Nicolas Bentley. They had enjoyed enormous success since 1946 with *How To Be an Alien* and its sequels, all published by André Deutsch. André, who had known Mikes in Budapest before he emigrated to Britain, was terribly suspicious of my 'Snob' venture. I had to reassure him that I wasn't poaching his stars, only borrowing them.

The Duke, much to the disapproval of a few other aristocrats, had opened up Woburn Abbey, his ancestral seat, to the public, and had written a book on running stately homes. Before inheriting his title he had been a rent collector, soldier, journalist and tireless self-promoter. Running Woburn was so expensive that he was constantly on the hustle for cash. In the 1960s he appeared, mostly in cameos as himself, in films or TV shows such as *The Golden Shot*, *The Liberace Show* and, bizarrely, *Coronation Street*. He had even allowed the film *Nudist Paradise* (1959) to be shot at Woburn, though I don't think he appeared in that one. Eventually, in the 1970s, he became a tax exile in Monaco, leaving his heir to run the estate.

In the run-up to publication I went to Woburn for a publicity meeting, and Wendy came along for the ride. When his third wife Nicole arrived to introduce herself she reprimanded the Duke for not having offered us coffee. It's not as if he would have had to make it himself—he had staff. Another time, when his agent gave Mikes and me lunch at the Ritz, the Duke and I both ordered roast pork. He made a terrible scene when they mistakenly gave me his outsize helping of crackling. He was shouting his head off—really the sort of thing you don't do, especially if you're a guest at the Ritz. The Duke's rudeness and lack of manners is a great irony—his book is partly about etiquette. Mikes himself was great fun—he certainly had a sense of humour and enough patience to handle an unpleasant and self-important aristocrat. In the book Mikes subtly sent up the Duke in revenge. A clever satirist, Mikes's book, with its brilliant illustrations, was a huge hit.

The other bestseller of 1965 was Violette Leduc's memoir *La Bâtarde*. At the time I could afford very good freelance public relations; in this case it was handled by Morley Richards, one of the grand old men of Fleet Street who had been a senior editor at the *Daily Express*. Morley arranged a literary lunch at Foyles, and we billeted Violette Leduc at the Savoy where we held a party in her honour. Violette was friendly though enigmatic. The book sold out, very quickly requiring a reprint. I wish I had been able to publish more of Leduc's books. To my annoyance, other than her marvellous novella *The Little Lady and the Fox Fur*, which we still have in print, the agent at Éditions Gallimard always let Granada buy them first.

It was in March 1965 that I attended another party at the Ritz for the launch of *Cosmopolitan* and was reunited with my boyhood friend Brian Braithwaite, the first best friend I ever had. I saw his name as host on the invitation and a few bells started ringing. By then he was publisher of *Harpers & Queen*, *Cosmopolitan*, *Country Living* and others. 'I think I went to school with that man!' I told my PR. Brian had invited me not knowing who I was—I'd still been Peter Offenstadt when he had known me at school. He'd been headhunted for a number of top magazine publishing jobs and was clearly very good at them. I'd been very upset when his family had moved to Twickenham when Brian was ten or eleven and he had left the school, so I was glad to be reunited with him, even though it took forty-seven years. As a boy

I never thought of getting his phone number and Twickenham had seemed a long way away. I had no idea where it was—it might as well have been the moon. People came and went. Over the course of my life most people have disappeared one way or another.

Brian had gained enormous experience in the trade, from managing advertising for the *Daily Mail*, *Evening News* and *Farmers Weekly* to launching *New Scientist* and becoming publisher for *Cosmopolitan* and *Good Housekeeping*. When he ran the advertising for the restaurant column in the *Evening News* he would visit all the London restaurateurs. They'd invite him in for lunch or a drink, so he got to know Victor Berlemont who ran the York Minster Pub in Dean Street which became the celebrated French House, often referred to as 'the French', when Berlemont's son Gaston ran it. Brian also wrote several books on the magazine and newspaper trade, a couple of which I published myself. *Women's Magazines: The First 300 Years* (1994) did very well, but *The Press Book* (2009) flopped. Brian and his wife would come to dinner now and then, and we've kept in touch ever since.

Another friend for a long time was journalist and author Ann Barr, who died in 2015. She had an awful Amazon parrot called Turkey. Disturbed by the kerfuffle at a party, Turkey bit me quite deeply on the hand despite the fact that I was trying to be friendly. Ann was famous for *The Official Sloane Ranger Handbook* (1982) and was for a time a neighbour of mine. Her obituary said she didn't suffer fools gladly—but does anyone? At any rate, she was one of the nicest, most generous people I have ever known. At the time I didn't know she was the heiress of Irn-Bru, a fluorescent-orange fizzy drink they have in Scotland that her grandfather invented. She was a brilliant journalist and worked with Brian Braithwaite at *Harpers & Queen* and *Nova*. At one point, Ann wrote an illustrated feature on 'happy marriages' and picked Wendy and me as an exemplar. It was a few months after Ben was born, and Marion and her mother were furious. I said, 'Well, what did you expect me to do?' I couldn't very well own up to the truth at the time.

Sue Grafton was another 1960s find. Before she became famous for her alphabet series of detective novels (from *A Is for Alibi* to *Y Is for Yesterday*—she didn't quite manage to get to Z) I published her first two novels, *Keziah Dane* (1967) and *The Lolly-Madonna War* (1969). I didn't think they were great literature, but they were certainly good enough to publish, and the second was made into a film. After she became successful as a screenwriter and detective novelist she didn't want the books reprinted, so the originals have become highly collectible. Fans pay a fortune for them. So I sold mine.

In 1969 I published Tariq Ali's first book, *The New Revolutionaries: A Handbook of the International Radical Left*. He had joined the International Marxist Group the year before and was very left wing, so we commissioned the book and got him to edit it with Michael Levien. It sold well internationally.

I have a photograph of Ali at one of our parties with Margaret Crosland, our translator and adviser, Peter Vansittart—who was a brilliant novelist and good friend—and Roland Topor, the French writer, cartoonist, actor and songwriter. Topor was immensely talented—his later drawings were animated for the cult 1973 science-fiction film *La Planète sauvage*. In 1968 we published a book of his *Stories and Drawings* which Margaret, who was also his agent, translated with David Le Vay. That's highly collectable now, too.

Another 1960s discovery I made was Anita Desai. I've been to India several times, first about fifty years ago as part of a world tour. She looked absolutely radiant, and we had something in common as her mother was German. We published her first two novels *Cry, the Peacock* (1963) and *Voices in the City* (1965). Initially Anita was appreciative but was very upset when I rejected a book I thought below standard. She spent three weeks in London and took it upon herself to write a book about Indians there. I thought it was unconvincing. I told her it couldn't be published, that to do so would harm her reputation. She took it very badly, making it clear that she expected me to publish everything she wrote without demur. More recently she has been very gracious about my decision. I wasn't particularly keen on her next book, a collection of stories, either, so recommended her to Heinemann who later hit the jackpot. In retrospect, it was a mistake of mine as she went on to garner all sorts of awards.

Publishing Marc Chagall's memoir *My Life* in 1965 brought terrible problems. I had to deal with his awful, smarmy partners and his wife and daughter. Things were so bad that litigation ensued. When I dealt with Salvador Dalí a few years later he was comparatively easy, despite his reputation for pottiness and avarice. Chagall's team hated the translation of the book—I can't remember how many drafts we went through. In the end they agreed to accept the judgement of Stephen Spender who pronounced the translation fine. It was, he said, Chagall's style that was arch. The trouble we took over the book proved worthwhile, however, as Chagall underwent something of a renaissance and the book was a success.

While some authors repay their publisher's time and investment, others don't. I published a couple of novels by Guatemalan author Miguel Ángel Asturias—*The Mulatta and Mister Fly* in 1963 and *The Cyclone* in 1967, the same year that he won the Nobel Prize for Literature. John Calder, who didn't want to publish him himself, had tipped me off that Asturias was available. Our publication of two of his books had undoubtedly helped him towards receiving the Nobel—it enabled the committee to read him in English. However, Asturias was ingratiating before the award and utterly arrogant, unpleasant and ungrateful afterwards. Although he was a good writer, I wished I'd never bothered.

One author who was very grateful to me was Dame Edith Sitwell, who died in 1964. I met her only once. In 1953 we brought out her novel *I Live Under a Black Sun* and have kept it in print ever since. It had been published by John Lehmann but was being remaindered. His decision certainly didn't sit well with Dame Edith: 'I've never been remaindered!' she wailed over the phone—she really was very upset. I can't remember who tipped me off, but I bought up all the old stock and got a small binder I knew to rebind them as Peter Owen books. She was so grateful that she invited Wendy and me to a large London tea party at the Sesame Club, in Grosvenor Street, Mayfair. A lot of very famous people were there, and, despite being anxious, I managed to chat to her for a bit. Dame Edith herself, a renowned eccentric, was formidable but gracious. Much later, in 1989, I republished her 1946 biography of Elizabeth I, *A Fanfare for Elizabeth*.

It was at Dame Edith's party that I first met Charles Osborne—an author who became head of the Arts Council literary section with powers to allocate money to publishers. It was said that if you took him to the opera, as John Calder did, he'd give you a grant. Eventually I published Osborne's book *Wagner on Music* (1970), which also curried favour. In those days that's how things worked. Years later I got very cross when someone I disliked took over the Arts Council—we loathed one another and he gave us no money even though, as a literary publisher, we were, with the closure of libraries, starting to feel the pinch and could have done with the council's support. I wrote to the *Daily Telegraph* and *The Times* pointing out that the Arts Council were happy to give huge grants to certain publishing houses run by well-heeled millionaires but not to those that really needed it. There was a terrible kerfuffle—a long, acrimonious public correspondence ensued in both papers. Of course I regretted it, even though what I said was true. I lost favour for years and felt that I had been blacklisted. These days we have an extremely good relationship with the Arts Council, but I did learn the hard way that you can never fight the establishment and win.

26

The Enigma of Anna Kavan

By the time I met Anna Kavan, one of the most striking writers I ever published, her work had been neglected and her existence pretty well forgotten. Diana Johns, a friend of mine who ran the Bodkins Bookshop in Kensington Church Street, told me one of her customers was a very distinguished writer who wasn't being published any more and suggested I look into it. Jonathan Cape had published much of Anna's earlier work but during and after the war, on the cusp of success, interest had waned.

Diana Johns was an excellent bookseller despite, while her husband went off gambling, drinking very heavily. One Christmas I volunteered to help out at the shop as she couldn't afford extra staff and needed to go away for a few days. She didn't brief me at all. I didn't know what anything cost, and quite a few well-known writers came in to buy books, picking up armfuls and telling me that Diana was happy for them to have them on credit. They were trying it on, of course, and never paid their accounts. Understandably Diana never asked me to deputise again.

Anna Kavan was one of the few Bodkins customers who was scrupulous about paying on the dot. Like my Uncle Rudi, Anna had contributed to the literary magazine *Horizon*, though I didn't make the connection at the time or recall her name. Somehow she had slipped under my literary radar. In the late 1960s, when I was handling all her work, I sent one of Anna's short stories to *Encounter* magazine. The managing editor Margot Walmsley couldn't believe it. 'Is it *the* Anna Kavan?' she wrote back. Anyone who remembered her as a literary figure had assumed she was dead. Sadly, she soon was.

In 1956 what Diana Johns told me of Anna and her work intrigued me enough to ask her to arrange a meeting. Anna was living in Peel Street at the time, not far from Diana's bookshop. My first impression was of a woman who was extremely poised and elegant, with startling bleached blonde hair and a husky voice. It was only much later I discovered that, for all her elegance, Anna was a heroin addict.

Anna had been born as Helen Woods in Cannes in 1901. Her wealthy British parents liked to travel, and Anna grew up feeling neglected. In David Callard's *The Case of Anna Kavan*, the biography I published in 1992, the author describes her as having been a timid, quiet girl nicknamed 'Mouse'. Callard seems to have got this idea from 'Mouse, Shoes'—one of the short stories in *A Bright Green Field* (1958), the first collection I published—without having any evidence that it was true. Many, like Callard, have assumed that Anna's fiction was more reliably autobiographical than it was and have been strangely reluctant to credit her with the powers of creativity and imagination she undoubtedly possessed. As a result, in the absence of trustworthy sources, much of what we know of Anna's life has been distorted by rumour, mythologising and wishful thinking. I published another biography, Jeremy Reed's *A Stranger on Earth: The Life and Work of Anna Kavan*, in 2006, but errors and myths are still widespread. I hope that future biographies will remedy this situation. In the meantime I'll set down here what I consider more or less reliable.

I think it's fair to say that Anna's life, at least as she saw it, was blighted by a more extreme version of the emotional neglect I experienced as a child. Anna was cared for by a nursemaid early in her life and was permitted to see her mother only for ten minutes before dinner. While still very young, Anna endured long, lonely stints at boarding-schools where her sense of abandonment grew. In 1911, when Anna was only ten, her father jumped from a ship and drowned at sea—a traumatic and permanent form of abandonment. At nineteen she married Donald Ferguson, a somewhat older man who claimed to be of aristocratic birth—a relative, he said, of the Earl of Marl and Kellie. Perhaps this impressed Anna and especially her mother who herself claimed descent from an Austrian count. The marriage was a disaster though, and Anna left Ferguson after the birth of Bryan, their son, in 1922. It was, however, while living with Ferguson in Burma that she began to write—her means of escape from an uncomfortable reality.

Beginning with *A Charmed Circle* in 1929, Jonathan Cape published Anna's first four novels under her original married name, Helen Ferguson. In everyday life Anna was calling herself Helen Edmonds, having taken the name of her lover, the painter Stuart Edmonds, whom she married in 1927. By then Anna was a drug addict. She is supposed to have claimed her tennis coach had introduced her to cocaine to improve her serve in a tournament. As for heroin, one of her short stories led some to believe her introduction to opiates came through consorting with daredevil racing drivers in Cannes who used it in their post-race come-down. The truth is likely to have been more prosaic: she was probably first prescribed either morphine or its derivative diamorphine (known as heroin) to relieve physical pain or mental distress. As a distraction from her troubles, and encouraged by her mother, Anna studied at London's Central School of Art. She proved a talented painter, and occasional prestigious exhibitions, though no great success, followed.

In 1935, during her marriage to Edmonds, a daughter was born but soon died. Kavan and Edmonds then adopted a girl, but, concerned by her mental fragility, the authorities ultimately denied Kavan permanent custody. After a decade of marriage Anna's relationship with Edmonds began to founder, and he eventually took another lover who became his third wife.

Kavan was always mentally fragile, regularly severely depressed, and often attempted suicide. By now her mother had married a wealthy gay South African who dyed his hair platinum blond and surrounded himself with pretty young men. In return for the fig leaf of heterosexuality she provided, he gave Anna's mother lavish funds for her travels and retained a suite at Claridge's for her personal use. Her mother also funded detoxification treatment for Anna at a London clinic. It failed to cure her appetite for the drug and was probably only intended to keep her addiction 'under control' by temporarily decreasing her tolerance. Anna thought of the heroin she was prescribed as a treatment for her depression rather than a cause. The experience of leaving a clinic is memorably dramatised in 'The Old Address', the first story of the posthumous collection *Julia and the Bazooka* (1970), 'bazooka' being her jocular term for her heroin syringe.

The ending of Anna's relationship with Edmonds triggered a suicide attempt. Two more suicide attempts were followed by hospitalisations. It was at a Swiss sanatorium—where she underwent insulin coma treatments similar to those undergone by my Uncle Rudi—that Anna accepted the permanence of her addiction and resolved to live alone. She bleached her auburn hair—ironically a simulacrum of her stepfather's—and reinvented herself as Anna Kavan—giving herself a new name and identity and an appearance that startled those who had known her before.

Though Jonathan Cape was enthusiastic about her work, Helen Ferguson's last two novels of the late 1930s, the mysterious *Goose Cross* and *Rich Get Rich*, were published by John Lane the Bodley Head, which Jonathan Cape and others were now financially backing. While the novels of her Helen Ferguson days are more naturalistic, they still contained what a reviewer in *Punch* referred to as 'an eerie originality' that came to typify the work of the more stylistically experimental Anna Kavan. Her new name, so much more than a pseudonym, was that of a character she had based upon herself who appeared in two Helen Ferguson novels *Let Me Alone* (1930) and *A Stranger Still* (1935).

In 1940 Jonathan Cape published the critically acclaimed collection *Asylum Piece*, the first of Anna's books under her new identity. She travelled widely with various companions for almost three years, writing continuously, and settled for a while with a partner in New Zealand where she enjoyed the desolate landscapes. She kept up her writing, noting down all her experiences as diaries and transmuting them into fiction. Encouragingly, her stories were in demand for magazines on both sides of the Atlantic. The war complicated and delayed her return to London, where she faced more tragic news. Her son Bryan Ferguson had joined the RAF at the beginning of the war. In 1942, aged just twenty, he was reported missing, presumed dead. During her marriage to Edmonds, Bryan had been looked after by his father's family but often stayed with his mother and stepfather during the school holidays. Though some claimed that Anna had been ambivalent about her son early on, there is no evidence for this, and she was clearly very upset by his death. In London Anna attempted suicide again and ended up in a psychiatric hospital under the care of Dr Karl Bluth. Their intense friendship dominated the rest of her life.

A German-born anti-fascist, Bluth had been friendly with Brecht and Heidegger and had written plays and criticism, including a commentary on Novalis. He fled Germany in 1934 and set up his London practice in Kensington. Peter Watson, who funded the literary magazine *Horizon*, was one of Bluth's patients and may have introduced him to Anna. Between 1943 and 1946 the magazine published numerous Anna Kavan book reviews and two articles, one her impression of New Zealand, the second a fictionalised study of a patient in the military psychiatric unit where she assisted for a short period. The piece was sympathetic to its subject and provocatively critical of his treatment there. Until heart problems intervened, Anna also provided secretarial and editorial assistance to Cyril Connolly at *Horizon*, where some of her stories, including 'I Am Lazarus' (1943), 'Face of My People' (1944) and 'The Professor' (1946), were published. Bluth himself contributed two essays to *Horizon*.

When I first visited her, Anna had recently subsidised the publication of her novel *A Scarcity of Love* (1956), but distribution was patchy and her publisher had gone bust. *I Am Lazarus* (1945), an acclaimed story collection which drew on her wartime experiences with military psychiatric patients, had been her last book with Jonathan Cape. The company had dropped her after Doubleday published her surreal 1947 novel *The House of Sleep* in the United States and it was resoundingly panned. The critics in the UK also responded badly to the British edition, published by Cassell the following year as *Sleep Has His House*.

Anna's only other publication in the 1940s was *The Horse's Tale* (1949). Co-written with Dr Bluth, and published by the experimental Gaberbocchus Press (which also published James Laughlin's poetry), the book is an allegory about a philosophical dancing horse who runs away from the circus to found the artistic school of 'Hoofism'. After a drunken episode at a party, the horse awakens in an asylum unsure whether he is a horse or a man.

I only met Bluth once or twice and found him very boring indeed. I thought *The Horse's Tale* was a bore, too. I didn't like it at all—certainly not enough to publish it. Bluth was a genuine doctor but an unconventional one. He also treated the poet David Gascoyne who had sent himself crackers through addiction to the amphetamine inhalers he first used to treat perennial catarrh. All these vulnerable people would line up for Bluth's injections of bull's blood, amphetamines and other dubious ingredients. I was pretty appalled when I heard about this, but such unorthodox treatments were not unique to Bluth. Max Jacobson, another eccentric German-born doctor in the United States, gave similarly noxious injections to Truman Capote, Tennessee Williams, President Kennedy and a whole troupe of celebrities.

Writing was always a precarious source of income, and Anna had survived mostly through family allowances and private enterprise. In the 1930s she had bred bulldogs. An excellent interior designer, in the 1950s she set up Kavan Properties and supplemented her income buying, refurbishing and converting houses. This kept her going while her work was neglected. The flat in Peel Street was made to her own design and was beautifully furnished with a mixture of modern items and antiques including a golden harp bequeathed by her mother, which Anna's maternal grandmother had once played at a Victorian charity concert.

I used to go to Anna's dinner parties now and then. The Welsh novelist Rhys Davies, probably her closest friend, was usually there, too. It was all very proper. It's remarkable that Anna was able to write so much so well despite her addiction. She was functional, and unless one knew she was an addict, one would never have guessed. I wouldn't have certainly—she always seemed sober and very well turned out.

Anna didn't drink much, just the occasional Dubonnet. It must be the only alcohol you can stomach with drugs, as it was also the only tipple Paul Bowles ever drank, and he was always stoned on cannabis. Conversation could sometimes be tricky with Anna. During a discussion about a new tenant for her downstairs flat I recommended a literary agent, an extremely pleasant woman, who was looking to rent somewhere. Anna excused herself and left the room for (I later discovered) a heroin fix. While we were alone Rhys told me not to pursue the matter, hissing, 'She doesn't like women!' She invited me for drinks on another occasion and half-heartedly added, 'Bring your wife if you'd like.' As a fan and a writer herself, Wendy was keen meet Anna, however, once we got there our host was polite but far from welcoming. Rhys also recalled a dinner party at which the novelist Olivia Manning was a guest. Anna snubbed her, preferring to peruse magazines rather than converse.

Anna was eccentric, I thought, rather than genuinely mad. She could be friendly and engaged or brittle and distant. Aside from Dr Bluth, she had a small support network of mainly gay male friends that she relied on for company and practical assistance when required. Anna did have some female friends—perhaps her closest were her lifelong friend Ann Ledbrook and

Ann's daughter Rose Knox-Peebles. Ann befriended Anna while they were at Malvern Girls' College during the First World War. The period of the 1918 influenza epidemic, which killed several fellow pupils, traumatised them both.

After she had grown up, Anna would not drive. She had enjoyed fast cars but was rumoured to have killed a pedestrian in a hit-and-run accident. This seems unlikely and is probably a mistaken reading of a story in the posthumous collection *Julia and the Bazooka*. Whatever the case, Rose became Anna's unofficial chauffeur and happily assisted with changing her typewriter ribbon and sundry other tasks. At other times deliverymen would often be inveigled into changing Anna's lightbulbs.

Anna claimed she had so many clothes, many of which she never wore, because she was frightened of saleswomen and never dared leave a shop without buying something. Much of her shopping was probably therapeutic. 'When I was a teenager I revelled in her cast-offs,' Rose told me, 'including a fabulous fur coat. They were far too grown-up for me, but I loved them and the faint scent they carried of Anna's favourite perfume.' Anna, thin and feeling constantly cold on account of her addiction, would wear her fur coats in all weathers. 'Her addiction, her need to inject,' Rose said, 'was just matter of fact, much as though she had diabetes.'

Soon after meeting her, Anna decided to give me the manuscript of *Eagles' Nest* which I published in 1957. This was followed by the story collection *A Bright Green Field* in 1958. We managed to get Anna a few reviews, but her oblique Kafkaesque style, her modernism, was out of step with the 'Angry Young Men' and kitchen-sink realism popular at the time. Anna was still little known, and her real breakthrough didn't come until shortly before her death.

27

The Cold World

Anna was nearly always very well behaved, but things began to deteriorate when Dr Bluth was hospitalised in 1963 for heart problems. His death in March the following year caused her great emotional disquiet, and she became more erratic. I was once at dinner with Rhys Davies when Anna got up abruptly and left to self-administer a dose of heroin. Again Rhys cautioned me away from our topic of conversation. The last time he'd upset her, he explained, she had hurled a whole roast chicken at him.

Much to Bluth's wife Theophila's annoyance and disgust, Anna occupied much of his time. She would often call him out in the middle of the night and relied on him both as a stabilising friend and a supplier of heroin. He continued to supply her with the drug even when she had defaulted on her medical bills. Anna regarded Bluth's death as a betrayal, claiming they had sworn a suicide pact, and begged Raymond Marriott, another friend, to spend as many evenings with her as he could endure. 'I will do my best to behave normally,' she told him. After Raymond and Rhys rescued her from yet another suicidal overdose she was furious, claiming they had forced her 'to live my life and go on suffering'. She wrote, 'I can't say how profoundly I resent their interference', and told me she was now merely 'waiting for death'. She still viewed renunciation of heroin as impossible. Karl Bluth's death had coincided with increased public and political concern over drug addiction. Fearing she would be forced to give it up, Anna began stockpiling heroin supplies.

Kavan was ambivalent about the burgeoning 1960s drug culture. She disdained its glorification and showed no interest in the underground scene and its literary representatives. She had smoked pot earlier in her life and tried it again in the 1960s, but, having endured a talk on marijuana, wrote to Raymond Marriott, 'What incredible rubbish is talked. Really, this drug business is beyond belief.' She took amphetamines frequently, though, and tried LSD. Sometimes she despaired of ever having taken heroin. At other times she declared that it had saved her life and kept her from madness. At her request Rhys Davies once took her to investigate the hippy scene in London clubs, but her interest was probably professional—she went more as an observer rather than a participant. Some of these experiences found their way into a few of the stories in *My Soul in China*, a posthumous collection I published in 1975. More often Anna would stay at home and watch television. She and Raymond, who had become her downstairs tenant, became devotees of the new BBC science-fiction television series *Doctor Who*.

By the time Bluth died Anna had completed an early draft of the novel she originally called *The Cold World*. The book, a metaphysical post-apocalyptic thriller which was to become her most celebrated novel, started out as something I had declined to publish. It seemed too long and unwieldy. Weidenfeld & Nicholson had planned to publish it after Francis King, their literary adviser, had recommended it. They got cold feet and, fearing it wouldn't sell, backed out. When I saw the manuscript again in March 1966 it still needed a lot of editing. I accepted it on the proviso that revisions were made.

The book was something of a departure for Anna, and, having made a few changes, she defended it, saying she couldn't write in the same way as her previous work. 'The world is quite different and so is my life in it,' she wrote. 'My writing changes with the conditions outside. This kind of adventure story seems to be in the air just now, which is probably why I wanted to write a book of that sort in my own language and with my own symbolism.' I thought the writing and characterisation too vague, but she didn't want to risk spoiling it with anything more concrete. 'I saw the story as one of those recurring dreams,' she wrote, 'which at times become a nightmare. This dreamlike atmosphere is the essence of the whole concept. Without it, the book would be meaningless. It is an effect very easily damaged or lost altogether.' Her letters were firm but polite. However, according to Rose Knox-Peebles Anna was really furious at my insistence that her book be edited and shortened. She had commissioned a nude photograph of herself and was resentful, too, when I refused to use it as her author portrait for the book.

Eventually Philip Inman, a friend of mine, said that he would edit *The Cold World* without a fee just because he admired her work and had nothing else to do. I had got to know Philip at the French House in Soho. He was keen and wealthy—the son of the first Baron Inman of Knaresborough—and wanted an entry into the publishing world. Had he not died by suicide in April 1968 he would have inherited his father's title.

Philip had written the initial reader's report describing the book as a cross between Kafka and *The Avengers*, the popular spy fantasy television show. Anna wrote to me saying, 'Considering Kafka's reputation and the success of *The Avengers*, I can't think why you don't want the book as it is!' She had made some tentative revisions but eventually agreed to work with Philip for much of the rest of the year on restructuring the novel. It was resubmitted in November 1966 as *The Ice World*. I felt the title was too similar to *The Ice Palace*, the Tarjei Vesaas masterpiece I had recently published, so gladly accepted her suggestion that it be retitled simply *Ice*. Contracts were issued, and we published the book in 1967. Much of the excised material was published posthumously in 1994 as *Mercury*, a sort of parallel novella abstracted from *The Cold World*, to which my friend Doris Lessing wrote a brief but enthusiastic foreword. *Ice* had strongly influenced Doris's 1982 novel *The Making of the Representative for Planet 8*.

Publicity for *Ice* was good. Dom Moraes, an Indian-born poet who was quite well-known at the time, interviewed Anna for the fashionable magazine *Nova*. The article paired her with Jean Rhys, describing them both as examples of 'great success and long obscurity'. Both writers admired one another. I sat with Anna during the interview, first in her house, then over lunch at La Chanterelle in London's Old Brompton Road. She answered Dom's questions but seemed fairly preoccupied and distant, giving the impression that she didn't care. I think she just disliked being interviewed. She had dressed beautifully and wouldn't have bothered to come to the lunch if she hadn't wanted to be there. She was also still grieving Karl Bluth's death, and at one point she turned to Moraes and said, 'I haven't felt anything for twenty years.' As to her sense of abstraction, she found socializing difficult and told Rhys, 'For an unsociable solitary person like myself, who has been alone all day in an unreal world of whatever I'm writing, to suddenly snap out of it ... and try to be sociable, requires a colossal effort.' Indeed, when Raymond was living in her ground-floor flat they would often exchange letters rather than converse.

In December 1968 we were giving a big party for Anaïs Nin at our house in Kenway Road. We had already held a press junket at the Savoy but invited Anna to the house because Nin was a fan. Anaïs had sent her admiring letters (which seemed only to annoy Anna) and later wrote enthusiastically of the British author in her study *The Novel of the Future* (1969). Anaïs also offered an introduction to *Ice*, but Anna rejected it. Like me I think Anna felt that she was the better writer of the two and was being patronised. By then Anna was living in the upper flat of a house she had herself designed and had built in Hillsleigh Road, near Holland Park in Kensington. Its interlocking rooms were painted white, and a lush secluded garden provided more private space.

Despite her hermetic lifestyle we had thought Anna might come to the party—she had indicated that she might—but we weren't particularly surprised when she didn't. By then she was quite unwell—a spinal condition and legs badly abscessed from botched injections meant frequent hospital attendances and admissions.

The morning after the party the police turned up on my doorstep saying they had bad news. For a terrible moment I thought something had happened to one of my children, but they said, 'Miss Kavan has committed suicide.' They had found our party invitation in her flat, which Raymond and Rhys had encouraged them to break into. She had been dead over twenty-four hours.

Anna was found lying across her bed using as a pillow the lacquered Chinese box in which she stashed her heroin. The police were wrong about the cause of death. The post-mortem revealed that her heart had failed. After decades of drug use and many suicide attempts her death was an accident. Scotland Yard's Drug Squad inspected the flat and found her heroin stockpile—enough, they said, to kill the entire street. She once told Raymond Marriott that she didn't give a damn what happened after her death. 'Why should I?' she wrote, 'It's nothing to do with me.' She did, however, care enough about her reputation to work extremely hard, while increasingly ill, at completing sufficient stories for a new collection and on what became *Ice*, her most celebrated novel. By a quirk of fate, the day of Anna's Golders Green funeral a telegram arrived from Doubleday, then one of the largest publishers in the United States, making an offer for *Ice* which Brian Aldiss, an admirer, had recommended to them.

Anna bequeathed her golden harp to Rose Knox-Peebles. She had continued to paint, therapeutically, resourcefully and imaginatively, throughout her life and Rhys and Raymond, her executors, gave me and others some of her paintings, including several haunting self-portraits. Others they kept, while a few—some depicting suicides and tortures—were so gruesome they destroyed them. Some of what survives strikes me as imaginative but still fairly grim.

In retrospect, I always preferred Anna Kavan to Anaïs Nin, both as a person and a writer. Though she could be cold, I liked her. She was devious but not to the same extent as Anaïs. Anna's work is much more imaginative and less immediately autobiographical. She effectively transmutes her experiences into something new and uniquely brilliant. Where Anna retains her mystery, Anaïs, through her voluminous journals, rendered herself utterly transparent. As with Anaïs, one never knew what was true in Anna's work. I suspect that most of what she wrote was fantasy. She once told me that she had tried and failed at writing autobiography and could only write fiction. Her husbands were unlikely to have been as boorish and monstrous as some of the men in her novels. Similarly, I doubt that Anna—unlike the narrator of her story 'A Visit'—ever experienced a leopard reclining beside her on her bed. No one knows the truth of Anna's relationship with her mother either. Ann Ledbrook claimed that she was, in fact, quite a pleasant woman. Despite Anna's often venomous antipathy—the product of her somewhat paranoid mind and unhappiness over her inheritance—she kept in her living-room a portrait her mother had commissioned of herself from Vladimir Tretchikoff. Many considered it hideous. Rhys recalled Anna glaring at the painting while berating her mother, though, paradoxically, Anna's surviving diaries often praise her kindness.

Anna's relationship with Karl Bluth was intense but probably not sexual. I think the heroin suppressed her appetite for sex, though there were unconfirmed rumours of Anna having had lesbian affairs. Anna and Bluth painted together, wrote together and wanted to die together. She thought they had a telepathic bond. Both died, literally, of broken hearts. Mrs Bluth, who attended Anna's funeral in a cold fury, blamed Anna's dependence on him for her husband's death. I shared a car to the funeral with Rhys and Raymond who were discussing Anna's £500 bequest to Mrs Bluth. 'Blood money!' one of them pronounced.

Diana Johns also came to the funeral. I don't know whether Anna really appreciated what Diana had done for her. It was she who had given me all the background and talked me into to publishing Anna. Once I realised joust how good she was, I snapped her up. She was a good find—perhaps our greatest modern classic, a writer who might conceivably be regarded as on a par with Virginia Woolf and Jean Rhys. Rhys Davies once told me that Anna always knew her work would endure. 'It's my life—I have to write,' she told me. 'There's nothing else.' Since her death I have published several posthumous novels, further collections of stories, and kept her books in print. Her work has been widely translated and disseminated. The Anna Kavan Society, founded in 2009, held its first conference in 2014, while Anna's paintings and novels have also inspired exhibitions, theatre, music and sound art. Her place in posterity is assured.

By the time of her death Anna had already incinerated most of her diaries and nearly all her correspondence, somewhat frustrating any attempt at a complete biography. Long before I published the two preliminary forays into Kavan biography by David Callard and Jeremy Reed, Brian Aldiss had wanted to write one. He gave up when he couldn't find enough information. Indeed, a character in one of Anna's short stories proclaims, 'I was about to become the world's best kept secret; one that would never be told. What a thrilling enigma for posterity I should be.'

28

Palaces, Kings and Killers

For the company's twentieth anniversary in April 1971 we celebrated with an event at the House of Lords. There is a photograph of me there, with Wendy and our daughters Antonia and Georgina. Wendy's wearing an outfit I bought for her in a Moroccan boutique in Tétouan. We all look pretty solemn—I don't know why. We also held an exhibition at the National Book League which was opened by Lord Goodman, then chairman of the Arts Council. Keith Cunningham, our regular designer, who created some of our best book jackets, designed the display.

A contemporary article in the *Daily Express*, presumably using one of our press releases, says the company was then 'worth over £300,000'—over £4 million today. Our annual turnover was half that, but turnover is not profit and, though we were undoubtedly successful, I never felt that rich. Our books were relatively pricey hardbacks, usually at least £2 which would be nearer £27 today. We'd had a bestseller in the 1960s with *The Duke of Bedford's Book of Snobs* and had other high-profile hits like Yoko Ono's *Grapefruit*, plus a good list of international literature, including five Nobel laureates (we've added five more since). I was still working hard but perhaps not as frantically as I had in the early days. By then I had a reliable staff of ten which included a young man called Dan Franklin.

Dan came to us straight from university. His tutor gave a reference which said that while most of his students were flashy, Dan was sincere. Initially we rejected him, but three months later the candidate we appointed ran off with the petty-cash box, so we brought Dan in as a sales assistant. He was actually very good at it—Dan is professional about whatever he does.

When he started, Dan worked as an assistant to Robin Gurland, our sales manager. Gurland started off well but became too big for his boots. He had relatives in South Africa and wanted me to pay all his expenses to go to see them despite coming from a fairly wealthy family. I remember they owned a Francis Bacon painting, so they can't have been poor. I think we said we'd offer a contribution to his expenses, but I felt that he was taking advantage really. At that time we had a bookkeeper called Mr Suzman, a German émigré who did very little work. There was nothing I could really put my finger on, but he seemed very cold and I didn't like him. Our production manager Beatrice Musgrave and another female colleague said he made passes at them. Suzman used to sit there reading a book; whenever anyone came in, he'd close it quickly and pretend to be working. I wouldn't have minded so much, but, though he probably had quite good taste, it was never one of our own books! Obviously he didn't need an assistant, but we took on Tony Lunn as a trainee, and Suzman made him do all the work so that he could idle time away with his nose in a book. We've had a few troublesome staff and swindlers over the course of time. The worst was someone who lost us money by messing up contracts and who embezzled quite a lot of money right under our noses. We caught him in time and got him to pay most of it back. Compared to that, people like Suzman were an irritant but less troublesome.

Dan Franklin was bright enough to know that if he was ever going to get into editorial work he'd have to achieve this by working up through sales and production. When one of our editors left, Beatrice Musgrave said that Dan would be hopeless as an editor, but I insisted we gave him a chance. He turned out to be extremely good. Between them Beatrice and Michael Levien taught him all he needed to know.

Some of the books Dan worked on needed a lot of rewriting, including Sandy Fawkes's *Killing Time* (1977) which became a big bestseller for us. Sandy had this tragi-comic sozzled life and was a regular in Soho pubs, especially the French and the Coach & Horses. Jeffrey Bernard was always mocking her in his column in *The Spectator*, but she never seemed to care. In 1974 she'd had a close encounter in the United States with a man who later turned out to be the prolific American serial killer Paul Knowles, the subject of her book. She'd crossed the Atlantic to try for a job at the *National Enquirer* but, having failed, went on a road trip down the Florida coast with a handsome young man she met in a bar. On her return she discovered that he'd killed at least eighteen people, two of them just before she picked him up. I read the manuscript while at Shrubland Hall, a health spa in Suffolk, with Gloria Ferris, my friend from the London Doubleday office. 'I'm reading this book,' I told Gloria. 'It's appalling! But the story is brilliant.' I wavered over commissioning it, but Gloria was adamant that I should. She was right—it became a huge bestseller and we sold the rights internationally. Francis Bacon joined us for the launch, but the book is so tawdry it's not one I flash around too much these days.

One of the most difficult books Dan worked on in the late 1970s was by Nesta MacDonald, another author I met at the Queen's Elm pub in Chelsea. Its landlord warned me not to go near her, but she seemed terribly plausible. She was writing a book on Isadora Duncan, the acclaimed dancer now famed mostly for her tragic, spectacular death. In 1927, as a passenger in an open-topped sports car, her long silk scarf got tangled in the wheels and yanked her out at high speed, breaking her neck in the process. Some say it almost decapitated her. Nesta was planning the definitive biography and had plenty of detailed material; she just couldn't write and wouldn't accept being edited. We had endless bother with her—she was impossible to deal with—and eventually palmed her off on another publisher. I did warn them of the difficulties, but they liked the book so much they thought it worth the risk. It never came out though—there was always something more to be discovered, and Nesta just wouldn't finish it.

Dan also worked with many of our great translators, including Joan Tate who translated books from Finnish and Norwegian like those of Knut Faldbakken. One of our most distinguished authors, Tarjei Vesaas, was mostly translated by Elizabeth Rokkan—a really outstanding English translator who had married a Norwegian and who became a professor of English at the University of Bergen. Translation isn't easy, especially literary translation, so you need someone with Elizabeth's skill to do justice to fiction as excellent as the work of Vesaas. In the 1960s Elizabeth also translated the novels of the equally acclaimed Norwegian writer Cora Sandel, including her semi-autobiographical Alberta trilogy.

Looking back over my publishing career, I still think the two really outstanding books we published at Peter Owen are Hesse's *Siddhartha*, and Tarjei Vesaas's *The Ice Palace*, which I first published in 1966. Elizabeth Rokkan contacted me about Vesaas, recommending this novel which had received the Nordic Council Prize—the highest Scandinavian award apart from the Nobel. Vesaas was then completely unknown outside Norway, but I saw the potential in the segment Elizabeth sent me and commissioned her to undertake the translation. We published eight or so of Vesaas's books in total, and they were all very well reviewed. For a while he was forgotten and slipped out of print for a few years. It shouldn't have happened, but we were rather late in starting our own paperback list, and, except for *The Ice Palace* which had been reprinted several times, hardback sales had petered out. After a while a small American publisher wanted the paperback rights to *The Birds*, Vesaas's second masterpiece, as it was required reading for college courses in the United States. I was happy to sell them, but he was a very small publisher and couldn't pay his royalties. I took the rights back, and we reprinted Vesaas as part of our contemporary classics in paperback. *The Ice Palace* sold pretty well but sales increased hugely when it became a cult classic after featuring on BBC Radio 4's *A Good Read* as an unknown masterpiece.

Vesaas (1897–1970) was a great writer—certainly as good as Hesse in my opinion. Like Hesse, some of the novels are minor but still quite outstanding.

We launched *The Birds* at the Norwegian Embassy in London in 1968. There is a publicity photograph of me with the Norwegian *chargé d'affaires*, Vesaas and Wendy. Vesaas came to London several times to help launch his books, and we often dined together. I thought he was a lovely man. He was a very unaffected country gentleman, quiet and unassuming. He spoke English fairly well, too. By the time he came over for the launch of *The Birds* he was very ill. I think he had cancer, though his Norwegian publishers said he had an ulcer. I was terribly grateful that he made the effort, because I knew he liked solitude and rural life. Given his state of health, he probably shouldn't have come, but he forced himself to speak at the embassy even though he hated that sort of thing. He did it to help us. I thought him a very unworldly and decent man. He was nominated for the Nobel Prize many times, but possibly his being Scandinavian was a disadvantage. He was asked whether he would like the prize and said it would have been a great nuisance to have won. Mind you, serious writers tend to say that—including Doris Lessing. The award must have increased her income enormously, but it wasn't worth the attention or intrusion, she felt. Authors can't get on with their work as they're being pestered all the time.

I knew Doris Lessing fairly well. She used to come to our launch parties and gave us generous quotes and endorsements for some of the books—she admired Anna Kavan in particular. She was always very helpful and was grateful to me for advising her when she decided to test the waters writing under the pseudonym Jane Somers. It was an experiment—she wanted to see if she could broach the border between popular and literary fiction. Originally she sent it to Jonathan Cape, her usual publishers, but their reader's report was very unenthusiastic, so they rejected it. Years later the novelist James Lasdun admitted he'd written the report, and expressed some regret. Jane Somers was described as the pseudonym of a 'well-known woman journalist', and Michael Joseph published the first of two books in 1983. It bombed under the pseudonym, so they brought it out under her own name not long after. It exposed just how difficult it is to get in print if you're an unknown, even if secretly you're a prize-winning author.

During Dan Franklin's editorial tenure we also contracted to publish the English translation of the autobiography of Olav V, King of Norway (1903–1991). The Norwegians were quite keen as was the King himself, but ultimately his advisers thought it was too naive and wouldn't work in the English language. In the text King Olav kept referring to his 'sainted mother', Queen Maud. Maud was the sister of our George V and the youngest daughter of Edward VII. Far from being saintly she was, as Dan Franklin put it, a tough old bag who loathed Norway and spent most of her time in England, leaving her husband, King Haakon VII, holding the baby! Despite the cachet it might have brought us, we decided against publication.

The only monarch we did actually publish was King Hussein of Jordan (1935–1999). The book, *My "War" with Israel* (1969), was written in conjunction with two journalists. It discussed the Arab-Israeli war and the ensuing Middle East crisis. I bought it from William Morrow, its publisher in the United States. It was very interesting, as he complained that the Egyptians had almost double-crossed him and didn't keep him informed. Hussein had advocated diplomacy rather than war and was distrusted by other Arab nations. It was quite a bitter book, but I suggested to the embassy that it might be a way of getting some sort of rapprochement. They told me it didn't work that way— that this could only be achieved through diplomatic channels— but I thought there was much more goodwill between the Israelis and Hussein than with other Arab leaders. He was educated at Harrow and Sandhurst and was somewhat anglicised. Although I never met him, I get the impression he was a nice honest man. Journalists called him PLK, Plucky Little King, because he carried on working despite always being threatened with assassination.

29

Confessions of a Mask

Over the decades I've enjoyed spending time in Japan and have published many Japanese authors in translation, from the tenth-century fable *The Tale of the Lady Ochikubo* (1970), to Wahei Tatematsu's modern classic *Frozen Dreams* (2012). Other novels have included Fumio Niwa's *The Buddha Tree* (1966) and several works by the highly-regarded Edwardian novelist Natsume Soseki. We published a few books by Japanese women too, including *The Twilight Years* by Sawako Ariyoshi. When it came to bringing out a novel by Chiyo Uno, who was an eminent author and fashion designer, I had wanted to meet her in Japan, but she was in hospital and refusing visitors. She had been something of a beauty and didn't want people to see her unwell. Perhaps it was fair enough—when we published her famed 1933 novel *Confessions of Love* in 1990 she was already ninety-three.

Uno was quite a daring and independent woman. Like Colette, whose books I also published, Uno's life was tumultuous and adventurous enough to inspire vivid and occasionally racy novels and a television dramatisation. I wish I had met her, but just meeting her agent involved quite a rigmarole. Wherever you go in Japan you're expected to bring a present of some sort. My translator and I bought the agent a lavish cake, but goodness knows what sort of gift *grande dame* Chiyo Uno would have expected had she agreed to receive us.

One of the first Japanese authors I published was Osamu Dazai. I had been offered the opportunity to publish Samuel Beckett's novel *Murphy* but felt it was unsaleable so plumped for the Dazai. 'Can't we publish the Jap *and* the Beckett novel?' Muriel Spark asked. I couldn't afford to do both at the time, but it was a terrible mistake as Dazai, good though he is, is all but forgotten now. The Beckett book went to John Calder, while I brought out Dazai's *The Setting Sun* in 1958 and *No Longer Human* the following year, both excellently translated by the Japanese scholar Donald Keene. Years later I also published *Crackling Mountain* (1990), a collection of Dazai stories translated by James O'Brien.

Strangely, so many Japanese authors I published killed themselves that it was almost a tradition. Akutagawa, whose satirical novella *Kappa* I published in 1970, had overdosed on barbiturates in 1927, Dazai had drowned himself in 1948, and Kawabata gassed himself in 1972 having been haunted by the spectre of Mishima who had opted for a more spectacular suicide a couple of years earlier. Perhaps each of them had struggled to conform in a very conformist society. Certainly many of the best authors are outsiders in some way, by temperament or birth. Yukio Mishima, one of the two most important Japanese authors I published, struggled with his sexuality, his vanity and a fancifully nostalgic imperial ideology. The other, Shusaku Endo, was a Catholic, something rare in Japan. He had also been raised in Manchuria and studied in Europe. Endo was in his own way deeply critical of contemporary Japan from his Christian standpoint and, like Mishima and Soseki before him, deplored Japan's growing materialism—its people quiescently festering, as he saw it, in a tepid spiritual mud-swamp.

I first travelled to Japan in the late 1950s. It was extraordinary in those days. There were still restaurants with signs saying 'Japanese Only', which I found disturbing. Some places were very welcoming, while others would throw you out as soon they saw you. One friend told me that you can live there fifty years and still not understand the people. I remember being in Japan when there was a large turn-out at the Tokyo Hall of Remembrance, apparently to celebrate the brutes who committed all sorts of horrors against prisoners of war. All these years later there's still great difficulty acknowledging the past. That's why Endo's *The Sea and Poison*, the first novel of his that I published, is so important. I think the Japanese have just about admitted to the case the book was based on—the torture and vivisection of American airmen they'd captured. But acknowledgement of the use of Chinese and Korean women as sex slaves is still pretty taboo. It's strange in that all the Japanese I've known have been seemed so honest, gentle and polite.

We published *Confessions of a Mask*, one of Mishima's most significant books, in 1960. The novel, especially its first two chapters on childhood, is a thinly disguised autobiography. Mishima describes a lonely childhood being brought up with girls by his paternal grandmother, a descendant of a shogun, who had herself been raised in an aristocratic environment. The grandmother, who sounds quite potty, wouldn't let Mishima out to play with other boys and kept him inside until he was around eleven. His father saw his interest in literature as a symptom of effeminacy and subjected him to bullying and other cruelties. All of this shaped his darkly poetic imagination. As an adult Mishima, who was small in stature and had been perceived as a weakling, began to practise martial arts and body-building. He also delved into the suppressed tradition of homoerotic relationships in samurai culture and, when staying in London, I'm told that Mishima would go to a gym at High Holborn to work out and to pick up men.

The translator of *Confessions* was the American publisher Oscar 'Tex' Meredith Weatherby who had studied Japanese before the war and who worked at the American consulate. During his wartime internment in Japan he had started translating to pass the time. His lover had been the photographer Tamotsu Yato. When albums of Yato's homoerotic photographs were published in the 1960s, his newly muscular friend Mishima furnished the introduction and even appeared in some of the photographs.

I thought Mishima conscientious and very likeable but terribly vain. He was extremely polite, spoke good English and betrayed no hint of the craziness and sadomasochism that stirred beneath his mask of friendliness and sophistication. At the time I had no idea about his extremely right-wing nationalist politics. If anything, Mishima seemed even more Europeanised than Endo, who spoke little English. While Endo had studied briefly in France, Mishima had immersed himself in European literature at home. When Mishima was in the UK for a book launch I said to him, 'You're going to get the next Nobel Prize for Japan, aren't you?' 'No,' he replied. 'Kawabata is the senior novelist. He will get it.' He was right—Yasanuri Kawabata was the first Japanese recipient in 1968.

I published Kawabata's novel *The Lake* in 1977 but only met him once. We spoke a little through an interpreter, but I took a dislike to him—he seemed extremely cold. I still think Mishima was the superior writer, but, while Mishima's politics and lifestyle might have been an issue, Kawabata was a harmless, uncontroversial Nobel choice. Mishima was certainly in contention for the Nobel, and his writing deserves it—perhaps he would have received it had he lived. Instead, Mishima chose to cut his life short.

Mishima wrote to me occasionally. I had met him several times, the first time in Tokyo shortly after we bought the English-language rights to *Confessions*. I dined with him the night I arrived there. I was amazed at his command of English and found him charming. The last handwritten letter he sent me gave no hint of what was to come—just a cordial note, written elegantly in black ink, asking about a mooted English production of his play *Madame de Sade* which I had published in 1968.

If there was anyone who got close to understanding Mishima and the bizarre end to his life, it was Henry Scott Stokes. I commissioned from him the 1975 book *The Life and Death of Yukio Mishima*, which Dan Franklin edited. It's certainly one of the most insightful biographies we've ever published. A journalist who was close to Mishima, Henry Scott Stokes lived in Japan at the time with a Japanese wife. In October 1970 he received a final letter from Mishima that, given his friend's theatricality, sounded ominous only in retrospect. Mishima was coming to the end of the final part of his quartet of novels *The Sea of Fertility*. He wrote to Henry, 'Finishing the long novel makes me feel as if it is the end of the world.' In the penultimate novel Mishima had asked whether there was any way 'to live honestly with Japan other than by rejecting everything.'

Mishima became very wealthy as a hugely admired writer in Japan. In his last years, romanticizing the imperial past, he expressed regret that the Emperor had been forced to renounce his divinity after the war. Spurred on by this new passion, he started his own right-wing youth militia in 1967, recruiting right-leaning university students drawn by his fame and charisma. It was all an elaborate bit of theatre really. Ordering his militia to swear to restore Emperor worship and the imperial Japan of old, he made them sign an oath in their own blood. Those who didn't faint sipped the leftovers from a cup, after which coffee and cakes were served. Mishima designed the group's flag and, at his own expense, commissioned fancy uniforms in which the eighty or so members could strut about.

In 1969 the group went to Camp Fuji where Mishima intended them to be trained by members of the Japanese army, despite soldiers being forbidden to engage in any political actions. Henry Scott Stokes, as Mishima's friend and a reporter to *The Times*, had been the only journalist invited to observe. He assumed that Mishima just wanted publicity but expressed puzzlement and anxiety in the published piece. The training exercise had been a bit of a joke, but the fervour of Mishima's recruits unnerved him. Mishima wrote that Japan had two choices: accept Westernisation or perish. Rejecting the post-war status quo he chose to perish in the most grimly flamboyant way he could imagine.

Mishima made an appointment with General Mashita for eleven in the morning on 25 November 1970, the publishing deadline for his last book and the anniversary of the date he began writing *Confessions of a Mask*, his early masterpiece. His co-conspirators had said goodbye to relatives and written their farewell poetry the night before. Mishima himself signed and dated the manuscript of his final novel, left two sealed letters (one each for Donald Keene and a second foreign scholar) and a brief note which read, 'Human life is limited, but I would like to live for ever.' At the appointed hour, having rehearsed their performance eight times, Mishima went with four students disciples to the headquarters of the Eastern Army in Tokyo and took General Mashita hostage before delivering from a balcony a speech appealing for the restoration to their 'true state' the army, the Emperor and Japan. His shambolic oration, in front of a crowd of mostly hostile soldiers, police and reporters, was partly drowned out by helicopters and heckling, with many of the crowd calling him an 'arsehole' and worse. Mishima then retreated to the General's office to commit *hara-kiri*. Lying in agony, after initial clumsy attempts, two of the students beheaded him. One of them, Mishima's deputy and probably his lover, was also beheaded.

Everyone in Japan, anyone who knew him, all of us were incredulous. Mishima must have been mad, it was felt. On the other hand, aged forty-five and in his prime, he had achieved all he wanted and saw before him only the fading of his health and literary powers. Like a character in his final novel, Mishima wanted to stop time before it devoured his beauty and while he was sufficiently vital.

Henry made his book an attempt to explain the enigma of Mishima and his final act. He surmises that in reality the Mishima Incident was a masquerade beneath which was a *shinju*—a lovers' suicide pact by Mishima and his deputy. In killing themselves for the Emperor and an idealised Japan, the two had rendered their relationship an honourable samurai sacrifice rather than a shameful secret.

After his death Mishima's family tried to suppress any discussion of his sexual involvement with men. His children even sued a publisher who had brought out a book quoting letters referencing his sexuality, despite it being a matter of record, not least through *Confessions of a Mask* and *Forbidden Colours*, his body-building photography and homoerotic fixations.

I had got to know Mishima moderately well, and I liked him very much. He was warm and friendly and seemed quite genuine. His novels are still some of the most accessible in Japanese literature, and there are many works still awaiting translation. Scott Stokes writes that Mishima only adopted right-wing politics in his last five years and had always regarded the factions who admired him as gangsters. Rather than as a fascist agitator, Scott Stokes wished to remember Mishima as a charming friend and literary giant who left behind him a fascinating legacy: thirty-six volumes of collected works.

30

There Goes Wendy Owen

In the 1960s and 1970s I enjoyed embracing fashion, perhaps a result of those early experiments in flamboyant clothing Grandma Betty and my mother foisted on me. Wendy and I once dressed up for a *Sunday Times* feature in which there are glamorous photos of me sporting a Sherlock Holmes Inverness cape. The invitation came through Molly Parkin who was very much part of the 1960s scene. An artist, journalist and novelist, Molly was the fashion editor for the *Sunday Times* from 1969—and managed to get banned by the BBC for swearing. In those days Wendy and I were part of the company image: me as the 'maverick publisher' and Wendy the successful novelist. There was nothing particularly calculated about it—it just happened.

Wendy had wanted to be an artist—early on she had designed a few book jackets for me—but when she took up writing in the early 1960s we found she had a real talent for it. She wrote short stories and plays first, then moved on to novels. Her first took her a couple of years to write, but, dissatisfied with the result, she threw it in the dustbin. Her next novel, *There Goes Davey Cohen*, was excellent. I thought Wendy, unlike Uncle Rudi, was really clever with story and dialogue so I took the manuscript to the Frankfurt Book Fair where William Miller, then at Granada, agreed with my verdict. Thinking I'd be accused of nepotism, I felt it would only be a hindrance if I published it myself, so Wendy sold the book via a literary agent to Hutchinson. It was published it in 1966, spent three weeks in the bestseller lists and was praised by many well-regarded critics and writers. Anthony Burgess, who sometimes came to our book launches, called it 'curiously haunting' and compared the ending to that of Flaubert's *Un Coeur Simple*, while Anaïs Nin praised Wendy's 'faultless ear' for dialogue, called her 'an expert portraitist' and admired her 'wonderfully exact touches on Spain—written in gold'. I was grateful to Marguerite Young, too, who described it as 'a jewel of a book which sparkles with wit', while Peter Hall said he 'loved its grotesque and disturbing comedy' and expressed interest in turning it into a film.

A funny, wistful look at a middle-aged Jewish couple abroad, *Davey Cohen* drew on experiences of our holidays in Spain and Morocco but otherwise is pure invention. My father, Arthur, needed much reassurance that the rather grim husband wasn't based on him. Though I have my doubts now, at the time Wendy insisted that the same character didn't depict me any more than the wife, who keeps thinking passers-by are film stars or people she knows, was her.

The trigger for the book occurred in Spain. We had returned to a favourite hotel only to find that it had gone to seed. Early one morning I was having my shoes cleaned and Wendy had a momentary fantasy that the man cleaning my shoes was Burt Lancaster. That and the grotty hotel were enough to spark her imagination, and she started jotting down the outline for the book while we were on a bus with an urgency that slightly unnerved me.

At home Wendy would write late at night or early in the morning while everyone else in the family was asleep. In the school holidays we would send the girls to stay with Wendy's parents for two or three weeks to give her time to write. Wendy had never learnt to type so wrote in longhand. She was imaginative, but her spelling and punctuation were poor. We got the manuscript professionally typed up and corrected. Sadly, Hutchinson didn't bother to edit the book properly, so her wonky Spanish phrases stayed that way.

When the book came out, a critic at the *Financial Times* judged Wendy one of the three best women writers of the decade alongside Emma Tennant, whose late work *The Beautiful Child* I was to publish in 2012, and Beryl Bainbridge. The title also helped helped sell the novel; Jewish readers would buy it to see what was about, thinking it might be antisemitic. Of course it wasn't.

When Panther wanted to bring out *Davey Cohen* in paperback I decided to publish Wendy's second novel myself now that she was established. There had been quite some competition for the book, and Wendy's agent kept putting up the price. In the end I paid a £500 advance (worth about £9,000 now), but, to my annoyance, she kept forgetting to bank it and the cheque lay around in the kitchen for weeks. In 1968, to celebrate the paperback launch of *Davey Cohen* and her new hardback novel *Whatever Happened to Ruby?*, we held a joint launch party at the Savoy. It was something we could afford in those days, especially as Panther stumped up half the cost. Wendy always looked very fashionable and glamorous at such events and enjoyed the acclaim.

Things really snowballed for her with interviews and features in every paper. Critics were enthusiastic about her second novel as well; I was told that Wendy had even been considered for the first Booker Prize longlist. Paul Bowles and Antonia White gave generous endorsements, and Auberon Waugh called it 'full of humour and genuinely moving'. The BBC invited Wendy to discuss the book's themes with Joan Bakewell and a headmistress on *Late Night Lineup*.

The book was partly an indictment of boarding schools inspired by unhappy experiences of the bullying other pupils had endured and perpetrated at her Catholic convent school in Somerset. She recalled how things had got off to a dramatic start for her there: on her first night the Germans bombed the town nearby, but she was more frightened by the nuns who whisked them down to a shelter. They'd had no time to don their wimples, and Wendy found their shaven heads terrifying. Half the nuns were saintly, she thought, the others sexually frustrated and vicious. The novel opened up a debate sadly still relevant now. One theme in the book is the abuse of a girl by a sleazy man. In some ways it was very much before its time.

When Wendy's career took off I was delighted for her, but the process of writing seemed to unhinge her and make her hyperactive. While she was writing *Davey Cohen*, I was pretty appalled. The necessity to immerse yourself in fantasy while you're creating can destabilise a person. Some novelists go a bit crazy I think. Feminism of the early 1970s also changed Wendy's perspective, and she became less content with her life. As a result, our marriage became increasingly unsteady.

31

Darkness Visible

I don't know who put me on to Unesco, but it turned out to be a godsend. Not many people knew that the international charity had started financially supporting literary translations, especially with the Unesco Catalogue of Representative Works which it launched in 1948. There was quite a lot of money for books it deemed suitable—in this case translations of books considered significant but little known outside their country of origin. Handily, as well as subsidizing translations, Unesco would also buy several hundred copies of each title it funded. For us it was a goldmine—it helped keep us going.

By the early 1970s I published about half the Unesco list and always had very good relations with its staff. At one point I was intrigued to meet the permanent Japanese delegate who turned out to be Yukio Mishima's brother. The contact I knew best at Unesco was Milton Rosenthal who was a very helpful man. He didn't necessarily agree with the titles I favoured, but he accepted my judgement. Endo was one of the authors who went through Unesco for a number of books, including our first of his, *The Sea and Poison* (1972). That was how I got to know Endo.

Milton was Jewish-American and lived in Paris. He and I became friendly enough that, on a trip to London, he once stayed with me for a week. Then he disappeared and no one knew where he was. His bank account wasn't moving despite his salary still being paid into it. Six months later it turned out that Milton's son had killed both his parents.

I knew he had a troubled son—Milton used to tell me how worried he was about the spoilt and irrational boy—but had no idea just how ill and deranged Daniel was. Milton's wife Leah reported her husband missing in 1981 a few days before she herself disappeared. Apparently Daniel had been a science student and was conducting strange experiments on chicken brains and embryos in a laboratory he'd knocked together in the living-room of his Hampshire bungalow. The suspicion was that Daniel, by then a paranoid schizophrenic aged twenty-seven, had gone to Paris to demand money from his father to fund more experiments and had killed Milton when he was refused.

Daniel had been convinced of his own genius but was renowned for leaving bloody messes—gruesome mixtures of flesh and feathers, the remains of his experiments—out in bags by the bins. Otherwise he'd bury bits in the garden in holes he dug with a spoon. The detectives surmised that, having dismembered his father and hidden parts of the torso in Wisebuys shopping bags in a forest outside Paris, Daniel had returned to Hampshire and killed and dismembered his mother when she threatened to raise the alarm. He was convicted of her murder in 1982 on the grounds of compelling forensic evidence, despite her remains never having been found. It was presumed that the Hedge End bin men had unwittingly aided him in their disposal.

Daniel ended up imprisoned in a high-security hospital alongside Ian Brady and other dangerous lunatics and was only charged with his father's murder in 2015. Milton's son has never admitted his guilt or fully explained what happened. Apparently he blames the CIA. I don't think they'll ever let him out—at least I fervently hope not. I think they never found poor Milton's head.

My relationship with Unesco survived Milton's death. I dealt with several people, most of whom were fine, but eventually the collaboration collapsed in the late 1990s when it decided to cease joint publishing. It's a shame, because it was a worthwhile scheme that got a lot of good international literature into print that wouldn't otherwise have been published. And, as I say, it was through Unesco that I discovered Endo—I might never have found him otherwise.

Recalling Milton brings to mind another friend of mine who met an untimely and suspicious death. Mike Dempsey was an editor at Granada who took on some of our paperback rights. He eventually left to manage punk rock bands, but, though our worlds were somewhat different, we often bumped into one another at the French House and he was friends with John Paine, too. I liked him and thought him a very good editor. Mike and I once went to Morocco together when he suddenly disappeared. He had seemed very jittery, and I was terrified he'd had some misadventure and would be found dead in a ditch. I was enormously relieved when he turned up a couple of hours before our flight was due to depart.

Some time later, Mike came to see me in something of a state claiming that he was being followed. I put it down to paranoia but was suspicious when the news came later that week that he had fallen to the bottom of a stairwell while changing a lightbulb on the landing outside his flat. This seemed unlikely as he was terrified of heights. The story went round the French that he had become addicted to cocaine, had got into debt with his dealers and been bumped off. Whatever had happened, it was very sad.

32

Shusaku Endo

Shusaku Endo was hardly known outside Japan when I started publishing him in the early 1970s. We soon became very good friends, and I think it's fair to say that I was responsible for creating Endo's international profile by promoting translations of his work and acting as his agent. He was unfailingly generous, always bringing me and the family gifts. He even gave me an autographed novel by Graham Greene, a mutual admirer. He was generous in another way, too. The driver I hired for him whenever he was over in London once asked the novelist whom he thought the best Japanese writer of the twentieth-century. Without hesitation Endo said it was Jun'ichiro Tanizaki, author of *The Makioka Sisters*. He didn't mention himself nor, surprisingly, Mishima or Kawabata.

Endo had been born in Tokyo in 1923—his father was a banker and his mother a violinist—but the family soon moved to Manchuria when his father took a job there. After his parents' divorce he returned to Japan to be brought up by his mother and her family. Under their influence he was baptised as a Catholic in 1934 and given the baptismal name Paul. In intensely nationalistic Japan he was bullied for his alien faith, an experience he explored in novels and stories of historic Christian persecution. As a university student in Japan he contributed to literary journals and, despite an early interest in studying medicine, gravitated towards literature, eventually becoming a lecturer. In the early 1950s he studied at the University of Lyon, but from that time on he was dogged by ill health including serious diseases of the liver, lungs and kidneys, most of which he kept secret. Painful medical treatments and long periods of hospitalisation found expression in his fiction. *The Sea and Poison* and *When I Whistle* (1979) feature unethical doctors, while many short stories, such as 'A Forty-Year-Old Man' from the collection *Stained Glass Elegies* (1984), feature a hospital setting. In Japan Endo's literary breakthrough came in 1955 with the award of the Akutagawa Prize. International acclaim took a while longer, but latterly he became a serious contender for the Nobel several years in succession.

After publishing *The Sea and Poison* (1972) and *Wonderful Fool* (1973) I wanted to get my hands on the rights to Endo's 1966 masterpiece, *Silence*. At the time the English translation rights were owned by an American university in Kyoto. Endo pleaded with the institution—he wanted an international publication in English—and after a long meeting they finally, reluctantly but generously, reverted the rights and let us publish it in the UK in 1976. *Silence* established his reputation outside Japan, and I followed this publication over the years with several more novels and short-story collections until his death in 1996.

It was hard work getting Endo off the ground at first. I had the devil's own job finding publishers to take international rights. No one in Europe or the United States seemed to want them at first. Not only was he little known, but some of the subject matter of his fiction wasn't obviously appealing. My American agent submitted Endo's *Silence* to Roger Straus in the early 1970s. Straus was the son of Gladys Guggenheim and a co-founder of the prestigious New York publisher Farrar, Straus and Giroux. Roger was regarded as one of the canniest publishers in the world, but on reading Endo's work he said, 'A talented writer—but he won't sell!' He was spectacularly wrong about that—but then Roger wasn't my biggest fan. For my firm's fiftieth anniversary we published *Everything Is Nice—and Other Fiction* (2001), an anthology of our best writers. To end the book, my editors asked for comments from authors, fellow publishers and fans. They were all very favourable and kind apart from the one by Roger Straus which was so pompous that my colleagues said I shouldn't use it. I thought it was quite good to have a quote that wasn't grovelling and, since it made him look rather stupid, we included it.

Endo and I decided that in order to establish a serious literary reputation for him we should downplay his lighter, more humorous writings. Most of Endo's novels were very serious explorations of faith and human propensity for cruelty, but he did write lighter work, much under the pen name Korian (the mountain lair of popular comic mythological characters Fox and Raccoon), some of which was quite funny. The only books we published that had something of that lighter side were a few of the short stories and the novel *Wonderful Fool* (1973), the story of Gaston Bonaparte's stay in Japan. Endo's work often tends towards the allegorical, and Gaston, a relation of the French Emperor, is one of Endo's innately good holy fools whose innocence and kindness transform all who meet him.

Despite the gravity of the themes in many of his most celebrated works, Endo had a mischievous sense of humour. His career as a columnist and in popular Japanese television remains largely unknown outside Japan, but he had enormous audiences there—he really was a major public figure and highly esteemed. Whichever country we visited, the Japanese ambassador there always gave a sumptuous dinner. Endo also had very good relations with the Japanese imperial court, perhaps partly because Empress Michiko had been brought up Catholic. Endo actually worked on getting us the publication rights to the Empress's poetry which they were publishing in a bilingual edition. In the end it went to a Japanese publisher, but Endo was, I think, very popular with the Emperor.

Once Endo's international reputation was established I started to campaign in earnest for his Nobel Prize candidacy. We travelled to Finland, Norway and Sweden together and met the Swedish Academy, where Endo came across very well. I knew we were up against serious opposition but thought we had a good chance despite being told by all those who cared to pontificate that Endo wouldn't win because of his popular television career and humorous books and because he was a Catholic. In Japan he had this dual nature—being regarded both as a serious intellectual and a playful clown. He knew his humorous mask might harm his reputation but liked to make others happy—it helped him deliver his more serious messages, he maintained. The Japanese literary establishment, which would have influenced the Nobel committee, was divided on Endo. He had hosted a witty night-time chat show for a while and was a guest on popular programmes such as *Hon mono wa dare da?!* ('Which One Is It?') and *Wakuwaku dobutsu rando* ('Thrilling Animal Land'), as well as appearing in an advert for Nescafé—so, in a way, you can see their point. It would be as if Samuel Beckett or Doris Lessing had regularly appeared on *Blankety Blank* or *It's a Knockout*.

By 1994 I was sure that Endo would win the Nobel. Roger Straus had his spies in Stockholm who tipped him off that Endo was definitely in the running. He thought it was almost certainly a choice between Endo or Seamus Heaney (who actually won it a year later). I'd got everything ready—publicity leaflets, adequate stock of all the books and so on—and felt confident enough to cable Endo that he was likely to win the award, so it was devastating when he didn't. In the end the Nobel Academy awarded it to Kenzaburo Oe—which I thought a mistake. I have always found his books unreadable, even in translation, and his sales did not benefit much from the publicity accrued from winning the prize. Endo's work has philosophical depth, but it is much more accessible than Oe's. The Japanese authorities tried to award Oe the Emperor's Medal, but he refused it, which was a great insult to the Emperor. Oe declared, 'I do not recognise any authority, any value, higher than democracy.' He didn't seem to mind being handed a Nobel gong and a massive cheque by the Swedish King though.

I suspect that *The Sea and Poison*, based as it was on the vivisection of prisoners of war by the Japanese in the Second World War, and *Silence*, which details the persecution, torture and execution of Christian missionaries in

Above left: Peter and his mother Winnie in 1929 (*Peter Owen Family*)

Above right: Peter's paternal grandparents Betty and Louis Offenstadt (*Peter Owen Family*)

Below left: Peter, aged two, in his orthopaedic boots, 1929 (*Peter Owen Family*)

Below right: Peter's parents Winnie and Arthur Offenstadt, late 1920s (*Peter Owen Family*)

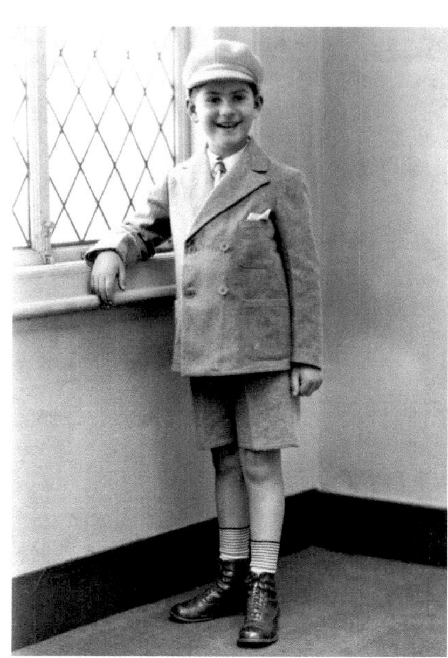

Above left: Peter in the snow, Nuremberg, 1932 (*Peter Owen Family*)

Above right: Peter in the new clothes his grandmother Sophie bought him on his arrival in London, 1933 (*Peter Owen Family*)

Below left: Rudolph Friedmann (Uncle Rudi) as a teenager in the late 1920s (*Peter Owen Family*)

Below right: Peter's maternal grandmother Sophie Friedmann née Pretzfelder (*Peter Owen Family*)

Above left: Peter, far right, with, from left, his Aunt Getta, her sister Grandma Betty, and his mother Winnie in Belgium, mid-1930s. (*Peter Owen Family*)

Above right: 'A couple of old cows'—drawing by Peter of his grandmothers Sophie and Betty (*James Nye Collection*)

Above left: Uncle Rudi with Peter in the 1930s, Brondesbury Park, London (*Peter Owen Family*)

Above right: Peter with his beloved nanny Liesl, c. 1936–7 (*Peter Owen Family*)

Above left: Peter in the late 1930s (*Peter Owen Family*)

Above right: Peter in RAF uniform, 1947 (*Peter Owen Family*)

Below left: Peter as a young publisher in the mid-1950s (*Peter Owen Family*)

Below right: Peter and Wendy Owen leaving Kensington Register Office after their wedding, July 1953 (*Peter Owen Family*)

Above left: The Men of Vision: Arthur Owen (front) and his brother-in-law Rudi Friedmann (*Peter Owen Family*)

Above right: Wendy Owen's 1954 dust-jacket design for the first edition of Hermann Hesse's *Siddhartha* (*Peter Owen Publishers*)

Below left: Jean Cocteau's drawing and appreciative note presented to Peter Owen to mark the signing of the contract for *Maalesh* in 1956(*Peter Owen Publishers*)

Below right: Wendy and Peter with baby Antonia, 1955 (*Peter Owen Family*)

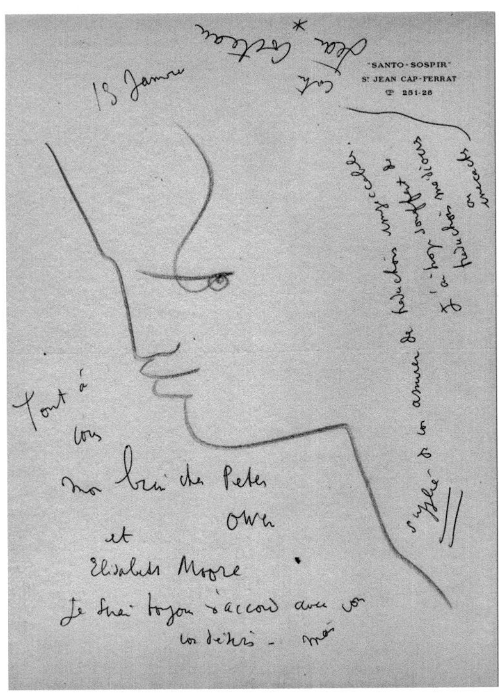
"SANTO-SOSPIR"
ST JEAN CAP-FERRAT
☎ 251-26

18 Janvier

Jean Cocteau

Tout à vous mon bien cher Peter Owen et Elisabeth Moore

Above left: Peter Owen, early 1960s (*Peter Owen Family*)

Above right: Jane Bowles and friends (*Peter Owen Publishers*)

Below left: Paul Bowles (*Peter Owen Publishers*)

Below right: Peter and Wendy Owen in Morocco, 1960s (*Peter Owen Family*)

Peter Owen in India with his author Anita Desai, 1963 (*Peter Owen Publishers*)

Peter Owen (seated, centre) with his staff at his office in Kendrick Mews on the occasion of the firm's twentieth anniversary in 1971. From left: Susan Paine, Peter's friend and, for some years, personal assistant, Michael Levien, senior editor, Sheila White, editor, Robin Horwitz, sales manager, and Beatrice Musgrave, production manager (*Peter Owen Publishers*)

Above: Peter and Wendy Owen, August 1964 (*Peter Owen Family*)

Below: The Japanese Ambassador (left) talking to Yukio Mishima and Wendy Owen at the London launch of Richard Corson's *Fashions in Hair*, 1965 (*Peter Owen Publishers*)

Above: Wendy (centre) with friends John and Susan Paine at a fancy dress party in the mid-1960s (*Peter Owen Family*)

Right: Anna Kavan at home, with her golden harp and, in the foreground, a copy of the first edition of her celebrated novel *Ice*, 1967 (*Peter Owen Publishers*)

Wendy Owen at home in Philbeach Gardens, Earl's Court, with her daughters Georgina (left) and Antonia, plus Mortitia, their first cat, January 1967 (*Terry Gibson, Daily Telegraph*)

Party at the Norwegian Embassy in 1968 celebrating the first English-language edition of *The Birds* by Tarjei Vesaas (second from left), with the Norwegian *chargé d'affaires* and Wendy and Peter Owen (*Peter Owen Publishers*)

A launch party Peter and his wife held in December 1968 for the French artist Roland Topor. From left, Roland Topor, Margaret Crosland, Tariq Ali, Wendy and Peter Owen and novelist Peter Vansittart. In addition to advising Peter Owen for many years, Margaret was a biographer and Topor's agent, as well as his translator. (*Peter Owen Publishers*)

Above left: Wendy and Peter Owen (left), with Anaïs Nin, Georgina Owen, and the actress Luise Rainer at a party celebrating publication of the third volume of Nin's *Journals*, 27 May 1970 (*Peter Owen Publishers*)

Above right: Wendy, Georgina, Peter and Antonia Owen at the House of Lords on 18 March 1971 attending a party held in celebration of the publishing firm's twentieth-anniversary (*Peter Owen Publishers*)

The opening of the firm's twentieth-anniversary exhibition at the National Book League in central London, 22 March 1971. From left, Keith Cunningham, book designer, Peter and Wendy Owen, Lord Goodman and Peter Vansittart (*Peter Owen Publishers*)

From left, 'Queen Mother of Tangier' the Honourable David Herbert, his sister-in-law Mary, Countess of Pembroke, Wendy Owen, Charles Farrell, Lady Katherine Farrell, Lord Norwich and Peter Owen at the launch of Herbert's memoir *Second Son*, 1972 (*Peter Owen Publishers*)

Above: From left, Octavian von Hofmannstahl, Cecil Beaton, Peter Owen (standing), Mary, Countess of Pembroke and Lady Elizabeth von Hofmannstahl at the launch party for David Herbert's memoir *Second Son* in 1972 (*Peter Owen Publishers*)

Below left: Peter Owen holding a copy of his English-language edition of Dali's only novel, *Hidden Faces*, 1973 (*Peter Owen Publishers*)

Below right: Peter wearing an Inverness cape, photographed by John Timbers, 1974 (*Peter Owen Publishers*)

Above and below: Wendy and Peter Owen photographed by John Timbers, 1974 (*Peter Owen Publishers*)

Peter Owen and Shusaku Endo, 1981 (*Peter Owen Publishers*)

From right: Peter Owen with Shusaku Endo enjoying his first time in a caravan on 18 April 1985. Its owner, the chauffeur Peter hired, is second from left with Dr Kato, Endo's personal physician. The photograph was taken by Endo's personal translator, Masako 'Mako' Kawashima. (*Peter Owen Publishers*)

Antonia Owen and her father perusing a manuscript in Peter's basement office at Kenway Road in 2001 (*Peter Owen Publishers*)

Above left: Peter Owen displays his OBE at Buckingham Palace with daughters Georgina (left) and Antonia, April 2014 (*Peter Owen Family*)

Above right: Peter Owen demonstrates his antique mechanical bird to his literary assistant, James Nye, August 2015 (*James Nye*)

Japan, may have caused some high-level national embarrassment. Writing *The Sea and Poison* struck me as particularly courageous as the events were so much closer in time. Perhaps Endo was never forgiven for exposing some of these dark episodes in Japanese history, even though both books have been made into Japanese films. But then Oe caused similar controversies with his 1970 essay about military involvement in coercing terrible mass suicides in Okinawa in 1945, so the rejection of Endo for the Nobel still remains puzzling as well as deeply disappointing.

Endo's career in television and popular journalism made him more wealthy than his serious novels did. I think it would be fair to say that he had more money than he knew what to do with, so he discussed the matter with me as a friend. Thinking the stock market too risky I set up savings accounts for him in London, as interest rates then were very favourable. Endo had plenty to live off in Japan and wanted some savings kept safely abroad as insurance. He told me that he feared a communist coup in Japan might result in the confiscation of his fortune at home.

Endo didn't make use of his London savings often but would occasionally dip into them for hotel bills or something frivolous. One day he was overtaken by a sudden passionate desire to own a grandfather clock. I took him to an antique shop in Chelsea where the dealer, spotting a Japanese buyer, immediately put up the price by several thousand pounds. I argued in vain. They had to take the clock apart and ship it to him at great expense. Another time Endo considered buying a flat in London. 'For God's sake, don't!' I begged him. 'If you're not going to stay in it much, it'll need looking after. It's pointless.' And then there was his sudden enthusiasm to buy a caravan in the UK—something he'd never seen but wanted to acquire. He was even more passionate about this, suggesting I could make use of it, too. However, I didn't want the responsibility. I knew it would have been endless bother. Eventually we went to inspect some caravans, and there are photographs of us sitting in one belonging to the regular chauffeur I hired for him. Ultimately Endo seemed content with that.

Another of Endo's indulgences was the Kiza Theatrical Company, Japan's largest amateur theatrical group. On one occasion he brought over to London a coachload of Japanese actors from the Kiza—all at his own expense—to put on a performance of *The Mikado* at the Jeannetta Cochrane Theatre in Holborn. The Japanese ambassador was to be the guest of honour. I wasn't involved, but Endo wrote to Dan Franklin, then working at Collins Harvill, asking him to get together an English group to perform an interlude. Assuming the whole thing to be some kind of elaborate joke, Dan teamed up with a couple of publishing friends to perform in drag. Endo found it terribly funny, bringing over a troupe of fifty, most of whom couldn't really sing. Dan describes it as one of the most wonderful experiences of his life. Goodness knows what the Japanese ambassador thought of it.

I know Endo liked me as much as I liked him. Mostly he lived in a big house outside Tokyo where I met his wife on one occasion. He also kept a flat in central Tokyo where he was kind enough to let me stay for a week. He used this flat, which was situated in a very upmarket area, for working and entertaining. It was well furnished and on the lid of his grand piano I remember there was a framed photo of him with the Emperor. 'Take as much as you want!' Endo said, indicating an enormous cupboard filled with every type of alcohol you could imagine. He had given up drinking entirely, on account of his health problems, and had renounced whisky in his thirties. On his visits to London we purchased for him non-alcoholic beer and wine, but in Japan, where he had kept his teetotalism quiet, he had built up a gargantuan hoard of booze, all of it gifted by friends and admirers. They used to send him everything—the best cognac, champagne and wine. I had a friend in Tokyo, an English literary agent, who came to see me once or twice while I was staying at the apartment. We did our best but didn't make much of a dent in Endo's stockpile. At first I was hesitant about drinking the champagne—I thought that might be pushing our luck—but on the last night I needed to write a letter, and it took so long it was too late to go out to dinner. In the end I helped myself to some of Endo's caviar and a bottle of his champagne. I thought he wouldn't mind—after all, he was a very good friend and an extremely nice man.

There was great excitement when the American director Martin Scorsese wanted to film *Silence*. He had bought the rights after reading the book in Japan in 1989, but none of us realised that we'd have such a long wait for the film to appear. Scorsese had been in Japan to play Van Gogh in a section of Kurosawa's film *Dreams*. Much impressed by the book, Scorsese perhaps realised that it would fit in with his other films on religious themes, *The Last Temptation of Christ* and, later, *Kundun*.

Scorsese wrote an introduction to a paperback edition for us and spent many years developing the script, sourcing funding, and trying to find the right time to make what was more a passion project than a commercial prospect. Filming started in January 2015, so I brought out a collectible hardback and auctioned the paperback rights. Penguin turned them down because we hadn't the e-book rights. When the contracts had been drawn up with Endo, no one had envisaged the existence of e-books, so his family now have these rights. In the end we received a high advance from Pan Macmillan, a company only too glad to have it on their list.

Several films of Endo's work had already been made in Japan, including a version of *The Sea and Poison* in 1986. *Silence* had been filmed in Japanese in 1971 and in Portuguese in 1996. This somewhat diminished the value of the *Silence* film rights when we sold them to Scorsese. I am told the Japanese version is shown on television every Christmas though, it strikes me as distinctly non-festive.

In 1973 Endo wrote *A Life of Jesus* to explain his own understanding of the subject to a Japanese readership largely unfamiliar with Christianity. I would have published a translation of this, but the rights weren't available. In the book Endo stresses the tender, maternal and forgiving aspects of Christ, perhaps borrowing elements from Jodo Buddhism.

Though Endo's Catholicism became central to him and to his writings, I think he was originally baptised to please his mother and her family. In time he realised the importance to him of his faith, something I've never had myself. For me, faith has always been a bit of a mystery; it just never made any sense. The way I see it, the historical Jesus was a good man who had some healing abilities and skill in oratory and who was labelled a prophet. But that's nothing to do with religion really—they weren't supernatural skills. Endo was the one person with whom I discussed faith. While I had never quizzed Muriel Spark or anyone in the West about their religious convictions, I thought as Endo was Japanese he might forgive my curiosity. I asked him why he had remained Roman Catholic throughout his life. Catholicism in Japan, he told me, has evolved rather differently. He simply regarded it as a very good way of living. Later in life he developed a broader outlook and became more reconciled with native Shinto and Buddhist traditions, including reincarnation. *Deep River* (1994), his last great novel, reflects this reconciliation with Japanese beliefs.

Endo was obviously disappointed to miss out on the Nobel Prize but was somewhat consoled by receiving the Order of Culture in 1995, the year before his death. He could add that to other distinguished awards he achieved, including the Akutagawa and Tanizaki prizes and the award of the Order of St Sylvester, a papal knighthood.

The sadness of Endo's death was amplified for me by his family's reaction. We had sold his books all over the world, and he was translated into every major language. As Endo's literary agent outside Japan I had worked hard for Endo, but the family seemed to think I would simply hand back the rights after he died. Protracted posthumous legal wrangling ensued which I found terribly upsetting. Thank goodness Endo's bank account had been moved back to Japan before he died and that he never bought a flat or caravan in the UK or doubtless I'd have been accused of trying to get my hands on them.

Endo's heirs brought in an extremely unpleasant American lawyer, but my solicitor Anthony Rubinstein handled matters very well. In the end he kept on throwing out their lawyer, because it got so silly. Anthony and I agreed that we would no longer respond to him. Ultimately the family agreed to appoint someone sensible, and we came to an agreement. The resulting contract was very complicated but left us with some publishing rights, some of them time limited, and fewer than we had enjoyed in the past.

Endo had been chronically ill for many years. Unlike Mishima, he didn't speak English very well and usually travelled in some style with Mako

Kawashima, his English-speaking secretary and translator. Mako was a lovely woman who spoke extremely good English and who was kind and attentive—but on his last two or three visits to London Endo added a doctor to his entourage, so I knew his health was seriously declining. The last time I saw him was on a trip to Tokyo. It was unusual because on every other occasion he or Mako had met me at the airport and there followed lots of dinners and meetings. This time I made my own way to my hotel. He visited me there and was using a walking-stick—I was terribly shocked at how much he'd aged since we had last got together.

I remember Shusaku Endo very fondly and still keep by my desk a photo of him, his mischievous smiling face framed by his trademark heavy spectacles. In my wallet I keep a copy of a generous letter Endo wrote me in which he thanks me for my hospitality and adds, 'Always I feel very sad when I have to say farewell to you. I truly appreciate you for your efforts in making me an international writer in the last ten years.' Along with Mishima, Endo was undoubtedly one of the great Japanese writers of the twentieth century and, in his case, a wonderfully kind and thoughtful man.

33

Tangerine Dreams

For the first few years of our marriage, while I was still working hard to establish the business, Wendy and I couldn't afford to go abroad often, other than hitch-hiking in France or in Germany. In 1961 we did manage to holiday in Tangier though. Inspired by films like *Casablanca*, I'd always had a romantic vision of North Africa. I thought it terribly exotic, particularly compared to the dull grey grind of London in the post-war years. Tangier was much more fun in those days—especially if you got to know other travellers and expatriates. All the swill of the world was there! We stayed in a cheap hotel and visited bars for Moroccan dinners with traditional dancing. Tangier was still quite a small city at that time, and one morning Wendy and I went for a walk to its outskirts. The view was breathtaking. 'This really is Africa!' I remember saying. It was, for visitors from Europe, an entirely different world.

Our first stay in Tangier was brief—just a stop *en route* to Marbella, then still unspoilt by mass tourism and over-development. But we had enjoyed our first taste of Tangier so much that we returned the following year with our friends John and Susan Paine and stayed at an English-run hotel in the middle of Tangier's old Kasbah where the Arabs lived. Laurence Olivier was there at one point with a handsome young man. They used to swim at the same spot we did and recommended a few restaurants to us. From there we went to Chaouen, a beautiful small town in the Rif mountains where the houses are painted various shades of blue, and stayed in a parador—a Spanish-style hotel—which was well run, pleasingly cheap and a few minutes' walk from a picturesque waterfall. While lounging by the pool drinking tea we got talking to another visitor, an American. Wendy and I mentioned that Paul Bowles's first novel, *The Sheltering Sky*, his disorientating, semi-autobiographical tale of travellers in North Africa, was a favourite novel of ours. He concurred and told us Bowles was still living in Tangier. Though he was renowned as a bit of a recluse—Paul and his wife were living in what he once described as 'distinguished obscurity' —we were determined to meet him. He had refused to have a phone in his flat, but the American Consulate gave us the number for his wife Jane, who invited us to tea.

Her fondest friend David Herbert described Jane Bowles as resembling 'an unpredictable marmoset'. In her face I could see remnants of youthful beauty somewhat ravaged by ill health. She was small and dark-haired and walked with a limp, the result of a tubercular knee in childhood. Sometimes she referred to herself in letters as 'crippy the dyke'. I liked Jane very much as I grew to know her. She was a little suspicious of me at first, but I came to see her as being as warm and caring as she was fragile and needy. At that first meeting, attended by Cherifa, her kaftan-wearing Moroccan servant and occasional lover, Jane surreptitiously vetted Wendy and me. She didn't want visitors bothering Paul and wasting his precious time. As it happened, Paul returned before we left, and I was able to explain in person how much I admired his work. He gave me a bundle of manuscript pages describing his life and experiences of Morocco, its people, music and culture. 'You can have it for publication if you like,' he said casually. I did like it, of course, and published it in 1963 as *Their Heads Are Green*. So began my relationship with Paul and Jane as both publisher and friend.

I returned to Tangier often and got to know Paul, Jane and many others in their motley circle of expatriates. Over the years I published several of Paul's books including, once I could acquire the rights, a new edition of *The Sheltering Sky*. The book had originally been commissioned by Doubleday and, discontented with the spirit-sapping materialism of United States, Paul had used the advance money to move to Morocco and write. Doubleday rejected the manuscript, something they lived to regret when British publisher John Lehmann published it in 1949 to great acclaim and enviable sales. James Laughlin of New Directions then snapped up the rights for an American edition. It wasn't until forty-one years later, in the twilight years of Paul's life, that Bernardo Bertolucci made the book into a film. Paul acted as adviser and even made a cameo appearance. The soundtrack included field recordings of indigenous musicians selected from the many he made for the US Library of Congress. Though Paul was later critical of the film, it did wonders for his finances—the foreign rights to all his books sold the world over. This made little difference to his lifestyle. He still had sacks hanging in the window in lieu of curtains until someone talked him into having an upholsterer make him a proper pair. Though he always lived in some style Paul wasn't possessive or materialistic—his existence was always fairly spartan.

Paul came from New England and spoke without a pronounced American accent. He was slight and elegant, with greying fair hair, a handsome face and excellent manners. Self-effacing and modest, he seemed that rarest of men, a perfect American gentleman. He had a small income from his family, dressed stylishly in silk shirts and, even when he wasn't wealthy, kept a chauffeur-driven black Jaguar convertible. He bought the car after his friend the artist Brion Gysin suggested one might be useful. His chauffeur probably didn't cost much to hire, and his hours weren't onerous as Paul would get up late—about two or three in the afternoon. However, every so often Paul would ask him to drive all the way to Switzerland to visit the dentist. You would have thought that there might have been someone competent nearer to home. The chauffeur inherited quite a lot of money when Paul died—pretty much the entire estate. But he was a loyal, decent man and very fond of Paul. He and Paul had been lovers, and Paul's bequest must have made him one of the richest men in Tangier.

Paul had settled in Tangier in 1947, and Jane joined him the following year. He had pursued a career in music long before he became established as a writer and first visited Morocco in 1931 on a jaunt with the composer Aaron Copland with whom he was studying. That visit had been prompted by Gertrude Stein who had befriended him in Paris where he had also met Ezra Pound and Jean Cocteau. Stein told him the sun always shone in Tangier, and he immediately fell in love with the colourful life he found there, the costumes, music and dancing. 'It was like a constant theatre,' he told me.

Eventually Paul made a little money from composition, writing film scores and incidental music for theatrical productions by Tennessee Williams and Orson Welles. Jane's lover Libby Holman commissioned Paul to compose an opera for her to sing based on Federico García Lorca's *Yerma*. It proved disastrous owing to the decline of Holman's voice. A ballet with costumes and sets by Salvador Dalí was another fiasco. Paul also composed some music for the Broadway debut of Jane's only play, *In the Summer House*, which drew on her complex relationship with her possessive mother. I had known little of Jane's literary career until a stay in Tangier when Paul suddenly said, 'What about Jane's book?' At the time her only novel, *Two Serious Ladies*, first published in 1943, was out of print and hardly known except in specialist circles in the United States where it was an underground classic. First editions were worth a thousand dollars—a signed copy even more—and neither Paul nor Jane had a copy they could lend me. However, the Bowleses' American poet friend Ruth Fainlight—who had once lived near them in Tangier for a while—kept a copy in London that Jane had autographed for her. Though we later became friends, at the time I hadn't yet met either Ruth or her husband Alan Sillitoe, and if it had been my precious book I would have been too suspicious to let it go. After a little persuasion Ruth generously lent it. Wendy and I both read it. She, especially, loved it, and I determined to buy the rights. I published it in 1965 with enthusiastic dust-jacket endorsements from Tennessee Williams, James Purdy, Francis Wyndham and Alan Sillitoe. Later editions featured an introduction written by Jane's friend and admirer Truman Capote. The book's critical reception was excellent, which cheered Jane a little.

I once asked Paul if his work had inspired Jane to start writing, but he said it was the other way round. Although he'd originally wanted to be a poet and had abandoned that for music, it was helping Jane edit *Two Serious Ladies* that had inspired him to start writing in earnest. Jane wrote slowly—*Two Serious Ladies* had taken her three years. She had written an earlier novel in French but had destroyed it. 'She wanted to destroy everything she wrote,' Paul told me. After we brought out our edition of *Two Serious Ladies*, Jane worked on a short-story collection but her progress was hampered by her ill health. Eventually Paul finished one of the stories and edited the collection, which we published in 1966 as *Plain Pleasures*.

I managed to sell *Plain Pleasures* to Farrar, Straus & Giroux in New York over lunch with Roger Straus and his son. Roger wanted more of Jane's work, and we both brought out a volume that included her play, novel and short stories. The reaction was enthusiastic both in the UK and in the United States. Our mutual friend David Herbert read her the reviews and asked Jane if she was excited by the acclaim. It had cheered her somewhat, but, she replied, 'It's too late. It all makes me realise what I was and what I have become.' In the copy she autographed for David she wrote, 'Of Dead Jane Bowles'. When he once offered to throw her a party, Jane told him he'd better hold it in a cemetery, 'because I'm dead'.

Jane had been vivacious and beautiful but was always rather insecure. She had a terrible stroke in 1957 when she was just forty and never fully recovered. On one of our visits Jane had just returned to Tangier from a mental-health clinic where she had endured electroshock treatment after a breakdown. Her depression had lifted somewhat, but the treatment worsened her powers of concentration and her ability to write. It has often been said that she was an alcoholic—not something I noticed, though perhaps she was taking a break from booze on medical advice. Her most prodigious drinking probably took place before her stroke. Although much improved, Jane still wasn't well enough to entertain, so others held dinner parties for her. Sitting next to her at a dinner I asked her whether she would have rather have been a cabbage than pursued her life as she did, writing when she could but experiencing excruciating mental-health problems. Without hesitation she replied, 'I would have chosen to be a cabbage.' She was no longer truly happy at all.

Jane was at that dinner on her own. Paul was suspicious of Moroccan restaurants and, although he occasionally dined at posher hotels and at private houses, he didn't attend such dinners unless there were guests he liked very much. So Wendy and I took Jane home in a taxi. She and Paul each had a flat on different floors of the same building, but, wanting company, Jane asked me to escort her to Paul's. Her beloved husband opened the door and said very coldly, 'You're downstairs. What are you doing here?' I was appalled—I'd never seen Paul like that before. He was usually so well-mannered and gentlemanly.

Considering what Jane had just been through it seemed heartless and very sad. I think Paul had a pot-smoking assignation with his protégé Mohammed Mrabet and would brook no interruption—not even from his lonely, fragile wife.

Paul and Jane's relationship was obviously unusual. Jane told me that she had always loved Paul—that he was the only man she had ever loved. They were both bisexual, and I understood that, though they still cared for one another deeply, after the first year or so of their marriage the relationship had become a platonic one. From then on they seem to have pursued mostly homosexual relationships. While Paul spent time with his male coterie, Jane pursued Cherifa, then a vendor in the grain market where she bought food for her parrot. Totally infatuated, Jane started visiting Cherifa three times a day, and the parrot grew fat from over-feeding. Eventually Cherifa gave in to Jane's charms. For Jane it can hardly have been worth it—Cherifa was extremely domineering and troublesome.

I got to know Jane pretty well, and she once told me that she had been on a train with James Agee, whom we also published. He was very attractive and wanted to sleep with her, but she had turned him down. 'Paul would have been too upset!' she said. I understood from this remark that Paul didn't mind so much if she slept with women but viewed as a betrayal her sleeping with men. I was somewhat chilled when she said to me, 'I'd rather have Paul on my side than against me.'

Besides Cherifa, Jane's loves included the glamorous American singer and actress Libby Holman, but it was to Helvetia Perkins, a lover she had met while living in Mexico, that, jointly with Paul and her mother, she dedicated *Two Serious Ladies*. By the time I knew her I don't think Jane was sleeping with anyone. Cherifa was still around, but Jane had told David Herbert that she had only slept with her once or twice anyway. To be honest, Cherifa seemed to me extremely unappealing—a dreadful woman. A 2014 article on Jane in the *New Yorker*, 'The Madness of Queen Jane', describes Cherifa as 'a gorgonish, hirsute grain seller with whom Jane fell madly in love'. I thought her a bit of a witch. She was so domineering that eventually Jane felt relief whenever Cherifa was absent. The writer Emilio Sanz de Soto recalls encountering Jane outside a café, tearful as she had lost her door key, fearful of the scene Cherifa would create on finding out, and blaming Paul for having gone on a trip and leaving her on her own. He helped Jane sort the contents of her bag, which, as well as the missing key, included a dead sparrow, a broken mirror and dozens of lentils. Cheered by the rediscovery of the key, Jane allowed Emilio to help her address the other discoveries. They gathered the lentils in a handkerchief and, to avoid bad luck, took a taxi to the seafront to cast the broken mirror into the sea. The sparrow was given a solemn burial behind Jane's apartment block. To celebrate these achievements Emilio treated Jane to a lunch *al fresco*. Suddenly radiant, Jane began to sing 'Lazy Afternoon', a favourite song. 'I shall always remember Jane like that,' Emilio said, 'magical, brilliant, spurring our hopes and illusions, and laughing, for ever laughing.'

34

Will I Go to Heaven?

Jane Bowles became a great friend and knowing her was often good fun. On one occasion, in about 1965, she was well enough to hold a party for her bibulous old pal Tennessee Williams. 'Tennessee's coming with a nice little drunk he picked up!' she told us. The 'nice little drunk' turned out to be a rather large middle-aged woman who was very pleasant but obviously a committed boozer. Wendy and I ended up sharing a taxi to Jane's with Tennessee and his new friend. On arrival Jane presented him with a bottle of cheap vodka she had procured over the Moroccan border in Ceuta. It was a good party—Jane had cooked superbly, and Wendy said it was the only Moroccan meal she really enjoyed—but I hardly spoke to Williams, apprehensive that he was so drunk he might turn on me. But when we left he came down to see us off in the taxi and was charming. Despite the fact that by then he had downed almost an entire bottle of vodka (I don't think his fat friend got much of a look-in) he wasn't slurring or stumbling—he could really hold his drink. I thanked him for publicity quotes that he had given us for Jane's novel. 'Oh, it was easy!' he said. 'It's my favourite book!'

On another occasion Jane said she could get us into this magnificent party but also, oddly, told us to dress down. Assuming it was a hippy gathering, I took her at her word and turned up in a casual shirt and no tie. Jane looked at me appalled. She thought one of Paul's silk cravats would sufficiently improve my tatty apparel, and we were able to set off to what turned out to be a pretty grand affair. It was the annual party of an Austrian baroness complete with two Moroccan bands and frenetic dancing. It seems that I passed muster, as the Baroness frequently invited us back.

At one of these parties I met George Andrews, an American living in Morocco who was terribly keen on cannabis. From him and Simon Vinkenoog I commissioned *The Book of Grass*, which came out in 1967 and did very well for a long time, going into many editions. Someone else I met there was

Marguerite McBey, an incredibly rich heiress of the First Bank in New York who had married the Scottish First World War artist James McBey, noted for his portrait of T. E. Lawrence. James wrote as well, and it was one of my mistakes not to have bought his memoir.

Marguerite was an imposing figure even in her seventies and eighties. With her high cheekbones and dyed black hair she had obviously been a beauty when young and was still very good-looking. She lived alone on Old Mountain in a mansion called El Foolk (The Ark) with a substantial daytime staff of cooks and maids, but at night had just a single watchman. I often feared for her safety—she was fabulously wealthy and had lots of expensive jewellery—but she seemed quite unworried. She was very sociable and also kept a beach house where everyone who was anyone partied. Tangier was full of cliques, many of them very snobby, and Marguerite's friends were mostly rich, well connected or titled. They were also largely gay or bisexual, and, once her husband died in 1959, Marguerite got herself a distinguished girlfriend in Lady Caroline, one of David Herbert's cousins. Caroline was married to Sir Michael Duff, the bisexual baronet, who was a renowned practical joker. In England his favourite prank had been to dress up as his godmother Queen Mary and pay people surprise visits in a chauffeur-driven car. He kept this up until the fateful day he bumped into Queen Mary herself in a neighbour's hall. I gather she wasn't amused.

I liked Marguerite McBey. She knew Paul pretty well and illustrated for us his 1991 book *Too Far From Home*, the first novel he had written in twenty-five years. Over drinks I once asked her about Paul and composer Aaron Copland. Paul had said of Copland, who was ten years older than him, that their relationship was 'strictly master and pupil', but at this Marguerite roared with laughter. I'd published *Without Stopping*, Paul's autobiography, in 1972 and Marguerite told me William Burroughs had dubbed it 'Without Telling'. Paul had so expurgated his life of anything personal that Marguerite said she occasionally read it to send herself to sleep.

Without Stopping had come about as a commission from Bill Targ, a senior editor at Putnam's. Paul was short of money so he agreed to it but then got cold feet. Not wanting to con anyone, he wrote to Bill warning him that he wasn't about to spill the beans on Jane or anyone else. He offered to withdraw, but Bill wanted the book badly enough to tell Paul to write what he wanted. To be honest, the result is pretty boring, though Paul did admit to one or two affairs with women, including one with Peggy Guggenheim. When I interviewed Paul for our book *Paul Bowles by His Friends* (1992) I had a list of questions that Jeremy Reed helped me draw up. When I asked him about love affairs Paul replied, 'With women? Not many.' He normally didn't give interviews, but I think he trusted me enough to grant it and was as candid as I expected—which was hardly at all.

The most detailed biography of Paul Bowles is by Virginia Spencer Carr who had also written about Carson McCullers. Virginia was incredibly diligent and made thirteen trips to Morocco in twelve years to conduct interviews. I sat in on a few of these which Paul, then over eighty and very ill, gave from his bed. He'd had cancer and was suffering from excruciating sciatica. I remember commenting that he had been very candid this time. He was contemplating the end of his life and told me that he wanted to put the record straight. Sadly, he appointed an executor and agent who refused to authorise the book and sabotaged it by forbidding any posthumous quotations from Paul's work or correspondence. It was a great pity. Paul, who died in 1999, had collaborated extensively with Virginia and had certainly wanted the book published. It came out in the United States in 2004, with my UK edition published the following year. Despite all the interference, it remains, in my view, the best biography of the author.

Paul had liked to encourage young authors in Tangier. I think he may have had affairs with some of them. Mohammed Mrabet, an extremely good-looking Moroccan storyteller and painter, was one of the most significant and enduring of his acolytes. Paul would record and translate Mrabet's stories, and in all they collaborated on fourteen books, a couple of which I published. I was suspicious of Mrabet, however, thinking him exploitative—something Paul more or less admitted. It was typical of Paul that he was fully aware but generously forgiving of the faults of others.

Paul liked to smoke quite a lot but disdained taking part in the transactions himself, leaving it to his more streetwise friends. Mrabet was possessive of Paul and always in attendance when I paid afternoon visits. He drove me back to my hotel a couple of times. I was somewhat apprehensive as he was pretty stoned. Somehow he got me back in one piece.

Mrabet met the Bowleses when he was twenty-one in around 1957. Eventually, on the proceeds of his relationship with Paul, he was able to build a house after which he spent less time with him, found himself a wife and started a family. He did invite Paul to dinner to view his home though, and Paul was astonished to find it furnished with a number of his own paintings and books. He presumed that Mrabet had 'borrowed' them from Jane's flat. Paul didn't do anything about it though—he didn't really care. He guarded his privacy so zealously at the time that when Mrabet wrote some notes for a book on him he actually paid him not to publish it.

At one point I remember Paul renting a bungalow in the grounds of a hotel on Old Mountain to work on Mrabet's books with him. Wendy and I were spending time with Jane, who could be terribly indecisive—that was one of her main problems—but at dinner at the Parade Club she had decided that we would visit Paul for a picnic the following day. She had two female companions at the time, Cherifa, her sometime lover and antagonist, and one of Cherifa's friends who acted as maid. They hated Mrabet, she said, and Jane didn't like him much either. During the trek to the bungalow she claimed that Mrabet's books were essentially Paul's work. 'He shouldn't be doing it,' she said; 'he should be doing his own work, not this stuff.' I suppose this may have arisen from Jane's animosity towards Mrabet—she resented his closeness to her husband. Paul told me he had to keep writing, that translations or collaborations were useful when he lacked inspiration of his own. To be fair, Mrabet must have had some talent. Friends tell me that his paintings are rather good and are sold in galleries, but I doubt his stories would have been published without Paul, who turned them into works of art.

Paul had always translated, mostly from Arabic, Spanish, French and Portuguese sources. His earlier translations had included the play *No Exit*, from Sartre's *Huis Clos*, which John Huston directed for the New York stage. As well a couple of his collaborations with Mrabet, I published his version of Isabelle Eberhardt's *The Oblivion Seekers*. Eberhardt, a fiercely independent, late-nineteenth-century Swiss explorer, appealed greatly to Paul. Dressed as a man, she pioneered travel to North Africa and immersed herself in Sufism, the mystical sect often regarded as heretical by orthodox Islam. Although she died young, she lived an extraordinarily adventurous life and eventually became a Muslim herself. Of Paul's living young friends, several of whom I published as well, he also translated Larbi Layachi, Abdeslam Boulaich, Rodrigo Rey Rosa and Mohamed Choukri. He was often terribly generous in taking no royalties himself on many of the books, leaving them all for his protégés.

Paul's own novels and stories often concern Westerners overwhelmed by North African culture or disoriented by exotic drugs or poison. This theme has echoes in his own life in Tangier—indeed he once claimed Cherifa had poisoned Jane. Perhaps she did, or maybe it was some sort of herbal folk medicine, but Paul insisted that Cherifa had plotted to get her hands on the house Jane bought for her in Medina by administering poison. When Millicent Dillon interviewed Mrabet for her book on Paul, Mrabet acknowledged his hatred of Cherifa and said that 'she was the dangerous one ... who had poisoned Jane and tried to poison Paul'. David Herbert, who was by then closer to Jane than Paul, told me this was all nonsense, but I suspect something really was going on.

Another strategy Cherifa attempted in order to magically induce Jane to give her money was to place a nasty mess of congealed blood, hair and other matter under a potted plant. Unaware of its sinister secret and wanting to keep an eye on the plant while Jane was in Málaga, Paul tried to move it to his flat. Cherifa flew at him in a rage, attempting to gouge out his eyes. The incident is echoed in David Cronenberg's film *Naked Lunch*, adapted from William Burroughs's novel. Of course Burroughs knew and admired the Bowleses and had similar interests to Paul. In the 1950s and 1960s many artists and dropouts, beatniks and hippies were drawn to Tangier by the climate and the easy availability of drugs, boys, booze or all three. For Burroughs, Paul and his descriptions of North Africa in *The Sheltering Sky* had been an additional inspiration. 'There is about Paul's writing, at its best, a palpable darkness, like underexposed film,' Burroughs wrote. 'I am forever indebted to Paul, for his writing that drew me to Tangier in 1953; and for his cherished friendship, then and since.'

Aside from Burroughs, over the decades he lived there Paul slowly became a magnet for other famous pilgrims. In 1967 he wrote to a friend that the Rolling Stones were in Marrakesh with Brion Gysin: 'They were here last week. Very much rolling (in money) and very stoned.' These visitors would come and go, and he was unfailingly welcoming, patient and civil with them, even the many who turned up at his door uninvited.

At one point Paul had a parrot he was fond of—it would call out 'Allah! Allah!'—but it eventually disappeared only to be rediscovered dead. Paul thought Cherifa had poisoned it, and, before Jane returned to Málaga permanently, the fear that Cherifa was poisoning them both finally prompted them to sack her. She died of cancer in around 1989, having sold the house Jane bought her to pay her medical bills. Perhaps Cherifa wasn't the only one who behaved suspiciously. Maybe Paul himself wasn't as gentlemanly as he seemed. After all, he told me that during the war, when he had been rejected for military service on psychiatric grounds, the report on him declared that he had a suspicious nature and a 'psychopathic personality' (other versions of this story call him 'psychoneurotic'). He regarded others as potential enemies and always locked his doors, a habit from childhood when he would lock his bedroom at night for fear his parents would kill him.

One disturbing rumour concerned Paul secretly slipping Tennessee Williams a Mickey Finn, or possibly *mahjoun*, to observe the effects with his mixture of clinical curiosity and authorial detachment. Even more sinister, in 2009 the film historian and critic Ronald Bergan claimed in the *Guardian* that, having watched the 1998 documentary *Let It Come Down: The Life of Paul Bowles*, he suddenly recalled a memory of Tangier he had repressed. As a teenage hitch-hiker in the late 1950s he and a friend arrived there tired and hungry. By chance they were befriended by the *St Trinian's* actor Richard Wattis who bought them food and beer, then offered to take them to see Paul Bowles. After Wattis left, Bergan alleges that Paul gave him and his friend, then just tipsy teenagers, some exotic cigarettes. The next thing he knew, Bergan woke up in a bed to find he'd been stripped naked and dressed in a *djellaba* while his less attractive friend had slept unmolested. The intervening hours were a complete blank. After his flashback, Bergan read Paul's entire oeuvre hoping to glean clues to the missing time. 'Bowles's best writing drew me into an exotic, perverse, nihilistic world in which one of the dominant themes was the destruction of innocence,' he wrote. 'What impressed me and disturbed me most was his second novel, *Let It Come Down* (1952), set almost entirely in Tangier among the louche ex-pat community. It ends with the main character, Nelson Dyar, a soulless American high on hashish, hammering a nail into the ear of his sleeping Arab friend.' Ronald Bergan might equally have cited *Up Above the World* (1966)—Paul's penultimate novel and the last until the novella *Too Far From Home*—in which an American couple are drugged into stupefaction and amnesia by their charming nemesis who suspects they know about the murder he has previously committed.

Whatever his flaws or possible misdemeanours Paul deeply loved his wife and saw that Jane, who endearingly called him 'dear Bubbles', was as comfortable as she could be until the very end. She had once had money—Jane was an only child whose mother was desperately fond of her and generous, too—but I know Paul struggled financially when Jane was ill. Her lengthy stays in sanatoriums, first in England and the United States, then Málaga, were expensive, and her writing brought in relatively little. Jane inspired deep affection in all of us and was an unusually interesting writer. Had she been well enough to write more, she would probably have been a major one. Eventually she deteriorated again, this time irretrievably, barely able to walk, often silent and indifferent. Paul returned her to Málaga to be looked after by nuns at the Clínica de Los Angeles. In 1970, her wild dancing at a hospital party and fury at her carers' attempts to restrain her caused another stroke, the first in a series. Aside from rare moments of lucidity, she barely spoke and hardly moved after that. Paul was distraught without her in Tangier. He and David Herbert travelled independently to see her, and I know they missed her terribly. She died in 1973 at the age of fifty-six after thirty-five years of idiosyncratic marriage. Paul, by then looking thin and unwell, told me it was the worst thing that had ever happened to him. He wrote very little of his own after her death, mostly translations and journal entries. 'There's no point,' he told me. 'There's no one to read it to.'

I liked Paul, but he was often so reserved and cultivated such a sense of mystery that I never quite knew what he was thinking. His imagination certainly went to dark places, but an image from our 1992 book *Paul Bowles by His Friends* lingers in my mind. In the last selection in the book, Gavin Young writes of Paul sitting on a tyre swing in his garden, swaying back and forth pushed by a Moroccan servant, 'a merrily giggling Paul whose only fear seems to be that, if things are going well and the sun is out, some disaster, by that very fact, must be imminent. I have never known a human being who so mistrusts happiness. The wonder is that mistrust doesn't put the kibosh on his delightful sense of humour.' Remarkably, Paul, who died in 1999 at the age of eighty-eight after living over half a century in Tangier, outlived Jane by twenty-six years.

We published *Paul Bowles by His Friends* for his eighty-second birthday with contributions from many admirers, including William Burroughs,

Francis Bacon, John Cage, Patricia Highsmith, David Herbert and Gore Vidal. We added the subtitle 'A Revealing Portrait', but it wasn't really. Paul was an expert at extreme discretion when it came to his own life and loves and was saving up any revelations for Virginia Spencer Carr's biography. He professed astonishment that anyone found him reticent or reclusive but also insisted that anything the reader wanted to know about him could be found in his books anyway, however transformed through literary alchemy. 'If you analyse it you will find out about the person,' he said, adding that, 'most writers live the dullest of lives'. He was modest about his success, saying that skill had little to do with it. 'What has happened in my career is all explained by one word—luck.'

The centrepiece of *Paul Bowles by His Friends* was the interview I conducted with Paul in Tangier which turned out to be the last time I saw him. I'd just been to Marrakesh alone and had a couple of days left in Tangier before returning home. Virginia was still interviewing him—I'd sat in a couple of times but felt a bit of a gooseberry. I went one last time only to find myself worrying how I would get back to my hotel. It was Ramadan, so people fasted all day. Everything in Tangier went a little haywire, and taxi services generally stopped until evening. Mid-afternoon I asked Paul if he thought I might get a taxi. He said, 'You might just as well ask me "Will I go to Heaven?"'

35

Tangerino Queen

Another friend Wendy and I made in Tangier was the Honourable David Alexander Reginald Herbert, second son of the 15th Earl of Pembroke. In the 1950s his friend Ian Fleming dubbed him 'the Queen Mother of Tangier', something that pleased and amused David—so much so that he once dared tell the Queen Mother his nickname. After a short pause she said she wouldn't mind in the least being referred to as the David Herbert of Clarence House! Of course it helped that she enjoyed gay company and even, against official advice, employed several gay members of staff. However, I don't suppose David would have dared mention it had not his sister, Lady Patricia Hambleden, been one of her closest friends and a lady-in-waiting.

Extremely well connected with the talented, the aristocratic, the rich and royal, David was a terrific snob but a very nice man and a superlative host. Much of social London used to visit Tangier in those days, and David made it his business to know when anyone of interest was visiting. No one ever turned down an invitation to his famous dinner parties—you knew you'd enjoy a decent free meal in brilliant company at the Pink House. David was also an incorrigible gossip and collector of anecdotes which came in handy for the books I eventually commissioned from him.

It was Jane Bowles who first introduced us. She and David were close friends to the extent that David had promised to marry her should Paul die first. Knowing I had published both the Bowleses, David was quite keen to have me at his gatherings, so Wendy and I went a number of times and got quite friendly with him. He was genuinely gregarious, but with me there was an ulterior motive. Eventually he announced, 'I'm writing my autobiography.' I read the manuscript and knew immediately that we should publish it. It was not the greatest writing, but the material was unbeatable. It featured everyone! Noël Coward, Cecil Beaton—practically everyone in the book was gay. David knew, and was friends with, all these extraordinary people including the Duke of Kent with whom he may have had an affair before the Duke's death in 1942.

David's family, the Pembrokes, is probably one of the oldest families in England, and his friendships within the higher echelons of the royal family included such divisive figures as Edward VIII, both as Prince of Wales and Duke of Windsor, and Wallis Simpson. David knew the Prince would make a disastrous king and once said a statue should be raised of Wallis Simpson for saving us from his reign. Looking back after all these years, I recall the newspaper headlines and ferment over the abdication in 1936. Edward VIII had been very popular with the working class, and there were street protests when he was forced to step down. Many aristocrats were enthusiastic about having a fascist-sympathising king, too. As for Wallis Simpson, aside from her two divorces, she had a fairly salacious history, including an affair with the Nazi minister von Ribbentrop. So it was lucky that things turned out as they did.

In total I published three of David Herbert's books: his memoir *Second Son* in 1972; a collection of anecdotes we called *Engaging Eccentrics: Recollections* in 1990; and *Relations and Revelations: Advice to Jemima* in 1992. The last of these, an amusing selection of reminiscences and opinions on life written for David's great-niece, I had wanted to call *Nobs and Snobs*. David quite liked my title, but our outraged editor Michael Levien objected so strongly that we settled on something less provocative. The book was pretty slight but sold well in Morocco because David constantly had house guests and would send them to Librairie des Colonnes, the large bookshop in Tangier which sold all the Tangerinos' books.

Though David's books weren't literary masterpieces the people in them really come to life. I could never understand quite how he managed it. I remember asking him, but he just grinned knowingly. It wasn't until years later that one of his friends admitted that he had ghostwritten them for him from notes typed up by another friend, Marjorie, Marchioness Tweeddale.

As he tells it in his first book, David first visited Tangier in the 1930s but settled there in 1946 after a stint as a wireless telegrapher in the Merchant Navy during the war. As the 'spare' rather than the heir, he enjoyed more freedom than his elder brother—but only after he'd deliberately failed to excel at Eton and other colleges he was sent to. While a student, he spent his pocket money illicitly hiring cars to be chauffeured with his chums to nightclubs and theatres, often sporting cloche hats, fur wraps and other purloined drag. During the General Strike of 1926 he was co-opted from school to work as a train guard, porter and track layer. The strikers viewed him as a blackleg and pelted him with rotten eggs and tomatoes.

Once reconciled to his unsuitability for the army career they had planned for him, his parents allowed David to pursue a career in acting. The writer, director and actor Elinor Glyn mentored him for his appearance as second romantic lead in her 1930 film entitled, ironically, *Knowing Men* and its follow-up *The Price of Things*. Both were disasters. David then became 'social secretary' to Otto Kahn, a wealthy international banker and womaniser he described as looking 'rather like a vole with bushy white eyebrows and moustache'. The job turned out to require David to escort interested young ladies from the nightclubs of Berlin up to Kahn's hotel suite and then back again once transactions were finished. Effectively he was a kind of pimp. He quickly gave up the role but fully relished the pre-war hedonistic Berlin night life which he described as 'an orgy of fun'.

Eventually he found himself broke and, having temporarily exhausted his family's financial indulgence, he started singing for his supper in night clubs dressed as a German sailor. After a brief stint back in England he went to New York and became friendly with the 'ambisextrous' actress Tallulah Bankhead. A job then arose as assistant to a classy interior designer doing up the houses of rich Americans who fawned over his aristocratic heritage. He also moonlighted as a portrait artist whose sitters included Rose, the mother of the future American President John F. Kennedy.

In the United States life for David seems to have been another hedonistic whirl amid the glitterati, fuelled during prohibition by bootleg booze and bathtub home brew. He returned to Britain only to set off again for Morocco to stay at El Minzah Hotel in Tangier. He made regular return visits until the war intervened. For gay and bisexual people, Morocco, despite being a Muslim country, was far more congenial in those days than the UK or the United States. So once the conflict was over David made Tangier his home, endearing himself to the natives and becoming *de facto* head of the Tangerinos—the community of Western migrants who settled there—for the remaining forty-nine years of his life.

In Tangier David could afford to entertain with ease. He had three or four servants including a chef trained in French cuisine who could cook quite decently. Food and wine were cheap. They used to go to Gibraltar or drive to Ceuta to get duty-free spirits, and it would cost next to nothing to have a dinner party for twenty people that in England would cost a fortune. His parties were great fun, but by the time I met David he sported an expensive toupée which, though quite convincing, I nevertheless found somewhat distracting. I tried not to stare at it during conversation, but often wished I could ask his advice for Peter Vansittart, another author and friend I published, whose own toupée was a real shocker. I could never find the right way to broach the subject though.

David's luxurious Pink House was furnished like an English country mansion with antiques that he'd bought or inherited. Over the fireplace was a Van Dyck portrait of one of his ancestors. There was a large and beautiful garden in which peacocks roamed, and a terrace where David's lunch and dinner parties were held. He had a parrot and in the garden kept a monkey. He had rescued it from ill treatment but was met with ingratitude. 'The monkey hates me!' he'd exclaim. The grounds also contained houses that he'd built for his loyal servants. He left them quite a bit of money in his will, too.

Paul and Jane Bowles's decaying apartments and furnishings were very modest in comparison to David's polished luxury. David recalled a party Jane threw in her tiny flat where their friend Sonia, 'a vast mountain of flesh', occupied the middle of the sofa all evening, not even rising to greet the guests despite it being the only seating. After all the other guests had gone, Jane thanked Sonia and gave her permission to move. Her bulk had been hiding a vast hole burnt in the middle of the sofa.

Wendy and I would often book into the Villa de France in Tangier, a wonderful hotel on a hill set in beautiful grounds. Gertrude Stein had stayed there, and Matisse was a fan, too, I understand. Paul who, like Jane, was very fastidious, once came to dinner with us there saying, 'It's one of the few places I go to because I know it's clean.' David Herbert—who knew all the gossip—boycotted the hotel and avoided any association with the German woman and her Dutch husband who ran it. David insisted—I don't know on what grounds—that they were appalling Nazis who had been involved in running the death camps during the war. The food was good though, as was the service. The couple gave every appearance of being nice and respectable people and had trained up all the Moroccan waiters, cooks and staff to a very high standard and ran it with Teutonic efficiency.

My sometime neighbour in London, Francis Bacon, also holidayed in Tangier. Francis could be charming but often behaved very badly, not caring what he said or who he offended. He was used to buying endless bottles of champagne and could have bought David Herbert a hundred times over. David obviously made allowances for Francis and was often concerned for his welfare, especially as he got roughed up frequently by rent boys. David once had a word with the chief of police. 'This is a very famous painter,' he said. 'Why is he always in a ditch in the morning? Can't you protect him?' The chief of police said, 'M'sieur! He like to be in the ditch!' The boys themselves had no beef with Bacon—he was a masochist and gladly paid them give him a thoroughly rotten time.

We held a colourful launch party in London for David's first book. As well as the author, guests included Cecil Beaton, Lady Diana Cooper and all David's titled friends and relatives—almost half of Debrett's Peerage. My friend the writer and novelist Elizabeth Berridge was dazzled by David and his entourage. 'We have a here a living legend!' she said. Of course with all those celebrated guests I wanted a decent photograph for *The Bookseller*. I took a gaggle of guests down to the dining room where my photographer wanted a formal line up. He was a press photographer who often did embassy parties and was certainly no Cecil Beaton. Beaton himself was in a pretty bad temper and, as my photographer faffed about, snarled at him, 'Snap, man! Snap!' I've always favoured candid shots myself rather than anything posed or self-conscious, and of course that's the way good photographers work.

During the party David's sister, Lady Patricia Hambleden, was looking after their mother Lady Beatrice, the Countess of Pembroke, who was ancient but still alive, just about. The poor old lady needed use of our lavatory, so Lady Patricia helped her upstairs—a tricky climb as we had a long and difficult staircase. I'm about the same age now as Lady Beatrice was then, and one doesn't realise what an ordeal such impediments can be for the elderly. However, she was pretty tough, the old Countess, and made it in time without losing her dignity. When she died a year or so later David was at home with his sister when the doorbell rang. It was the day after their mother's funeral and cremation. David went to the door and said, 'Is this another package for the Countess of Pembroke?' And the delivery man said, 'No. This *is* the Countess of Pembroke.' He was delivering her ashes.

36

Anaïs Nin

If anyone had a significantly more complex love life than mine, or indeed anyone else I've ever known, it was Anaïs Nin. Margaret Crosland, the translator of Jean Cocteau and the Marquis de Sade, first recommended that I publish Anaïs back in the late 1950s. I had known the author by repute and wrote to request a meeting. I received a cordial response and an invitation to dinner with Anaïs and her husband at their elegant apartment in Greenwich Village, New York. In due course I published some of her novels and short stories, but initially they didn't sell particularly well. She encouraged me to publish the first one, *Children of the Albatross* (1959), by saying that Lawrence Durrell, genuinely a fan of her work, would write an introduction. I knew Durrell vaguely and later published his translation of Royidis's romantic biography of Pope Joan. Durrell hadn't known anything about an introduction and certainly wasn't falling over himself to help out, but Anaïs and her husband invited him to meet them in Paris and wined and dined him into agreement. His endorsement certainly helped, but it wasn't until we started publishing her deeply personal journals from 1966 onwards that sales and press interest grew enormously.

Anaïs mentions Wendy and me in her seventh journal:

> Summer 1970. Peter Owen and his wife Wendy. He wears a yellow laced shirt and a tie embroidered with bangles. She came to the airport wearing a red feather boa in the style of Clara Bow. They drink until I fear they will disintegrate before my eyes. Wendy said in a genuine Cockney accent, 'You're a lady. Peter should have married a lady like you!'

Wendy, who had a great sense of humour, found this hilarious, but I wasn't quite so amused. On this occasion I wasn't drunk because I was driving, and Wendy, who had been born in Hampshire, was privately educated, had a cut-glass accent and never spoke like a Cockney. But then, as we were to discover, Anaïs was a great inventor of fiction.

There is a photograph of Wendy and me standing with Anaïs taken in May 1970 at the launch of the third volume of her journals, not long after we had collected her from the airport. It was shot in our back garden in Earl's Court at a party given in the author's honour. Wendy is on my right, while Anaïs is pictured in the middle looking down at my younger daughter Georgina. Beyond Georgina is Anaïs's great friend, the charming Oscar-winning actor Luise Rainer. We all look very elegant, and Anaïs has an arm affectionately draped round my daughter's shoulder. The pose was almost certainly for the camera as I suspect Anaïs didn't much care for children. My elder daughter Antonia was by then an independent-minded teenager who had swiftly gained an unfavourable impression of Anaïs as self-absorbed and self-regarding. She preferred to shut herself in her bedroom for the duration of the party. She may have been right, but at the time I was completely besotted with Anaïs, as were so many who came into contact with her. With her radiant beauty came a terrible vanity, so it is likely that she is looking down at Georgina in the photograph to show herself in the best possible light. When Anaïs started to object to being photographed in the garden, Luise Rainer chided her, 'Don't be silly. I don't mind.' Anaïs usually insisted on demanding the right of veto on all photographs and had insisted that the press photographs taken after a party we held for her at the Savoy were touched up. This photo, then, is a rare one of her *au naturel*, though by this time she had already had some discreet facelifts. If she had known the subsequent popularity of the photograph she would have been furious.

During her visit there were various press junkets, and Anaïs complained that the Fleet Street interviewers were 'as brutal and malicious as in the States', which may or may not have been true. She also complained that one woman journalist 'wrote the most hostile review ... Because it was cold and I put my hand in my cape for the photographer, she said I was hiding my freckles to appear younger. The entire review full of venom.' We took Anaïs to the Press Club where women had recently been admitted for the first time. 'I was met at the door by a man so old I was afraid he would die before my eyes,' she recorded later. 'He said in a quavering voice, "You must realise this is a privilege, not a right!" I found the feminist women fiercer than the Americans because they have less freedom.' She went on, 'Because I listened to his wife's griefs with sympathy, one critic wrote that I was a fierce liberationist. The drinking is staggering. The interviewer who took me to lunch drank until he could no longer control the tape-recorder. He wanted to know whether Henry Miller was as good a lover as he purported to be in his novels.'

There is some truth in this last anecdote. I took Anaïs to lunch with Peter Grosvenor, the literary editor of the *Daily Express*, who was a friend of mine. Though he could be prissy at times, he was a very good interviewer. Perhaps emboldened by drink he asked Anaïs if Miller had been a considerate lover. She needn't have replied, and later recorded her disgust at this line of questioning, but I recall that she said he was no good in bed at all, despite the fact that she had always claimed elsewhere he was a true Casanova and that she was nuts about him. Grosvenor couldn't use this nugget in the *Daily Express*—in those days it was too salacious for its readers—so he gave it to the *Sunday Times* instead.

It was during a previous visit in 1968 that we held a party at our house to which both Anaïs and another major author, Anna Kavan, had been invited. Anaïs writes of hearing that Anna 'all dressed to come to the reception' had died 'holding a heroin needle after giving herself an overdose', though the coroner concluded differently. Anaïs goes on to say:

> My intuition is that the English in general do not understand or like my work. I met some exceptional young people from Cambridge and there we harmonised. The young are natural, warm and spontaneous ... Left London feeling it was the most hostile place for my work.

She was wrong—its denizens generally found her fascinating and inexplicably exotic, if something of an enigma. We were all puzzled, however, by her mixture of *hauteur* and charm.

Anaïs was born in 1903 to Cuban parents in the western Parisian suburb of Neuilly-sur-Seine. The fifth book of hers, which we published in 1968, was an edition of her short-story collection *Under a Glass Bell* with woodcuts by her husband Hugh Guiler. She had been forced to bring out her own edition in 1944 because no commercial publisher would touch it. To do so she set up a her own imprint which she called Gemor Press—a sort of play on the name of Gonzalo Moré, a Peruvian bohemian and armchair radical with whom she was enjoying a sexual relationship more passionate and explosive than the one she was simultaneously conducting with Henry Miller. When the Second World War caused her to flee France and live in New York she employed Moré to work with her in publishing. He, however, proved utterly unreliable. Most of his work for her was very poor, as he was lazy, a boozer and drug-taker with artistic aspirations and nothing to show for them. Anaïs ended up doing most of the work herself. She became disillusioned with Moré and began to fantasise about murdering his wife, the exotic dancer and manipulatively psychosomatic invalid Helba Huara, who Anaïs blamed for corroding his spirit. Her tortuous love affair with Gonzalo Moré became the basis for her novel *The Four-Chambered Heart,* while Helba inspired the character of the dancer in *The House of Incest.*

Anaïs, while in France, had dreamt of living on a houseboat and made the dream a reality by renting one on the Seine as a love-nest for trysts with Moré.

The Four-Chambered Heart, which I published in 1959, features the symbolic houseboat; so do stories from *Under a Glass Bell*, which had originally been published by Tambimuttu's Poetry London in 1947. Far from being the idyllic paradise and ship of her dreams described in Anaïs's books, her biographer Deirdre Bair said the houseboat was cold, damp and leaky. Indeed, Gonzalo Moré had to be bribed to go there!

Most women I knew disliked Anaïs. She nearly always made a beeline for their husbands if she thought it might advance her professionally. The Canadian novelist Elizabeth Smart, who never said anything nasty about anyone, was not a fan. Anaïs had had a go at seducing her lover, the boorish drunken poet George Barker, who once threatened to beat me up at a party for reasons that elude me even now. Anaïs frequently made a play for men, and Barker was one with whom she did eventually have an affair. Unless a woman—a feminist or a major admirer—could further her career she showed far less interest in them. Beautiful though she undoubtedly was, I would not have liked to have been married to her. She may have been ladylike but she was certainly no lady when it came to relationships.

I never found out what my friend Gunther Stuhlmann, Anaïs's agent and the editor of her journals, truly felt about her. Obviously he admired her work, but all of his girlfriends hated her. Anaïs was out of action when I was in New York once—she was in hospital—and Gunther's then girlfriend asked bitchily, 'Why don't you ask her whether it's cancer or a facelift?' Like the Duchess of Windsor, Anaïs had cosmetic surgery. She looked pretty good as she aged. She was very elegant and radiated great charm. But as one French publisher said to me years later, 'She never smiled with her eyes; just with her lips.' Marie Pierre, the second wife of André Bay, a senior editor at Editions Stock whom I knew very well, hated her. She told me, 'I disliked her before she came to Paris and before I met her. After we met I disliked her a lot more!' Anaïs plainly didn't make an effort with her. One time Marie was pregnant and had morning sickness. They were at a dinner party at a restaurant, and she had to leave the table. Anaïs said to her coldly, 'One does not do that.' But André was besotted with Anaïs despite being very much a man-of-the-world Frenchman. Anaïs had got on well with his first wife so probably had it in for Marie Pierre anyway.

By 1970 Wendy had decided that she liked Anaïs who had obviously made an effort to work on her. Wendy didn't realise then what Anaïs would say about us in Volume 7 of her journals—that we were always drunk. Although an inveterate liar, Anaïs could be painfully honest when it came to others' work. She was complimentary about Wendy's two novels and must have genuinely liked them. She certainly didn't mince her words about a work of fiction by Gunther Stuhlmann's lovely wife Barbara, who not surprisingly also loathed her. Barbara's novel was, to be frank, a pretty undistinguished, run-of-the-mill one about Greenwich Village, and the publicity quote Anaïs gave read, 'This is a good picture of Greenwich Village.' That was all she had to say! Paul Bowles, who usually had a kind word for everyone, also disliked Anaïs. He had known her in New York during the war after she fled Paris. He and his beloved wife Jane were in Greenwich Village when Jane found herself accosted. Paul didn't recognise Anaïs, but there was a lengthy conversation between Jane and a strange female, and he asked Jane, 'Who was that little woman you were talking to?' She replied, 'It was Anaïs Nin telling me what a lousy writer I am!' Paul never forgave Anaïs for that and from then on she would appear in his nightmares, head shaved and wrapped in newspaper.

Elizabeth Smart and Paul Bowles had both divined the truth: Anaïs was actually quite unpleasant. When Anaïs came to London I asked her about Paul and Jane. I said, 'What did you say to Jane that on that occasion that so upset her?' She replied, 'I was just pointing out the defects in the book, one writer to another.' But it wasn't her business to do so—she hadn't been asked her opinion. Jane lacked confidence, was insecure and chronically ill, so it was quite the wrong thing to say. I really don't think if you meet someone in the street it's your business to have a go at their writing.

It's hard to comprehend the sort of life Anaïs chose to lead. She was famously the lover of Henry Miller in 1930s Paris and was certainly attracted to Miller's second wife June, while at the same time being married to and supported by Hugh Guiler, an American-born banker she had wed in Havana in 1923. I think it's fair to say that the journals are partly a record of her nymphomania. She fixated on many of her lovers, sometimes several simultaneously. Clearly at one point in 1933 she was desperate to marry Miller but admits in the journals that to separate from Guiler would cause him great distress and that, anyway, without his financial support she and Miller 'would starve together'.

Hugh Guiler illustrated some of his wife's books with attractive woodcuts under the pseudonym Ian Hugo, a name he also used as an experimental film-maker from the 1940s onward. He wanted to keep his life as a successful and respectable banker separate from his life as an artist and as husband of the notorious writer. We knew him simply as Hugo, and I found him a very cordial man, completely devoted to his wife despite her extreme disloyalty. I felt sorry for him. In her diary of January 1933 she writes, 'I hate lies, double lives, continuous insincerity, shifting, transition, deceits.' Yet she goes on to record how she deceived and manipulated Hugo and others for the rest of her life. There is a story in Nin's unexpurgated journal *Incest* of how she engaged in sex with Henry Miller when Hugo came back unexpectedly, so Miller, like a character in a domestic farce, hid in the guest room. In fact she records Miller doing this at least three times in 1933. I think she liked the sense of danger, excitement and power that these situations provided for her.

I could not claim to have known Henry Miller well, but I met him once in New York at the offices of Barney Rosset of Grove Press which published Miller's *Sexus* and *Tropic of Cancer* when no one else would touch them. I was standing there watching a grubby old tramp being screamed at by Barney's secretary. It was Henry Miller gone to seed. I liked him though. As well as publishing his *Letters to Anaïs Nin* (1965), one of the first books I published was Miller's *The Books in My Life* in 1952. Much later I realised that many of the authors he had chosen had made it on to our list. I went after the novels of Hermann Hesse after reading his book, and Anaïs Nin, Lawrence Durrell, Rabindranath Tagore and Blaise Cendrars were others whom I subsequently published. Whatever his faults, Henry Miller had good taste in literature.

We don't know how much factual content there is in Anaïs's journal *Incest*, which covers the period 1932–34, and includes much of her affair with Miller. Anaïs's brother said it was fiction, but I am inclined to believe the most shocking revelation of the book—that she slept with her father—is true or at least represents a partial truth. Her parents were separated, and she had been psychoanalysed by Otto Rank with whom she studied and had also had a sexual relationship. Rank was the love her life, Gunther once told me. It wasn't just Otto Rank though; she also seduced René Allendy, the French pioneer of psychoanalysis. She persuaded her brother to go to Allendy for therapy, too, but the shrink spent the entire session telling him how deeply in love he was with Anaïs. She had this strong attraction to father figures, so perhaps sleeping with her own father was a way of getting over her Electra complex. Or perhaps it was just a Freudian fantasy she confided to the journals that she knew would eventually be published. One gathers that her father, a pianist and composer, was very like her—narcissistic and with similar defects. What she claims he did was despicable. Her brother, the composer Joaquín Nin-Culmell, maintained that the incest story was untrue, but then he would hardly know unless Anaïs and her father had decided to make it a *ménage à trois*.

Looking back, it's remarkable that Anaïs found time or energy to write anything. She was having sexual relationships with Henry Miller, Antonin Artaud, Gonzalo Moré, probably her own father, her cousin, and then—to keep him quiet—Hugo as well, and there are likely to have been other individuals on the side. In the unexpurgated journals such as *Fire* and *Incest* she sometimes recounts having sex three or four times a day with different people.

Anaïs always wanted to be a famous writer and really worked at it. Apart from the sex, her addiction was to fame. Drink and drugs were of no interest—it was fame she craved. Wanting to keep her wits about her, Anaïs hardly drank alcohol at all. Elizabeth Taylor was exceptional in that respect—most women renowned for their beauty, if they are keen to remain attractive, do not drink a great deal. Anaïs might have had the odd glass of wine, but she kept her looks through a combination of dietary self-restraint and facelifts. Being sober must have been vital. She was a master—a mistress—of manipulation, and sobriety helped her keep the upper hand.

I was once told that Hugo had no idea Anaïs was a bigamist who had married Rupert Pole in 1955. I can't believe that—I'm sure it's not true. Hugo was paying all the bills, keeping Henry Miller, keeping all these people Anaïs cultivated as lovers, friends or admirers. I imagine he must have had some inkling. He was a perfect gentleman, and I think she treated him pretty badly. But perhaps Hugo didn't mind about her infidelities so long as he could be part of her life and as long as she depended on him.

Early on we discovered how fierce Anaïs could be in protecting those parts of her life she and Hugo wanted kept secret. During her first visit to London a very tough journalist from the *Financial Times* had found out that the film-maker and artist Ian Hugo was in fact the respected banker Hugh Guiler and was married to Anaïs. This was mentioned in a review of the first volume of her journals. Hugo saw it and prompted Anaïs to send a telegram with the words 'NO HUSBAND'. He didn't want publicity and felt it was bad for business. Anaïs, too, was very upset at any printed mention linking her with him and wrote me a terse letter to which I had to respond with a grovelling apology. She was fortunate, indeed dependent on the fact that Hugo did have a well-paid if rather stuffy job. With Nin as his wife he had plenty of extra expenses. Her brother Joaquín described Henry Miller as 'a professional sponger'. In one of the journals she wrote, 'Henry needs a new winter coat. But Hugo is so mean.' In fact Hugo was anything but mean! He paid for Henry Miller and all those other people with whom she associated, and, of course, it's very easy to be financially generous when it's someone else's money. Hugo also knowingly gave monetary support to Gonzalo Moré for a time, having done so unwittingly for far longer.

Because of the strict instructions to excise any references to her first husband it was only after his death in 1985 that the unexpurgated diaries could be published. Hugo's role in Anaïs's life is thus little known or appreciated, though she did once describe him as her 'fixed centre, core… my home, my refuge'.

As for Rupert Pole, the husband Anaïs bigamously married on the West Coast, the story is that he thought she was divorced from Hugo. She was manipulative and perhaps a sufficiently good liar to pull the wool over his eyes, but I don't think either husband could have been so stupid as not to realise what was going on. It's more likely that they pretended they didn't know—to themselves and to her.

Long before it became public, Paul Bowles told me that Anaïs was a bigamist who had married both a banker and a PE teacher. In fact Pole was a former actor with a degree in forestry from the University of California, Berkeley, who worked as a forester and a high school science teacher. Anaïs lived and sponged off Hugo in New York and would head off to California supposedly to write. There she would see Pole who, after her death, became her literary executor and edited the later unexpurgated versions of the journals until his own death in 2006.

To keep her two parallel lives going—her 'bicoastal trapeze act', as she dubbed it—she had to tell elaborate lies which she jotted down on index cards and kept in what she called her 'box of lies'. She had cheque books in both her married names. It was only through their tax returns, when both husbands tried to claim her as a dependent, that they officially found out the truth. Anaïs annulled her marriage to Pole in 1966 but continued to live with him until her death eleven years later. I think Hugo loved her too much and forgave her. He was simply in her thrall and was devoted to her.

We never found Anaïs a difficult author to work with, although she could be fierce and prickly on occasion. In one of her last letters to me, written in May 1975, she says:

> I just had five month's fight with cancer, three months in the hospital, and [am] just recovering while still under chemotherapy treatments here in Los Angeles. It has been a slow recovery this time. All I do is work quietly on Volume 6 and walk and swim to regain my health, visit the hospital ... I am appalled at the bad taste of the paperback covers. Gaudy and vulgar. Is there anything that can be done? Will my reaction affect them at all? Of all the translations, publications from all over the world the English paperback is the ugliest.

She concludes by offering her warmest greetings. I had to reply that I had no control over the paperbacks, published as they were by another company entirely.

Anaïs died in 1977 and her ashes were scattered in Mermaid Cove, Santa Monica Bay. Hugo's ashes joined them when he died in 1985. Immediately after Anaïs's death her bestsellers became the posthumous publications *Delta of Venus* and *Little Birds*—the erotic stories she had written for cash in the 1940s for a private collector. I published neither. I don't think anyone can accuse me of being prudish—after all, I have published some quite extreme writing by all sorts of writers, including the Marquis de Sade and Apollinaire. I simply didn't like them. They were, I felt, essentially exploiting the market for soft porn. I still feel that as far as quality literature went we published Anaïs's best work.

The American editor Gunther Stuhlmann always got the best publishers in Europe for Anaïs, and she is still highly regarded. I'm on record, however, as saying that Anna Kavan is, ultimately, more important and had greater imaginative power. I think Jane Bowles might have been a better writer, too. It is claimed that Anaïs anticipated feminism, and she certainly blazed a trail for sexually emancipated women's writing, though personally I think she was too dependent on men. She could undoubtedly write well. Her prose was very good, but her work is too self-centred, too narcissistic in my view. The journals, however reflective, are a rehash of her life and vice versa, whereas Kavan had much greater capacity for transmutation and inspired invention. I think *Anaïs* has staying power though, and the sheer quantity and psychological complexity of her work, with all its frankness, manipulativeness and self-deceit, will keep readers, critics and psychologists engaged for many years to come. Even with her newly unexpurgated journals we still haven't got the whole Anaïs. She was so complicated. Now there's a new generation discovering her work, and it's gratifying to find that it is undergoing something of a renaissance.

37

Engaging Eccentrics

Anaïs Nin may have been a manipulative nymphomaniac, but she had interesting literary taste. As well as admiring Anna Kavan and D. H. Lawrence, she was a fan of Marguerite Young. Anaïs and Marguerite were neighbours at one point and remained friends afterwards, perhaps because Marguerite was comparatively plain and therefore no threat. Anaïs must have been one of the select few enthusiasts who read Marguerite's enormous 1965 tome *Miss Macintosh, My Darling* all the way through. She wrote about the book in her study *The Novel of the Future*, which also discussed her admiration for Anna Kavan.

Miss Macintosh took Marguerite eighteen years to write, and by then the manuscript was nearly 3,500 pages long. Editors managed to whittle it down to about 1,200 pages for the published version—a bit more than *Atlas Shrugged* but well short of *À la recherche du temps perdu*. Legend has it that seven suitcases full of manuscript were lost at a French railway station only to be retrieved by seven porters, each pushing a barrow. One character in the novel, the opium lady, was based on a rich addict Marguerite knew who had been bedridden for years but who was an admired patron of literature in Chicago. The opium gave her vivid dreams and hallucinations, and Marguerite claimed to have been with her while a school of blue fish swam over the bed and once heard her chatting with the decapitated head of John the Baptist. There was also, apparently, a golden bird—the spirit of an ancient Greek philosopher no less—perching on her bedpost. Furthermore, she entertained imaginary elephants and blackbirds as big as men—though not all at the same time, I think.

Miss Macintosh, My Darling wasn't critically successful but developed a cult following. We published it in Britain in 1966 and Anaïs wrote an introduction for a paperback edition. We quoted her in the book's blurb: 'A book I want by my bedside. It is vast, it is human, and it is illimitable.' Marguerite was talented but, I thought, a terrible bore actually—the sort of person one wouldn't want to get stuck with at a party.

As a publisher I engaged many eccentrics and mavericks other than Marguerite Young. As I've mentioned, I published Yoko Ono's *Grapefruit* in 1970. She was probably the author I most disliked. Ono had first issued the book in Tokyo in 1964 in a limited edition under her own imprint. It consists of a set of Zen-like performance art instructions inspired by the American composer John Cage, one of the original dedicatees, with whom Ono's first husband, Toshi Ichiyanagi, had studied. There wasn't much to the book really—just odd phrases and photographs of people's bottoms—but it sold thanks to Lennon. The original edition is now worth a fortune, with my second edition fairly valuable too.

When our edition came out in 1970 we held a signing at Selfridges. Fans were queuing up round the block, mainly because John Lennon was there in an Afghan coat. He had written an introduction for it and contributed a few drawings, so it was an opportunity for fans to meet him and ask for his autograph. I can't think anyone was as interested in either Ono or her book. To be honest, I thought the book didn't amount to much and ended up saying so to its author at the launch party we held upstairs afterwards. It's true that I did get a bit merry before I said my piece, but I wasn't rude. Besides, she had taken to phoning me up in the middle of the night to give me notes, to ask about sales and telling me what to do, which I found tiresome and thoughtless. In the end I told her, 'You're good at writing pop songs and I'm good at publishing, so why don't you do your thing and I'll do mine!' She never bothered me again.

Before the book came out the company's editor and production manager Beatrice Musgrave and I went to see Lennon and Ono at the Apple headquarters in Savile Row. We liked Lennon but found Ono pretty unpleasant. She was sitting at a long desk, arrogant and expressionless, scoffing great spoonfuls of caviar from an enormous Fortnum & Mason's pot. Beatrice knew that it was worth £40 a jar (about £600 today) because her wealthy uncle used to buy it. We were put out that Ono didn't have the grace to offer us any, nor any other refreshments.

I had met Lennon before at several parties held by a man from *Art & Artists* magazine. Yoko Ono used to attend them with Anthony Cox, her second husband, before their 1969 divorce. I also knew a couple who had offered to put Ono up for a while only for her to stay two years! They said she behaved appallingly and treated her daughter Kyoko very badly indeed. All in all, Ono struck me as a complete phoney. She was so unprepossessing too—what Lennon saw in her God only knows!

In *Grapefruit* one of Ono's performance art recipes is entitled 'Painting to Be Stepped On'. The instruction is simply to 'Leave a piece of canvas or finished painting on the floor or in the street'. I once unwittingly fulfilled these instructions, more or less. One evening, after a particularly bibulous session at the French House, I parted with friends after buying a painting from the artist Francis Souza. When I arrived home I was horrified to realise that I'd left it in a telephone box while calling for a taxi. Doubtless it was stolen, or trampled on by some philistine. Undamaged, it would be worth a small fortune today.

Another of my eccentrics, one I liked significantly more than Yoko Ono, was Ithell Colquhoun whom I first met in the early 1950s at a gathering of writers and artists in a Soho pub. A very attractive woman in her forties, with ash-blonde hair and an endearing giggle, it turned out that she was a very fine surrealist painter who also dabbled in poetry and prose. Ithell had been born in India, but her fairly well-to-do family had returned to England a few years later. She trained at the Cheltenham School of Arts and Crafts and then at the Slade in London where her talent was first recognised.

After I married Wendy in 1953 Ithell often visited us for coffee. With a mutual interest in art, she and Wendy become firm friends, and she regularly joined us at bottle parties throughout the 1950s and 1960s. Wendy and I also used to visit Ithell in her Hampstead studio where we sat as she chatted engagingly, sometimes dressed in a kaftan, surrounded by somewhat bleak landscape paintings of Cornwall, most of which were emblazoned with her trademark phallic symbols. Ithell lived mostly in Hampstead but often retired to enjoy the solitude of her Cornish cottage. She moved there permanently by the early 1970s on doctor's orders.

I published a handful of her poems and pieces of prose poetry in the first two *Springtime* anthologies of 1953 and 1958. The titles of some of those poems—'Magical Sequence', 'The Wax Image', 'Divination' and 'Amulet'—illustrate her enthusiasm for occultism and mythology, themes her artwork also explores. Her encounters in Paris in the 1930s with the paintings of Salvador Dalí and other surrealists also influenced her imagery and technique. To the surrealist obsessions with dreams and Freudianism, Ithell added enthusiasm for Jung and secret magical societies. She often employed automatic writing, chance and coincidence in her work. I knew little of the occult side of her life, though she once told me Aleister Crowley had attempted to seduce her. Unwilling to accept her refusal, he ended up pursuing her all around the house. Crowley was also an acquaintance of Anna Kavan, a fellow drug user, and her doctor Karl Bluth.

Ithell was definitely one of the most progressive writers I knew. *Osmazone*, a rare anthology of her writing, included texts using found material (like a list of varieties of condom), as well as poems celebrating the anus and other orifices. The collection was published in 1983, but many of the texts were written as early as the 1940s. None of these more adventurous texts found their way into any of my publications. I did commission from Ithell a couple of evocative illustrated travelogues though. The *Times Literary Supplement* described the first, *The Crying of the Wind: Ireland* (1954), as 'rare and beautiful'. Like the second book, *The Living Stones of Cornwall* (1957), it foreshadowed the subjective approach to landscape and myth that many later psychogeographical writers were to take. They sold pretty well and became highly prized by collectors.

As well as some of her poems, *Springtime Two* also contained an extract from her novel *Goose of Hermogenes*, a strange alchemical gothic novella. She had written it long ago and often asked me to publish it in the early days of our friendship. I was cautious about publishing such an unusual book but felt it so memorable and resonant I took the plunge in 1961, despite opposition from editors Muriel Spark and Michael Levien. Reviews were positive though, and it later sold well in paperback editions.

Looking back, I realise that, as well as being very good company, Ithell was an exceptionally creative and gifted artist. One of many women surrealist artists who was relatively neglected in life, it is pleasing to find a resurgence of interest in her work and the issuance of biographies and previously unpublished work. Several paintings, prints and drawings are now in national collections, including the National Portrait Gallery, the Victoria and Albert Museum and the Tate Gallery. I wish now I had taken up the offer to buy a painting she offered at a very reasonable price. It certainly wouldn't have been something I'd have left in a telephone box.

It was through Ithell that I first met Peter Vansittart when she invited Wendy and me to a PEN Club dinner at the Rembrandt Hotel in South Kensington, later the scene of my final tryst with Eleanor. Peter had taught at fairly progressive schools for decades before becoming a full-time writer. He had an extraordinary memory for historical detail, and his knowledge was as vast as it was deep. By 1968, when I signed him up for *The Story Teller*, a novel spanning five hundred years of history, Peter had already written over a dozen novels for other publishers and was critically lauded as one of the finest British historical novelists. Over the course of our friendship I published over a dozen more of his novels, as well as a couple of history books and a memoir.

Our editor Dan Franklin thought Peter Vansittart a wonderful man who was easy to work with and the most impressive of our list's English novelists. Michael Levien thought much the same and especially admired *Pastimes of a Red Summer* (1969), one of Peter's most readable novels. He remembered Peter catching sight of the original commissioning report in which Michael, though recommending publication, noted a lack of action. He said Peter was affronted by this, but I know he was modest enough to accept his own weaknesses—he also once admitted he was too remote from ordinary life to render dialogue well.

Michael also recalled that Peter was peculiarly uninterested in making his environment comfortable or pleasant. His ramshackle Hampstead flat was almost always devoid of food. When he stayed with Peter at the cottage in

Suffolk he had inherited from his mother, Michael found the bed sheets were filthy, there was no working oven and the whole place was uncomfortably spartan. However much he liked Peter it wasn't an experience he cared to repeat.

Peter was a good friend and his books, though never bestsellers, were critically admired and always sold well enough. I made little money on them but never lost any either. He retired from writing in 2007 with the publication of *Secret Protocols*, an ambitious and imaginative story set in the Second World War and one of his more accessible books. He died the following year at the age of eighty-eight.

38

Erté

Throughout our marriage Wendy and I liked to keep up with the London art scene and attend gallery openings. In the late 1960s and 1970s the Grosvenor Gallery in St James's Street, Piccadilly, was one of the posh ones. It was run by Eric Estorick, a rather brash American who nevertheless knew his stuff. He represented Francis N. Souza, an artist I admired. Eventually I came to own a couple of Souza's paintings, having accidentally abandoned a third in a telephone box. Sneakily, I bought them from the artist himself, thus depriving Eric of his percentage. Despite his occasional disagreeableness, Wendy and I got on reasonably well with Eric and his wife Salome.

One of Eric's greatest triumphs was managing to unearth the Russian-born artist and designer Erté. They had met in Paris in 1967, and Eric realised there was nothing in print on Erté and that his art-deco style was enjoying something of a renaissance. Wendy and I were really taken with Erté's work, too, so when Eric said he wanted to commission a biography of Erté for his birthday I leapt at the chance. Of course Eric was doing himself a great favour, too—he became Erté's international agent and made a fortune.

By the time I got to know Erté he had practically been forgotten. He was born Roman Petrovich Tyrtov in 1892 to a distinguished Russian family and adopted his pseudonym (based on the French pronunciation of his initials R. T.) so as to avoid embarrassing them when he took up a career as an artist and designer in Paris. He was probably right to do so—I remember him sashaying about campily in a mink coat! He was a very nice man, though, and pretty easy to deal with when it came to working on *Erté—Things I Remember*, the memoir we published. Eric was unbelievably brash, though. I remember attending a meeting with him and Erté at the gallery to discuss the as yet unfinished manuscript. As far I know Erté wasn't deaf, but Eric said to me in a loud voice, 'I've got nothing in writing. What if the old boy dies on me?' It was awful! Despite this, I know the Estoricks were fond of him and otherwise treated him quite decently.

We had a launch and signing of Erté's book at Harvey Nichols in Knightsbridge where the large stock of copies ran out very quickly. My sales manager had to pop back to the office for more stock, as the queues for signed copies were building up almost on a par with those for Yoko Ono's *Grapefruit*. The book had been edited by Beatrice Musgrave, and she and I once asked Eric if there was to be anything in the book that revealed Erté was gay. Eric said he'd written just a couple of lines on this, but that Erté had scribbled on the manuscript, 'No! No! Never will I permit this!' He was still worried about his mother, I think—though she must have been long dead. Erté himself was around eighty-three at the time.

The London launch was followed by a party in my garden. Wendy and I had separated by then, but she came to the party, enthralled as we all were by Erté and his fashionable fans. I remember rising to the occasion by wearing a black-and-gold embroidered Moroccan shirt which Erté admired greatly. It was one of many shirts I had made by a tailor just off the Medina in Tangier.

I was friends with the fashion designer Thea Porter, and when the Erté book came out in 1975 she was really keen to meet him. She took Erté and me out to dinner in Paris, and I got him to sign my book and include a little drawing. Beatrice had told me she didn't think he'd be able to draw off the cuff, but of course he could. At the end of the evening he returned to the Paris suburb where he lived while I went back to Thea's for a nightcap.

Thea was an innovative designer who had been born and raised in the Middle East and who brought her taste for Arabesque and Indian fabrics to fashionable boutiques in London, New York and Paris. That night a button came off my coat and I was a somewhat worried about losing it. I asked her, 'Could you sew it on for me?' 'I can't sew! I don't sew!' came the reply. I couldn't have made a bigger *faux pas* had I asked Coco Chanel to darn my socks. As I headed down the stairs I heard some shrieks and screams. Perturbed, I called up to ask Thea if she was all right. It seems that her boyfriend was beating her up, but presumably it was what she wanted because she called down saying 'Yes!' quite cheerfully.

As well as Erté's drawing in my copy of his book, I own an original gouache by him. I bought it neither from Eric nor Erté but very cheaply from a chap I knew at the Queen's Elm pub in Chelsea who usually dealt in silver. He knew of my interest in the painter and that I was publishing his book and just happened to have bought a mixed consignment in which, by luck, was this work of art by Erté.

Although the artist lived to a ripe old age—he died in 1990 aged ninety-seven—I didn't see him again after that Paris dinner with Thea. The Estoricks had genuinely cared about Erté and had expected to be left everything—all the drawings, rights and so on—in his will. But, like Paul Bowles, Erté left everything to his chauffeur.

39

Hello, Dalí

Members of my family have been publishing works by Salvador Dalí for nearly seventy years. Uncle Rudi, like Dalí an enthusiastic Freudian, took an interest in the painter's work and, with my father, first published *The Secret Life of Salvador Dalí* at Vision Press in 1948. There were several reprints and editions over the next three decades, and they also published *Dalí on Modern Art* in 1958. I remember Rudi, who mostly collected out of a love of art, not for commercial value, owned a rare copy of Lautréamont's *Les Chants de Maldoror* illustrated with actual Dalí lithographs. After Rudi died I auctioned it at Sotheby's where it fetched £500 (perhaps close to £10,000 today).

Dalí's American friend Caresse Crosby had encouraged him to write *The Secret Life of Salvador Dalí* while he was staying with her. A wealthy heiress, she scandalised convention with her open marriage and the recklessly hedonistic lifestyle she pursued in the artistic circles of Paris and the United States. She was a poet, editor and publisher, too, and her Black Sun Press published beautiful deluxe limited editions of works by Proust, Pound, Hemingway and others, all of which are highly prized by collectors today. Blessed with a capacious bosom, she also had the distinction of gaining the first patent for her inspired invention, the modern brassière.

When Dalí's memoir was first published he was well-known, even infamous in some circles. By the time I came to republish *Hidden Faces*, his only novel, in 1973 he was probably the most famous contemporary artist in the world aside from Picasso. When I discovered the rights were available, I knew I had to have it. Like *The Secret Life*, *Hidden Faces* had been translated by Haakon Chevalier, a professor of French literature at the University of California, Berkeley. An American born to French and Norwegian parents, Chevalier was an interesting man. He was a friend of the atom bomb pioneer Robert Oppenheimer and had also served as an official translator at the Nuremberg trials of 1945. Left-leaning in his politics, he was suspected of passing information from Oppenheimer to the Russians. As a result, Oppenheimer lost his security clearance while Chevalier lost his job and the prospect of further employment. He eventually left the United States for France where he carried on translating until his death. When I met Chevalier he told me he'd written pretty much written Dalí's books. He said he'd used Dalí's material, but it was such gibberish he had to assemble it into something coherent. Maybe this is true. Chevalier certainly didn't strike me as someone prone to lying and exaggeration.

Hidden Faces had been written at the New Hampshire residence of the choreographer and ballet impresario George de Cuevas, the Marquis de Piedrablanca y Guana, and his wife Margaret, the granddaughter of John D. Rockefeller. Both were Dalí fans and patrons. Dalí worked hard at the novel for four months, producing what Chevalier described as a 'lush jungle' of over-ripe prose detailing the decadence and decay of wealthy aristocrats. In the epilogue, written in autumn 1943, Dalí describes Hitler awaiting defeat and death accompanied by selections from Wagner played at ear-shattering volume. To be honest, I think surrealist painter Giorgio de Chirico's *Hebdomeros*, which we published in 1968 in a translation by Margaret Crosland, was by far the better novel by an artist.

In negotiations for the rights to *Hidden Faces* I usually saw Dalí by his penis-shaped pool or in his drawing-room at his home in Port Lligat, near Cadaqués, on the Costa Brava of Spain. His shtick included referring to himself in the third person. 'Dalí loves money!' he'd exclaim. 'Have you brought any?' He was famed for his avariciousness, and, as early as 1939, the leading surrealist André Breton anagrammatised 'Salvador Dalí' as 'Avida Dollars'—which sounds like the French *avide à dollars* (greedy for dollars). Apparently, Dalí regularly doodled on cheques when paying restaurant bills, knowing that the owners would thus never cash them. Before our meetings I was briefed by Captain Moore, the rather awful man the artist had there as a secretary. Peter Moore had gradually wrested control of Dalí's affairs and is thought to have faked at least 10,000 lithographs and stolen and altered original paintings. Thanks to him, there's a huge problem with Dalí fakes, especially prints, because of all those blank sheets of paper Moore got him to sign.

Captain Moore was a London Irishman Dalí had picked up. He told me that when I brought the title pages for Dalí to sign I would need to bring some cash, too. He was right. Dalí's first question to Moore on our arrival was 'Did he bring anything?' The answer was yes—I brought with me advance payments on the international rights we had already sold. Every time I went to see Dalí—and I went three or four times—it was the same story; I had to bring him some cash.

The first time I visited Dalí in Cadaqués was in 1972, and by his phallic pool we discussed the American rights to *Hidden Faces*. We needed a release from

Dial Press who had originally published the book in New York in 1944. I saw Dalí snap out of his camp genius routine and become serious and businesslike. 'Remember, I am the son of a notary, and I know these things!' he said. I'd had the foresight to take with me the first 1942 Dial Press edition of *The Secret Life of Salvador Dalí* that Rudi and Arthur had used as a basis for their own edition. I asked Dalí to sign it, and he did so, extravagantly writing 'Pour Peter Owen Hommage de Dalí 1972' and adding a drawing of Don Quixote in a desert landscape. At least I knew this and the other books I asked Dalí to sign in my presence were authentic.

Certainly Dalí didn't do all the work on his paintings and hadn't since at least the early 1950s. A picture was wheeled in when I was at his house on one occasion—he was quite brazen about it—and Dalí said, 'He's done well today!' By then Dalí was rich and lazy and had someone else do the rotten donkey-work of actually painting, especially layouts and geometric design. The work they brought in was a painting of Franco's granddaughter. There are photos of Dalí presenting it to Franco and his granddaughter in November 1972, though a lot of sources state that it wasn't finished till 1974. I don't suppose buyers at the time ever dreamt that another painter would be doing much of the work. Franco certainly would have assumed that Dalí had painted it in its entirety, not some hack—but I suppose that's what the old masters did, too.

Dalí was unscrupulous, mercenary and avaricious—in fact I would say he probably was not a very nice man. When *The Secret Life of Salvador Dalí* came out, George Orwell reviewed it and described him as a brilliant draughtsman but a 'disgusting human being'. I would have to agree. Dalí was often a greedy, insincere showman, though I don't think he was vicious. I suspect it was his wife Gala who trained him to take advantage of as many people as he could, in any way he could.

I met Gala only once at the Hôtel San Régis in Paris where they had rented a suite. I was invited to attend what I thought was going to be a private meeting, but his whole entourage of pseuds and hangers-on were there. Dalí and Gala were just about to leave, but I had a brief talk with them. At the time I didn't know of her reputation for unpleasantness, but on meeting her I immediately felt a sense of something evil. She was originally married to the poet Paul Éluard but was completely mercenary and decided the infatuated Dalí was a better bet. Eventually Dalí bought her a castle in which to retire, but she still managed to manipulate him from afar.

Though I never met Babou, Dalí's famous pet ocelot, I saw several times a very glamorous, attractive girl at his house. When I asked a porter at my hotel about her he giggled and said, 'That's not a girl—it's a man!' Her name was Amanda Lear, and she often denied that she had been assigned as male at birth. The rumour was that Dalí had sponsored her reassignment operation in Casablanca. If so, they did a jolly good job, because I saw her topless at

Dalí's pool, and she looked quite stunning. Dalí first met Amanda while she was a fine-art student and was clearly transfixed. She became a close friend, travelling with him and Gala abroad and spending every summer with him in Cadaqués for the next fifteen years.

When the painting of Franco's granddaughter was wheeled out, the James Bond film producer Harry Saltzman was there. We had been served sparkling wine they tried to pass off as champagne—it really was the cheapest, foulest stuff you could get—I know because I mistakenly bought some. A bossy woman came in and asked us all to leave as Saltzman wanted to discuss commissioning a deck of tarot cards from Dalí for the film *Live and Let Die*. In the end Saltzman used another artist, but Dalí did go on to design his own tarot deck—there had been a lucrative resurgence in trendy occultism.

Dalí had been commissioned to sign our title pages for *Hidden Faces*. As requested, we drew pencil lines for him to add his signature, otherwise it would have gone all over the place as he was doing the job while in bed. We had also asked for a couple of line illustrations to print in the novel. When the pictures arrived I was appalled. It looked as though he had scribbled these in bed as well or got his cleaner to do them. We omitted them from some later editions, as many international publishers simply didn't want them included. The autographed copies were very desirable though. When it came to getting the signed pages out of the country without Spanish customs officers impounding them as works of art or applying a vast surcharge, I came up with a simple solution. I knew my suitcase would be searched or risked getting lost in transit, so, on my return flight from Barcelona to London I took all 160 signed pages as hand-luggage in a bland-looking paper bag. Fortunately no one thought of checking it. Dalí was impressed with the ruse.

Hidden Faces was the toast of the Frankfurt Book Fair in 1973. This was where all the international rights deals were done. It was a huge publishing event. The previous editions, published during the war by Dial Press in 1944 and by Nicholson & Watson in London in 1947, had been hardly noticed, so this was a major relaunch. At Peter Owen, alongside our standard edition, we cannily produced a limited edition of a hundred deluxe copies each signed by Dalí, bound in gilt-stamped white vellum in a slipcase, and with a special twenty page insert, 'Postface to Hidden Faces' containing 'Objective Chance and Reverie'. It's a load of drivel but unique to that edition of the book. I don't know what it's about, and I'm not sure Dalí did either. Of course the special limited edition is worth a fortune these days. We originally sold them for £35 (over £400 now, adjusted for inflation). These days they sell for up to £3,000 to collectors.

Dalí was really quite arrogant and casual about certain things. Had Gala still been in control rather than Peter Moore she might have saved him an unfortunate legal case. It turned out that the name of one of the main characters in *Hidden Faces* was very similar to someone of means in Paris. I don't know whether he had used the name accidentally—he didn't know the individual but may have read her name somewhere. She had consulted a lawyer who had written to Dalí saying that she would be minded to drop any action were Dalí to meet her and donate a signed print. Dalí chose to ignore the issue completely. André Bay of Éditions Stock and I urged him to comply, but he couldn't care less. In the end he was legally compelled to pay her quite a lot of money *and* give her a signed print all due to his obduracy and arrogance. Had he not complied she'd have really taken him to the cleaners.

Paul Bowles told me of his own experiences with Dalí. As he recalled in his memoir, *Without Stopping*, Paul was commissioned to compose music for the 1944 ballet *Sentimental Colloquy*—inspired by a short poem by Verlaine—for which Dalí was hired to design sets and costumes. Paul attended the première only to be aghast that Dalí had betrayed the spirit of Verlaine's poem, his work entirely at odds with Paul's music. The ballet's stars had armpit hair extensions extending to the floor and men on bicycles often collided with them, their yard-long beards getting tangled in the spokes. All the while the cast were menaced by an enormous mechanical tortoise encrusted with coloured lights.

Paul had first met Salvador and Gala at a formal dinner in 1943 and hadn't been impressed with what he saw as their determined *faux* eccentricity. Dalí declared that a tossed salad reminded him of Switzerland and revelled in an anecdote about a St Bernard attacking and devouring a child it was supposed to be rescuing. Gala had repeatedly insisted that she desired nothing more than to become Paul's pet parrot. To that end he must, she said, purchase a large aviary, shut her in it and chuck bird seed at her while whistling constantly. Paul politely declined her request.

40

Just Me and the Rodents

From a personal point of view the 1970s were very disruptive. My marriage finally broke down irrevocably. It takes a while. You see the cracks appear but don't realise they can only get worse. People would tell Wendy and me we were well matched and shouldn't separate. Others would hear one side of the story and be judgmental. But you can only really tell what it's like from the inside.

I was reading recently about Vivien Leigh and Laurence Olivier. One day she told him that she didn't love him any more. 'We were like brother and sister, just as she always wanted,' Olivier said. 'But fortunately occasional incest was allowed.' That's how things became for Wendy and me.

When I first left home as a bachelor I advertised for a flat-share. I ended up in a cheap flat in Philbeach Gardens, Earl's Court, with a man who'd been in the Royal Pioneer Corps and, like me, had a German background. After I married, Wendy and I rented accommodation at 149 Holland Road, near Shepherd's Bush. We had just one bedroom but put up a partition in the corner for Antonia once she arrived. When she started to crawl, my mother paid for fitted carpets so that she wouldn't get splinters from the bare boards.

I don't suppose I was a particularly good father. I was unsuited to domesticity and easily became bored. Perhaps because of my own odd childhood I found I couldn't spend much time playing with the children or sharing their interests. Once, when Antonia was two, I made the effort to dress up as Father Christmas in a borrowed red dressing-gown and cotton-wool beard. She fervently believed in Santa but wasn't fooled. 'It's Daddy!' she pronounced. I never tried it again.

By the time Georgina, my second child, arrived in October 1960, Wendy and I were better prepared. We managed to move to an upstairs maisonette at 42 Philbeach Gardens, near the Earl's Court Exhibition Centre. As a former tenant, the landlord let me rent in the building without the need for an extortionate new deposit. We rented out the third bedroom to a lodger,

Miss Milward, who was always happy to babysit in the evening so long as Wendy prepared the girls' dinner in advance. Opposite our flat there was a large communal garden where the girls could play and make friends.

I had learnt to drive in 1960, so, pootling along in our secondhand Morris Minor, I could drop Antonia and Georgie at their school which was near my office in South Kensington. Wendy was unable to learn to drive due to her epilepsy but would collect the girls from school and take them home to Philbeach Gardens by tube. She was undoubtedly a conscientious, loving parent while the girls were growing up and spent much more time with them than me. She made sure to take them out at weekends and during school holidays to playgrounds, local parks and funfairs, as well as to plays and pantomimes, museums and exhibitions, and to the cinema. Wendy also bought the girls a white budgerigar called Lychee. At the time we had a cat called Morticia, too, a rather unsociable tortoiseshell stray who one day suddenly swatted Lychee when she was on Georgie's lap. We tried to revive the poor bird but eventually had to have her euthanised. Having already disgraced herself once already, after Morticia took to shredding the upholstery we put her up for adoption.

While I was working late or out with friends, Wendy was always there to put the girls to bed, often inventing imaginative and funny bedtime stories to help them sleep. She also encouraged the girls in music—Antonia learnt the guitar, while Georgie took up the flute and became quite accomplished. During the summer I would accompany the family to the Serpentine Lido in Hyde Park where we would picnic, swim and sunbathe. Swimming, mainly in pools and lidos, was, for many decades, my favoured form of exercise until around 2010 when recurring hip problems put the kibosh on that little bit of joy.

Things did improve for Wendy and me during the 1960s—we had some really joyous times—but the harm had already been done, and things deteriorated in the 1970s. For its 'Relative Values' magazine feature I told *The Sunday Times* that I had thought it would be interesting to have children but had found it a bit like getting married: you think it's going to be fun and then come all the problems and responsibilities.

It was terribly difficult for women to pursue careers in those days if they had children. Wendy adored the girls but, once she started writing in earnest, juggling home life with a career as a novelist must have been stressful. I suppose that's why so many of the other women writers I knew—Anna Kavan, Kathleen Raine, Muriel Spark and Doris Lessing, for instance—got others to do much of the parenting for them. When Wendy and I first met we had a lot of fun together and enjoyed one another's company. We were very close. She was much less shy than me—she had a more extravert personality, and was lively and entertaining. Though we'd weathered a great deal through the years, we seemed to grow inexorably further apart. We had many friends but were both becoming a little lonely in our relationship. We just didn't talk about it until there was a big rift. We separated for a bit in the mid-1970s, had some marriage-guidance counselling and got back together for a while. I tried very hard and we were very close for about six months, but in the end it didn't work.

Although Wendy was a very nice girl when I first met her, in the last couple of years of our twenty-three year marriage she no longer seemed to me the person I had wed. At the end I realised I didn't even like her any more—and you can't love someone you don't like. By the early 1970s she was starting to drink quite heavily—at home or in the pub. Unlike me she had never been a heavy drinker before, but alcohol didn't combine well with her anti-epilepsy barbiturates, and, as I spent more time away on business trips, in pubs with my friends, or with Marion and Ben, she started drinking regularly at home, especially while writing fiction. A couple of times Wendy said, 'I don't think you love me any more.' I thought it best not to reply, because the answer was that I didn't—and I think perhaps she felt the same.

In early 1976 my father Arthur managed to catch flu from my mother and then a heart attack finished him off. They had celebrated their golden-wedding anniversary at the Savoy the previous August. He'd sold off Vision Press and had retired, spending some of his time raising funds for the Jewish charity B'nai B'rith. He and Winnie often attended B'nai B'rith events at the Dorchester and Grosvenor hotels, and he became head of the Jewish lodge he still attended.

I certainly wasn't grief-stricken when my father died but my mother was, of course, upset. They had only recently moved from Wembley, where she had fallen downstairs and broken her leg badly, to a small flat in St John's Wood. Winnie was fond of Arthur, even though he often teased her when she put on weight. If she asked for a second helping of pudding he'd shout, 'Up go the balloons!' I had never really had much close contact with my father so never developed any real empathy. Early on I decided I didn't particularly like him. Aside from a lifelong aversion to semolina and porridge, my childhood left me scarred by a lack of affection and Arthur's frequent outbursts of shouting. My mother never shouted back but would bring up historical grievances which merely provoked and prolonged these episodes. I suppose my father felt he had a lot to shout about. He didn't really want to be bothered with a child—especially after he lost the Nuremberg factory during the rise of the Nazis. He was often in a bad mood at home and would even start shouting when out, often in restaurants, much to our embarrassment.

My father had enjoyed affairs as a young married man in Germany and probably pursued a few when he moved to London. He certainly had an eye for the ladies and was fond of Wendy who told Antonia he once patted her knee in his car when giving her a lift. I think he may have picked up women in the West End—Winnie was certainly suspicious of him. When they rowed it was sometimes because my mother had raised the topic of other women—real or imaginary—but more often the two themes were the wickedness of their respective mothers and money, of which my mother was always kept short. She told me she often had to resort to hurriedly helping herself from my father's pockets when he went to the lavatory.

Though they quarrelled like cat and dog and the marriage was often unhappy, I think my parents actually had been in love. My father was extremely lucky but was also genuinely in love with Winnie. Had he not needed the Friedmann fortune when the German factory faced trouble I think he would still have married her. She was in love with him, too, and pretty tenacious—she'd had to be, as her father wasn't hugely keen on the match.

Sophie, Winnie's mother, always loathed my father and throughout my parents' marriage kept up a campaign of vilification, urging my mother to leave 'the bloke' (as she called him) in spite of the considerable shame attached to divorce in those days. On one occasion my parents were holidaying in Eastbourne and Arthur's mother Betty was due to visit. 'How long will the old witch be staying?' my mother asked. My father was furious about this slur and retrieved a particularly vicious denunciatory letter Sophie had written about him which Winnie had torn up but stupidly thrown on an unlit fire. He carefully reassembled it, then had it photographed for use as evidence of his mother-in-law's manipulativeness should divorce proceedings ensue. I thought this was a disgusting thing to do, though nothing ever came of it.

Despite the friction, my parents remained very fond of each other, and I don't think they ever seriously considered divorce. Before the war I remember Winnie telling me how difficult it was for a divorced woman in those days. I suppose my parents had been through a great deal, too. They had been in love when they married, though my mother was glad when they were forced to leave Germany, a country she'd never much liked. It was an odd relationship, though, and my father certainly wasn't a model husband. Winnie told me that their life was much better once 'those silly old women', their manipulative and constantly feuding mothers Sophie and Betty, had died.

Wendy and I stayed together too long really. I knew divorce would be a terrible headache in every way—the house, the children and the money—and have always been fearful of confrontation, so I just put up with it. We tried not to row because all those arguments between my parents I had overheard when I was a child had so badly affected me. I knew rows would be harmful to our children, so hoped the girls would sense little of the tension. Wendy and I should not have bottled things up, but I managed for a while by taking weekends off and going away on my own. Unfortunately, my leaving her at home gave her too much time to drink alone.

Early in our marriage Wendy and I rarely drank much at home. We did go to a lot of parties though. Unless you're very strong-minded you really can't go partying and not drink, and Wendy couldn't hold her drink well. Her father hadn't let her drink at home, and, because of her epilepsy, both her consultant and Uncle Bobby warned her that combining alcohol with medication might kill her. Bobby knew that we were both drinking too much, but I found that if we went out for dinner and had wine I couldn't really tell Wendy to only have just half a glass. So, while I had been the more significant drinker to begin with, her drinking gradually crept up. When she was writing, drinking helped the flow. She'd sit up half the night quite often drinking all the while. She was warned it was suicidal. Wendy knew the price of drinking but kept forgetting it.

In the 1960s, apart from the publishing parties to which we were invited and Sunday roast lunches where we might have a glass of wine or two, the one time in the week that Wendy would imbibe was mid Saturday morning. Ernest and Barbara Hardy—friends of ours who lived opposite us in Philbeach Gardens—sometimes joined by the progressive local vicar, would come over to sample our lethal gin fizzes, while their children, Julia and Kate, would play with ours. As a result, family lunches were nearly always postponed and sometimes abandoned altogether. We probably chatted a little about books and arts—the vicar loved literature, and Barbara was a talented literary critic, academic and novelist who became one of my award-winning authors—so we were able to kid ourselves that these boozy sessions were actually literary salons.

Part of the joy of those sessions was undoubtedly relief and a renewed sense of freedom. From the mid 1950s, Grandma Betty had insisted that, alongside my parents and children, Wendy and I visit her for lunch at her flat in West Hampstead every single Saturday. By 1960, Wendy and my mother agreed that they were fed up with this arrangement. It was terribly boring as Betty refused to speak anything but German. Wendy and Antonia couldn't understand a word she said, and eventually Winnie informed my father that she had never liked her mother-in-law and that he would from then on have to visit his mother alone. Our liberation from this onerous obligation was certainly something we could all drink to.

In the end it was Wendy who petitioned for a divorce and proceedings were already underway before my father died. By then I had left home—I couldn't take any more. I'd bought the house in Holland Park Avenue as office premises and lived in the basement flat to begin with. I took over the entire house and moved the business to 73 Kenway Road in 1976 after Wendy and the girls had moved out. At one point, when Wendy asked me back, I talked to Helen Joyce, one of our best friends, about what to do. I'd tried it before—things would be all right for a couple of days and then she'd be drinking again. Helen advised against returning. They had been out together, and Helen warned me that Wendy was having too good a time. So I told Wendy I wasn't coming back until she stopped drinking—or at least stopped the kind of drinking she was doing. It was at that point she said she wanted a divorce and to be on her own.

As an immigrant outsider in England, George Mikes, in his huge hit *How To Be an Alien*, observed that 'continental people have a sex life; the English have hot-water bottles'. Obviously he and I mixed in somewhat different circles. Throughout my marriage I did look elsewhere for 'comfort'. Wendy told once me, 'I don't care so much about physical faithfulness on your part as long as you don't get involved on an emotional level—and I don't want to know about it.' I know now that, though unhappy about them, she had been philosophical about my early extramarital affairs. At the time she said that were she to name a co-respondent in the divorce it would be the publishing business, not the women I'd had relationships with. As the influence of feminism grew, she became less willing to tolerate them. We were pretty poor in the beginning, so I worked long hours and brought work home. I suspect I became somewhat unsympathetic. Wendy would have been at home all day, doing housework and caring for the children, and would want to chat, but I needed to work. I probably told her to shut up sometimes—occasionally things got pretty heated—but, especially in a small property, there was no real way of separating home life and business back then.

Towards the end of the marriage Wendy had an affair too. It would have been better had she not told me. She had picked up a man who I thought was a 'bit of rough' and beneath her. After she had told me about the affair she said, 'Don't leave me. I'll drink myself to death if you do.' I was very upset. Aside from the odd insignificant crush, Wendy and Eleanor were the two real loves of my life. I always seem to go for slightly dotty or eccentric women though—probably because the alternatives were boring. More complex, intelligent people have a tendency to instability, I think.

By the time we divorced, Antonia had left home and gone to university. Contemplating her parents, Georgina was quite upset. She didn't know whether she wanted to live with either of us. She tried living with Wendy, but her mother's bothersome drunken acquaintances would often drop by. When Georgie moved in with me I was out every night. By that time she had a boyfriend whose mother liked her and who had a home big enough to accommodate a full-time guest. I paid her to help out, and, since her children were all boys, she rather liked having a girl around the house and they remained close for years.

Before he died my father had told me it would be a good way out financially if I gave Wendy the basement flat at Holland Park, which was an absurd idea. Obviously I needed to provide for her, but I didn't want her living in such close proximity. So, after living in her own property in London for a while, Wendy moved to Chichester before finally relocating to live near Georgina in Devizes.

When the divorce came through in October 1976 I became a bit of a pariah. It was almost as if my friends thought divorce was infectious. Lots of friendships cooled off. Even many close friends, from whom I would have expected more support, left me to my own devices. I was left on my own but didn't mind back then. At the beginning I was too relieved to feel lonely. I'd been camping out in the house in Holland Park, so at this stage moved back into Kenway Road. Georgina's pet hamster had got lost there some months before. I think, as they both belong to the mouse family, it must have joined the mice under the floorboards. So for a while it was just me and the rodents.

41

Publishing, Censorship and Apollinaire

Recalling the 1951 debacle at Peter Nevill, when customs had impounded Maude Hutchins' novel *A Diary of Love* on the grounds that it was obscene, I thought I'd better consult my solicitor before publishing Leonard de Saint-Yves' selected translations from the writings of the Marquis de Sade. Despite de Sade's literary reputation I was advised that it was risky—one might get away only with stating certain acts had taken place as long as no graphic descriptions were given. As a result, when we published the book in 1953 the text ended up reminiscent of Morse code with dots and dashes almost outweighing the original text. I have always been doubtful whether any book, play or film could influence anyone to behave in a manner alien to their nature, but hoped that it wasn't one of my editions of de Sade that found its way into the Moors murderers' reading list alongside Nietzsche, Dostoevsky and *Mein Kampf.*

Things changed for book publishers when Penguin won the 1960 *Lady Chatterley's Lover* trial. Despite this, there were still limits on what you could get away with putting into print. I had thought of publishing Henry Miller's debut novel *Tropic of Cancer* in 1963, but Norman St John-Stevas advised against it. Six months later he announced it was now permissible, but by then I had lost interest and John Calder brought it out. The book would have caused even greater controversy had Miller kept his original title, *Crazy Cock*. It was first published in Paris in 1934 with money that Miller's lover Anaïs Nin borrowed from Otto Rank. Somehow I doubt she paid him back. Attempts to publish it elsewhere led to legal challenges, and for many years it was widely banned in the United Sates, the UK and Canada. In the 1960s support from literary luminaries, including T. S. Eliot, dissuaded Scotland Yard from trying to seize copies or mount prosecutions.

I was kept informed regarding the infamous 1971 *Oz* magazine trial for obscenity and would probably have agreed to stand witness for the defence had John Mortimer asked me. One publication I certainly wouldn't have endorsed was Hubert Selby Jr's *Last Exit To Brooklyn.* Calder & Boyars bought the rights and published it in 1966. It sold like hot cakes, but a trial found them guilty under the Obscene Publications Act. John Mortimer defended them and won on appeal in 1968, but I thought the book was revolting and would never have published it myself.

Nowadays one can publish anything, but I believe strongly that just because you can doesn't mean you should. A publisher must ask whether a book has literary merit. If you strongly disapprove of a book you shouldn't publish it. I'm not in any way prissy, but I do think publishers should exercise self-discipline and go by their own moral codes. The books I strongly object to are true crime ones. I told Gloria Ferris she shouldn't have acted as agent for the author of a book on the Yorkshire Ripper. It was a pretty disgusting book, but when the rights were auctioned the publishers were mostly disciplined and there was just one offer.

Support for one risqué book I did publish came from a surprising source. One of my regular haunts was the Queen's Elm in Chelsea, the literary pub. Laurie Lee, who came to some of our book launches, used to spend quite a bit of time there as he was, like me, a friend of the landlord. When the landlord got married, his reception was, not surprisingly, a fairly drunken affair and I ended up chatting to Laurie Lee. I'm not quite sure how we got on to the subject, but we started discussing Apollinaire's 1907 pornographic novella *Les Onze Mille Verges or The Amorous Adventures of Prince Mony Vibescu*. We had published a bowdlerised translation in 1976. 'Oh! It's my favourite book,' Laurie said, 'but you've desecrated it! You've cut the best bits out!' We had published the Apollinaire under legal supervision because I feared prosecution—so what we cut out would have been fairly exotic when you consider the book includes paedophilia, coprophilia and necrophilia. Most of the cuts were passages that involved extreme violence. I said to Laurie, 'Can I quote you on the blurb for the book?' He was aghast. 'No! No! I'm a family author!' Apollinaire's literary reputation was better served years later when we published David Hunter's study *Apollinaire in the Great War* (2015) in which *Les Onze Mille Verges* appears only in a couple of footnotes.

As well as my own edition of *Les Onze Mille Verges* I think Laurie Lee must have known the 1953 Olympia Press version translated by Alexander Trocchi. It was published in France where, though officially banned for many decades, censorship was more lax. Beatrice Musgrave had found a copy and brought it to my attention. We knew we'd have to make cuts but still felt it worth publishing. Our translation was by Nina Rootes who also translated Blaise Cendrars for us.

Les Onze Mille Verges was a funny spoof, but when it came to *Les Exploits d'un jeune Don Juan*, Apollinaire's second book in this vein, I thought it was pretty poor and rather dreary. More recently, for those that require it, the unexpurgated *Les Onze Mille Verges* has been published by others. I was right to be cautious in 1976 though—the risk to publishers of bringing out controversial material was genuine. Indeed the following year there was even a successful blasphemy prosecution involving James Kirkup, a writer I published much later.

42

Dracula's Daughter

After my divorce from Wendy I slowly made new friendships. One of these was with Jenny Botsford who remains a very good friend. Jenny and I were never properly an item, but we shared some good times together. Her husband had died when their two children were quite small so she had trained as a teacher because it allowed her to spend the school holidays with them. During term-time in the early 1970s she tutored child actors during filming at Elstree Studios but eventually ended up working in public relations. Though she later set up on her own, I first encountered her when she was working for a publicist in Great Marlborough Street.

Soon after we met, I took Jenny to lunch at the opening of Mr Chow's, a smart Chinese restaurant in Knightsbridge. Her boss was annoyed as we were out for the whole afternoon. We also often went to Poon's, a Chinese restaurant in Soho which, in dining terms, was going from the sublime to the ridiculous. It was cheap and cheerful, but the food was pretty good. They had quite a roomy lavatory at Poon's, and a builder friend of mine used to use it as a fornication booth. Posh generals' daughters would fancy him as bit of rough. He was a prolific philanderer whose wife knew only a tiny fraction of his illicit liaisons. He was also a bit of a rogue and attempted to make himself non-existent for tax-evasion purposes. It didn't work very well, and he was constantly worried they'd catch up with him. On at least one occasion he did a flit over the garden wall with his accounts in a briefcase to avoid the inspectors.

Jenny and I also went to the wonderful Pizza On The Park parties that Peter Boizot, the founder of PizzaExpress, held at Hyde Park Corner. At my regular Thursday nights at the French House I'd often bump into Jenny. I also took her to the Queen's Elm where I introduced her to Laurie Lee and Beryl Bainbridge. On one occasion Jenny and I were at the Colony Room in Dean Street when the Scottish psychiatrist R. D. Laing, supposedly one of our greatest contemporary minds, was standing behind the door. He got banged on the head every time it opened. He never moved out of the way, and it always seemed to take him by surprise.

During this period I had a three-month affair with an extraordinary American girlfriend who dressed entirely in black. She also wore black make-up and green nail varnish. John Paine and I nicknamed her DD—Dracula's Daughter. She had studied painting at the Chelsea School of Art and lived in Clapham in a house her mother bought for her. The house, where she had her own studio, was always a terrible mess. DD was a very nice woman but had no idea how to look after anything. She didn't cook—I don't think she knew how to—she just bought food in. Her family in New York was one of the top one-hundred richest families in the United States. She told Duggie Fields, a contemporary at Chelsea, that she was friends with the American financier Asher Edelman who was involved in showing and investing in art, and would introduce him. The introduction never took place. Edelman, incidentally, was supposedly one of the inspirations for the rapacious businessman Gordon Gekko in the 1987 film *Wall Street*.

All DD cared about was painting. She was, she said, very influenced by the renaissance painter Mantegna but, lacking confidence, never showed her work to anyone. There was something of a mystery about her family. The only clue she had was a photo of her mother as a child standing in front of an old château. DD said her relatives would never discuss it, but I gathered her mother was the illegitimate offspring of a branch of the Belgian royal family. They fornicated all over the place and would presumably have settled money on any resulting children to keep them quiet. She didn't know for sure, but it's possible that her father was a Belgian prince. Duggie Fields also said he had the impression DD was part Native American. He found sharing a studio with her at Chelsea unnerving. 'It felt like most of the time she just sat watching me,' he recalled. 'It continued the whole time we were sharing. It was very odd, very awkward. We barely spoke to one another, and every time I looked up she was staring at me!'

DD was into pop music, especially Lene Lovich who inspired her dress sense. In fact at one time DD thought she might write a book on her, but Lene started to find DD's imitation of her style and constant presence more worrisome than flattering and felt she was becoming rather obsessed. The book never happened.

DD used to smoke using a long cigarette-holder like the one in the famous photo of Audrey Hepburn. Gloria Ferris made out that DD once attempted to put her eye out with it. I told her this was nonsense. 'She may not particularly like you, but she's not going to poke your eye out!' DD wasn't vicious, just a bit distracted and probably short-sighted. Come to think of it, she did dislike most of my friends.

After I dumped DD she somehow seemed to know exactly what I was up to. 'You're still seeing that Jenny person!' she hissed down the phone. I assume that she'd had me followed by a private detective. She was certainly quite naive and told me at the outset that she wanted to see how 'ordinary people' lived.

Most of my relationships at the time were a bit like this—neither deep nor long-lasting. I asked DD to dinner a few months after we split up, and she was very cold. She said she hadn't liked her experiences of 'real life'. Ordinary people were overrated, she thought, so she went back to painting, living like a hermit in her messy studio. No one seems to have heard of her since. Antonia recalls her last impression was of DD disappearing into a taxi clutching a tiny kitten.

43

The Passionate Penis

Perhaps it was inevitable, but over the last six decades I've published many gay, lesbian and bisexual authors, including Monique Wittig, Violette Leduc, Marcel Proust, Jean Cocteau, André Gide, Paul and Jane Bowles and Yukio Mishima. I also published an important non-fiction book on the science of sexuality, *Born Gay: The Psychology of Sex Orientation* by the distinguished psychologist Glenn D. Wilson and his former student Qazi Rahman. It was first published in 2005 and has gone through several printings. It suggests that sexuality is constitutional and that, though there are genetic factors involved in sexual orientation, antenatal ones are also important.

I met the American novelist James Purdy in New York through my friend John Cromwell and his boyfriend Wassily and published Purdy's work from the late 1980s onwards. He was a good writer, though his books were probably all too similar. Through James Purdy's recommendation I also published Noel Virtue, another gay writer. Noel had been born in New Zealand into a Plymouth Brethren family but had moved to the UK in 1967 to become a zookeeper. He retired from this in the late 1970s to concentrate on writing. We published Noel's novels—most of which drew on his early life in New Zealand—through the late 1980s and early 1990s. At his best he was very good—*The Redemption of Elsdon Bird* is particularly fine.

I also published several books in the 1990s by James Kirkup, the English poet and writer infamous for his poem 'The Love That Dares to Speak Its Name'. Published in *Gay News*, the poem describes a Roman centurion's feelings for the dying Christ and became the subject of a blasphemy trial in 1977. James had translated quite an important Japanese textbook which gave him a niche in Japan where he became a professor of English literature at Kyoto University. He approached us with his novels. Kirkup understood Japan but used exaggeration for comic effect. I remember *Gaijin On the Ginza* (1991), about an actress and a gay colonel, being quite funny. I was told he ended up living in Andorra because it was a good pick-up joint for waiters.

A more significant gay author I published was Jean Cocteau. For one specific book I went on a mission in the early 1990s to Maison Jean Cocteau in Milly-la-Forêt. Cocteau's heir and former lover Édouard Dermit showed me around the house, now a Cocteau museum. I stayed in the village and visited Cocteau's tomb in the nearby chapel Saint-Blaise-des-Simples which Cocteau had decorated in his beautiful, idiosyncratic way. My mission was to collect a cache of Cocteau's gay erotica drawings and courier them back to England for publication.

Édouard Dermit, together with actor Jean Marais, another muse and lover, looked after Cocteau's posthumous legacy, but it was Dermit who became his adopted son and heir. When I met him, Dermit would have been about sixty-five but had been in his early twenties when Cocteau had first employed him as a gardener. He was handsome and, through working as a miner, had developed the sort of physique Cocteau most admired. Much enamoured, Cocteau had nurtured him as an actor and painter, and Dermit ended up the star of several of his films. On account of the value of the items I was collecting, Dermit and I didn't want to risk their being impounded by customs or lost in transit. He was also concerned that the local villagers shouldn't get wind of their existence either, so the whole operation had to be very discreet. We published the erotic drawings as *The Passionate Penis* in 1993, and it's something of a collector's item now. Occasionally in the French House I'd whip out a photocopy of one of the illustrations, a generously endowed sailor perhaps, to astonish my friends.

My long association with Cocteau as his British publisher began in the 1950s when I brought out two of his memoirs, *Maalesh: A Theatrical Tour of the Middle East* (1956) and *Opium: The Diary of a Cure* (1957). *Opium* was co-translated by Margaret Crosland who had first contacted me at Peter Nevill. She had written a biography of Cocteau which Peter Nevill published in 1955. An extremely gifted and prolific translator of French, it was she who encouraged me to approach Anaïs Nin, as well as suggesting translations of de Sade, editing *The Passionate Penis*, and several other Cocteau books.

The only time I met Cocteau was in 1960 when he was in England for Princess Margaret's wedding to the Earl of Snowdon. Margaret Crosland came with me. Desperate to meet him, Diana Johns also tagged along. The encounter at his hotel was short and fairly uneventful, but he seemed very pleasant, friendly and courteous. Jean Cocteau died three years later due, some say, to shock at the news of the death of his friend Édith Piaf, whose autobiography I published in 1965. I still treasure the signed drawing Cocteau sent me in gratitude for commissioning translations and publishing his unique work.

44

Inhabiting Shadows

I was somewhat taken aback when when I first met the writer and poet Jeremy Reed. A friend of his had driven him to my door in a Rolls-Royce Silver Cloud. Jeremy's appearance was no less striking. He was wearing purple eyeliner, heavy foundation and black nail varnish, and looked something like a rock star. He explained that he had just come from one of his performances at St Mary's College, University of London. I had invited him over that afternoon to discuss publishing a book of his. It became clear that he was sensitive, intelligent and hugely creative. We became firm friends.

It was often hard to find anything I actually wanted to publish, so I was always putting feelers out for work by talented and interesting writers. I had met the Blake scholar and poet Kathleen Raine in the 1940s via Tambimuttu and had always hoped she might offer me something of hers. Nothing came of it, though Kathleen did contribute to, and act as consultant for, our 1989 tribute to Tambi. I reminded her to put anything my way she thought worth publishing, and that's how I came to meet Jeremy.

Jeremy grew up in Jersey and, somewhat like me, had a pretty difficult background as an only child, though I don't think he was neglected as much as I was. His mother was kind and supportive, though she never understood his work—she liked to have his books but would never read them. His father had wanted to be a pilot and was frustrated and unhappy working at an office job as an accountant. He had no interest in culture and never read any books as far as Jeremy could tell. I think his father was pretty unpleasant. Like my Uncle Rudi, Jeremy was a child far above his parents' intellectual level. They simply had no way of comprehending him. Jeremy was quite relieved when, while he was at university, his father died. He never went back to Jersey after that except to visit his mother.

Jeremy's interests were purely contemporary, so he was attracted by the Essex University courses on American literature where he completed an MA on Robert

Lowell and a PhD on Hart Crane. Having moved to London, he upset a lot of the poetry establishment by actually performing his work rather than just reading it, often in heavy make-up, sometimes in collaboration with other artists and musicians. He gained quite a following and was then, as now, always writing.

Jeremy's poetry had been published from the early 1970s, and he won the 1985 Somerset Maugham Award for his collection *By the Fisheries*. This, along with a couple of novels, had been published by Jonathan Cape under the editorship of Tom Maschler. Maschler had a stellar career. He had been born in Berlin but originally lived in Vienna where his father had established himself in the book trade. The family fled to England after the Nazis annexed Austria in 1938. Early experiences with André Deutsch and Penguin were followed by Maschler becoming a pioneering literary director at Cape. He edited Hemingway's last manuscript and bought in works by Joseph Heller, Doris Lessing, Gabriel García Márquez and many other great writers. As an author Jeremy was in very distinguished company.

When Random House swallowed up Cape and Maschler moved on, Jeremy was looking for a new publisher. He had come to know a lot of interesting poets and writers, including Kathleen Raine to whom he often read his work. One of his books caught her ear. 'It's Peter's sort of thing,' she told him, 'good non-fiction with an unusual slant.' When the text of *Madness: The Price of Poetry* arrived with Kathleen's endorsement, I very much liked the book and invited Jeremy over to discuss it before publication. With studies of John Clare, Baudelaire, Gascoyne, Rilke, Rimbaud and others, the book, published in 1989, still stands up today as an insightful study of the relationship between poetic genius and mental suffering. Seamus Heaney praised it as being 'full of rich and careful writing, dense with pleasure in words that pleasure the world and waken us to its lovely surprises'.

Over the years I've published over a dozen of Jeremy's books, including novels, poetry and criticism. When I first asked him for a novel he came up with *Inhabiting Shadows* (1990), a semi-autobiographical novel about his alienated schooldays in Jersey. Then came *Delirium* (1991) composed for the centenary of Rimbaud's death, followed by a very good trilogy about mad French characters—*Isidore* (1991) about Lautréamont, *When the Whip Comes Down* (1992) about de Sade and *Chasing Black Rainbows* (1994) about Artaud. J. G. Ballard particularly admired that early trilogy and was generous with quotes. Jeremy became friendly with Ballard and features him in *Diamond Nebula* (1995), a post-apocalyptic science-fiction novel in which Andy Warhol and David Bowie also appear. *Diamond Nebula* has something of a cult following and, since one of the organisers was a fan, Jeremy was invited to perform at the Victoria and Albert Museum Bowie exhibition on the strength of it.

A recurring theme in Jeremy's work is the idea of the past colliding with the present or future. A reincarnated Christopher Marlowe, for example, appears in Jeremy's dystopian novel *The Grid* (2008), while similar temporal disruptions appear in *Boy Caesar* (2004) which centres on the infamous boy emperor Heliogabalus.

Jeremy had a terrible breakdown in the early 1990s. He'd been put on tranquillisers in his teens by a doctor in Jersey and became dependent on them, buying them on the street or getting multiple prescriptions. They were the sort the Germans invented to keep the occupied countries quiet and were very addictive. Many who took them became very ill. Jeremy stopped by going cold turkey, which was disastrous. He was terribly ill. I was able to help with his breakdown but knew nothing about withdrawal from medical drugs and was unable to offer as much help in this respect.

As part of his recovery Jeremy went to see Joe Berke, a prestigious psychiatrist who had qualified in the United States and then come to London to work with R. D. Laing in his experimental therapeutic community. One of his patients was Mary Barnes, who had been diagnosed with schizophrenia and who, after reading Laing's book *The Divided Self*, joined the community. Laing had her regress to a childlike state and paint with faeces on the walls before progressing to more conventional media. She emerged having discovered a talent for painting and, with Joe, wrote a book about her experience. I commissioned a couple of books from Joe Berke myself: *Counter Culture* (1970) and *The Cannabis Experience* (1974).

Joe Berke's approach to therapy was similar to Laing's, and he wouldn't have been my choice of therapist. I don't think Jeremy's treatment included painting faecal murals, but, whatever it involved, Joe was an enormous help and successfully weaned Jeremy off tranquillisers.

People often don't realise how devastating breakdowns are. Jeremy and I agree that we are still scarred by our experiences. You can forget what some illnesses are like, but you never really forget a breakdown and depression. Even though writing was always a useful distraction for Jeremy, it still impressed me that he was able to be so productive throughout this difficult period. One result of his continued creativity was the book *Bitter Blue* (1994), an important but underrated book on addiction and creativity that discusses Anna Kavan, Jean Cocteau and other creative addicts.

Jeremy's most recent non-fiction book for us, *The Dilly* (2014) concerns the rent boys that used to ply their trade around Piccadilly in the days before the internet became a more useful marketplace. The only other book on the subject, published in 1974, was rather homophobic and unsympathetic in tone. Jeremy was able to interview many former Dilly boys, some now in their fifties and sixties, who told him they were mostly wanted for companionship—so many men were lonely in a homophobic world. The former Dilly boys were glad to be able to talk about their experiences, and it made for a very good book.

45

Just One Vodkatini

Though I should have been much more cautious, I did marry a second time to a lovely woman who, for reasons which should become obvious, I'll refer to as Ruth, rather than use her real name. Though we remained friendly, the marriage was mercifully short.

Finding a new love match proved difficult after life with Wendy soured. I had started dating but didn't find it easy to begin a new relationship while finishing another. I had been going to the French House a little more by then because money was no longer such an issue. John Paine often took me to those Soho sessions, and I got to know quite a few of the regulars. Gradually I became bored with that scene—going out with different people all the time, many of whom I didn't especially like. But I grew more and more isolated and more and more lonely. People don't realise that one can really become *pathologically* lonely. It was better during the week when I was working, but at the weekend my sense of isolation started up again. Steadily it worsened.

I was watching a lot of television to distract myself and pass the time. I'd often note the names of the cast. It's strange to think now but I remember a 1961 episode of *Maigret* that introduced Ruth as an actress, and, at the time, thinking what a pretty girl she was. I forgot all about it until ten or so years later when I met her at a west London pub. In the 1960s she was married to a theatrical production designer who was much in demand having worked on West End hits. She had married him much against her father's wishes, packing in her university course to do so. By the time I met her, she had left her first husband and was living with the pub's landlord.

The pub was an excellent establishment apart from the house wine, which was absolutely foul. It was a period when I started drinking pretty heavily, and Ruth and I became friends. Sometimes I used to drive to the pub at lunchtime as my office wasn't far away. It proved a bad idea. I once had a prang with a trade unionist's car on my way back, and he really wasn't happy. Somehow I got away with a warning. If the police had breathalysed me they would have had me bang to rights. I was more careful after that but eventually gave up driving completely. I never enjoyed it anyway and was too much of a liability behind the wheel.

Ruth was at the pub every day. Her boyfriend was an engaging raconteur who hosted both the lunchtime and evening sessions, so she wouldn't have seen him otherwise. At that time Ruth was determined to marry him but couldn't get a divorce from her first husband who was Catholic. Ironically I remember she once said, 'If he doesn't marry me I'll marry you!' It didn't cross my mind at the time that she would. Eventually, after eleven years, she got the divorce she wanted and married him. She was good friends with Guy Hamilton, one of the James Bond film directors, and his actress wife Kerima who told Ruth her second marriage wouldn't work. 'You and he are too bohemian and slapdash', she said. She was right in a way, though Ruth stayed with him until he died. One day he suddenly fell over in the pub—he tripped over some dodgy wiring, I think—and ruptured his spleen. They patched him up at a private hospital, and Ruth made him promise to give up his evening sessions, especially the after-hours lock-ins. But it was the beginning of the end. He was in hospital for a while and hadn't been able to drink anything, so went cold turkey, which can't have helped. The couple planned to retire to Brighton when he was discharged, but it never happened—in fact he didn't really want to go. He had a heart attack not long after and died in 1986.

I was never actually in love with Ruth, but she was a lovely woman and, since both of us were extremely lonely I thought we might enjoy a marriage of convenience. I invited my friend Jenny Botsford and her partner to dinner with me and Ruth to see whether they approved of the match. Jenny said she had no idea but that I should go ahead if I liked her enough. When I proposed, Ruth accepted. In retrospect, of course, I should never have asked—I hadn't known her well enough by then.

I quickly started to regret the proposal and did my best to delay the wedding and discourage Ruth from going ahead. I reminded her that marriage to me would mean that she would lose her widow's pension, but she said, 'Oh! It's nothing. It hardly keeps me in make-up!' Ruth and I had the same doctor who was widely broadcasting the news of our engagement—in Chelsea, Soho and the entire West End of London. It was becoming embarrassing for her—for both of us. People used to come up to me at the French, giggling, and ask when I was going to 'make an honest woman' of her. In the end she went to the Kensington Register Office and booked the ceremony herself. I felt I had to go through with it, though I was practically dragged there screaming.

So it was that Ruth and I married in May 1987. It was pretty disorganised. We had lunch at a restaurant afterwards with Antonia and a few close friends, but there were no photographs. Ruth hated being photographed anyway. I suppose she didn't like the effects of ageing on her looks. The one photo I had of her she took back and tore up. The atmosphere that day, though not exactly grim, certainly wasn't joyous. I knew it was a mistake and shouldn't have gone through with it. The only guests were Antonia, Winnie, Beatrice Musgrave and Ruth's friend Joan, the widow of ITN newsreader and enthusiastic off-screen boozer Reggie Bosanquet.

Though I'd had an inkling before I proposed, I didn't know—and probably didn't want to know—that Ruth was an alcoholic. I don't know how I could have been so naive. I once tackled her on the subject when she was with a friend, and they both said her drinking was merely a response to her second husband's death, that she was simply grieving. But it wasn't that; she was an alcoholic just as Wendy had been. Ruth's father had not let her drink, though he'd taken her to endless theatrical parties when she was trying to become an actress. She'd had a few acting roles, but her daily lunchtime visits to the pub catapulted her into alcoholism. The wine there was so bad, and her consumption of it so prolific, that she got a stomach ulcer.

I thought Ruth might get better in time as she got over her bereavement, but it became obvious she never would. I once told her she was an alcoholic, and she slapped my face. There was something in the family—perhaps a genetic predisposition. It was clear she was never especially well balanced. She had perhaps been spoilt in her youth—there was too much money and indulgence in her family.

At the beginning Ruth and I would just meet up at weekends or go on holiday for a week or two. I never knew where all the drink she got through was coming from, and it took me months to work it out. She used to get more and more drunk, but I could never spot a bottle. She used teacups and coffee mugs, and I'd ask her what she was drinking. She'd say it was tea, but once she'd left the room I'd give it a sniff and it was clearly vodka. I'd look all over the place—in cupboards, in the oven and other obvious places. It turned out she was hiding the bottles in the dustbin.

It is so distressing when someone you care for is lying—both to you and themselves. Once I took her on a trip to Morocco to stay at a hotel in Marrakesh. She had bought the usual duty free bottle of vodka and drank the whole lot in a morning. We probably had a fair amount of wine at lunch, too. I was going out to dinner in the evening and asked her if she wanted to come. I knew she was fairly inebriated so was relieved when she said she was going to bed instead. When I came back from the restaurant the hotel porters were falling over themselves laughing in the foyer. 'We've just had to carry your wife upstairs!' they told me. 'She was so drunk!' She had been in the bar drinking Brandy Alexanders all evening—a potent concoction of brandy mixed with cream and crème de cacao—and she had told me she never drank brandy! She really was horribly drunk. It was about ten in the evening by then, and her supper tray came up. On it was a bottle of wine. And that was it—that was the end. I knew I had made a terrible mistake and got involved with another alcoholic. As planned, I went off to Tangier the next morning for a few days to interview Paul Bowles. I went on my own, and it gave me space to think what I should do.

I imagine that Ruth had started drinking during her first marriage. They used to go to parties pretty much every night, and the champagne flowed. It was all very high end—she used to answer the phone and it would be someone like Sir Laurence Olivier asking for her husband. She desperately wanted to be an actress—she still had a wardrobe of actressy dresses when she was married to me. Unfortunately, though she was extremely pretty, she was a fairly run-of-the-mill actress with, I thought, no particular charisma. I think her father had had it in mind that she should marry into the Irish aristocracy or landowning gentry. Whether her life would have turned out any differently I honestly don't know—but it was such a waste! Perhaps she would still have drunk through boredom, but I do think she could have done more and led a more fulfilling life. She had also wanted to be a photographer—a field in which she showed some promise. She wanted to be all kinds of things but lacked confidence.

At one point Ruth had a minor stroke and went into a hospital for a couple of weeks, which meant a period of enforced sobriety. One of her friends was a top nurse who kept any eye on her but who told me that as soon as Ruth came out of hospital she had asked her to get her a bottle of vodka. The friend said, 'No. I'm not going to get you anything. If you're well enough you can get it yourself.' Almost immediately, Ruth went back on the booze. I knew I couldn't be seen in public with her. There had been an incident when I took her to an event at the Ritz—a private party for the son of Ernst Rowohlt, a distinguished German publisher. She looked fine—she had one of her film-star dresses on—but she and another guest got terribly drunk and made a spectacle of themselves on the dance floor—a pair of spectacles, I suppose. I felt so embarrassed. Many of the guests had also seen Wendy a bit 'overly refreshed' in the drinks department. They may even have thought it was the same woman. Ruth would always get terribly drunk at parties and claim she'd just had 'one vodkatini' when she'd had at least six. It sent me berserk.

After we married, Ruth never gave up her flat to move into Holland Park with me. She came for a while but never really intended to stay. She maintained that my house, which was 150 years old, was haunted and it bothered her that the area had been the stomping ground of the Notting Hill Ripper. I felt both excuses were codswallop. It was true that a cleaner of mine had claimed the house was haunted, and this did scare some burly builders enough that they wouldn't go in alone, but I always found it a friendly house. Fortunately Ruth had kept on her rented flat overlooking Kensington High Street. I don't think she got a divorce settlement from her first husband and was putting all three of the sons she had with him through private school. She had inherited a good deal of family money, though much of it had been lost during the Troubles in Ireland where her family came from. So she had less money than she might have had once, but though she wasn't rolling in it she was still fairly well heeled. When her second husband was in a private hospital he couldn't afford the bill; I think it was over £20,000. So Ruth had funded his treatment by selling a modern Italian painting that she had inherited.

Once it became clear that we were never going to have a fulfilling marriage together my solicitor advised me to divorce as soon as I could. 'She can't take you for anything at the moment,' he said, 'but the longer you leave it the worse it could get.' So I filed for divorce, and Ruth behaved very graciously. She didn't ask anything of me financially—and I don't think she'd have got it if she had. The divorce was finalised in summer 1992. Ruth and I remained friends and I often used to take her to Sunday lunch, though eventually things fizzled out. I had to move house in 2012 and fell ill myself, and Ruth began to develop dementia and went into care. I never felt any ill will towards her. She wasn't an unpleasant person by any means, though she could be difficult when very drunk. The divorce wasn't problematic. Our marriage had been a mistake.

The last telephone call I had with Ruth was very odd. With her dementia, it seemed to me that she had gone back to the past, to the time she was married to her first husband, and had forgotten about her second husband who had been the love of her life. I'm not sure, in her mind, how I fitted into this. In the end, one thing my relationship with Ruth did was cure me of any desire to be married. I don't believe in marriage now—I think it's much better to live with someone, and when it's finished it's finished. My marriage to Ruth also convinced me that there are worse things than being lonely.

46

Jeffrey Bernard Is Defunct

In the early days I didn't drink much. I couldn't afford it. Once the firm was established in the mid-1960s I had both more time and money to spend at regular haunts in Soho—the Colony Room Club and the French House—or at the Queen's Elm in Chelsea. When we were first married, Wendy's father once asked her what our weekly drink bill was. She told him that we could barely afford to drink at all! Now and then we'd stretch to some Merrydown cider or cheap wine while her affluent father was spending the equivalent of an average salary on wine, whisky and gin every week. He probably imagined us sitting down to dinner with apéritifs and classy French wines with brandy and cigars to follow.

In the beginning I wasn't into the pub scene—I was working too hard and preferred to save the little money I had for holidays and things I'd enjoy more. Occasionally I would go to a pub or club such as the Carte de France in Soho, a sleazy bohemian place at the lower end of the market. The Gargoyle Club, opposite the Colony in Dean Street, was classier and more expensive. I certainly didn't go to the Colony until years later when my friend John Paine, who'd joined the club in the early 1950s, took me there.

Francis Bacon, who was very friendly with John, made several paintings of Muriel Belcher, the Colony's proprietor. She was famous for cheerily greeting customers with 'Hello, cunty!', and early on had paid Francis ten pounds a week to bring in people he liked. Charles Laughton, Dylan Thomas, Louis MacNeice, E. M. Forster, Tallulah Bankhead and Frank Auerbach were just a few of the famous names who also turned up. My friend John Paine, then a very fit and good-looking builder, recalls Francis getting a bit fruity with him. 'He used to chat up all the blokes and put his arm round you, that kind of thing,' John told me. 'I didn't take any notice—no one did.' Francis was a keen gambler and would come to the Colony with five pound notes falling from his pockets. People would reach down and pocket them, but he was so wealthy by then I'm sure he didn't mind. He would often take people from the Colony, including John, to a restaurant and pay the entire bill. He'd be greatly angered if anyone else tried to pay. Molly Parkin saw the Colony as 'a character-building, glorious hell-hole. Everyone left their careers at the roadside before clambering the stairs and plunging into questionable behaviour.' Brian Patten called it 'a small urinal full of fractious old geezers bitching about each other'.

By the time I encountered Jeffrey Bernard, one such old geezer, he was pretty much a Soho institution. I've still no idea why people were so enthusiastic about him. I suppose his 'Low Life' column in *The Spectator*, described by Jonathan Meades as a 'suicide note in weekly instalments', was quite amusing, but there was nothing of any great depth. Personally I thought him an objectionable little man and disliked him intensely. He was the youngest and nastiest of three brothers who were in Soho all the time. Jeffrey and I quickly developed a mutual loathing. I remember once chatting to John Paine and another friend, the publisher Michael Dempsey, outside the French. Jeffrey Bernard spotted me and came over spoiling for a fight. He got so excitable that he offered to beat up John and Mike as well. 'Don't get involved', John warned me. 'He used to be a boxer!' I wasn't tempted to oblige Jeffrey anyway, but if he'd hit me I would have bloody well punched him back!

Jeffrey's father was an architect who designed hotels such as the Regent Palace and all the Lyons Corner Houses, so there was money to send his sons to private school. But the whole Bernard family were mad. Years later, when Peter O'Toole was performing the title role in the Keith Waterhouse stage play *Jeffrey Bernard Is Unwell*, Gloria Ferris and I went to see it. The play takes place in the Coach & Horses where Jeffrey is locked in overnight, having fallen asleep in the lavatory. I thought it was boring—just some bloke getting drunk and becoming bothersome. The play received terrific reviews, but I found it tragic and would have walked out but hadn't wanted to offend Gloria.

Jeffrey Bernard was mostly a Coach & Horses man—he wasn't popular at the French, though he did frequent the Colony. He attempted to dry out a few times but found it too miserable an experience. I remember one evening in the French when Francis Bacon was terribly drunk. He had a dinner date with his biographer, the art critic David Sylvester, at one of those very posh French restaurants in Soho—the sort you had to be pretty rich to get in. A friend and I escorted Francis to the restaurant as we weren't sure whether he'd make it otherwise. Francis had sobered up a bit by the time we arrived and at the back was Jeffrey Bernard sitting miserably alone and obviously missing the drink terribly. I don't know how he could afford to be there. He wasn't eating or drinking, but the owner obviously knew him and took pity.

I got on much better with Jeffrey's brother Oliver, a poet and translator, and published his memoir *Getting Over It: A Sortie into the Bohemian Beginnings of Oliver, Bruce and Jeffrey Bernard* (1992). Oliver, who made the Penguin translations of Rimbaud, was the sanest Bernard of the lot. The third brother, Bruce, a writer and photographer, was also very nice—just a bit mad. He objected to our use of a photograph of the three brothers as children on the cover of Oliver's book and for no good reason became thoroughly difficult about it. Oliver himself had supplied the photograph, so it was pretty ridiculous for him to have objected.

My friend Lorraine, a Canadian who worked at *The Spectator* and later looked after me at home for a while when my mobility declined, used to take Jeffrey around in a wheelchair. I remember attending the annual *Daily Telegraph* bash at the Burlington Gallery and seeing Lorraine wheeling in an incredibly shrivelled old man. I took it to be her grandfather, but it was Jeffrey Bernard, then in his early sixties but looking more like ninety and rapidly approaching his demise. As usual he threatened to beat me up. By then he'd had a leg amputated, so was hardly in a condition to make good the threat.

Some people become mellow and quiet when drunk, others loud and aggressive. I would put the poet George Barker—who once threatened to beat me up at a party—in the latter category. He could be disarmingly friendly, as he was when I last saw him at Elizabeth Smart's memorial service, or terrifyingly belligerent. Elizabeth, who wrote so movingly of her infatuation with Barker in her novel *By Grand Central Station I Sat Down and Wept*, had four children by him, though he sired many more elsewhere. He had so many children—at least fifteen—and was so indifferent to them that he claimed he didn't even know their names. He also treated his women pretty contemptuously. I think the Bernard brothers were sometimes paid to babysit and in this way became friendly with George and his wife Elspeth.

Barker enjoyed his reputation for wild behaviour. Jeremy Reed once told me of a thoroughly alarming encounter. Asa Benveniste, who hand-printed books for his Trigram Press and was an admirer of Jeremy's work, took him to see George. The poet was living in squalor at Bintry House, which Graham Greene had bought for him, in Itteringham, Norfolk. When Jeremy arrived, their host was taking amphetamines and drinking neat brandy by the bucketful. They got on well, but when the booze ran out George decided to head off by car to the village pub for replenishments only to drive straight into a ditch instead. They continued on foot and managed to wangle another bottle of brandy on credit. Back at Bintry House, Barker insisted Elspeth read him some A. E. Housman, only to rip the book from her hands and throw it in the fire. When Elspeth put a record on the player downstairs, her furious husband jumped up and down on the machine, smashing it to smithereens. At that, Benveniste thought a retreat might be in order before fisticuffs ensued.

You would meet all sorts of people in Soho in those days. There were lots of recording studios in the area, so you'd meet quite famous actors who would drop in after recording a voice-over for lavatory cleaner or chocolate bars and so on. One regular I liked very much was Tom Baker. I knew him during his *Doctor Who* years—a very nice man, not affected at all—and we'd talk socially as one does at a drinking club. Another Soho pal was John Hurt, who was also friendly with the Bernard brothers and frequented the Colony where we used to chat. He drank very heavily in those days, but, though he was a friendly drunk, he eventually reformed and was ultimately knighted. He was a brilliant actor, and my second wife Ruth claimed to have been in a play with him. He couldn't remember her though, and, knowing Ruth, I'm not sure she really knew him either. Once he had achieved sobriety, John missed his bibulous chats with Peter O'Toole and Jeffrey Bernard and those endless sessions with Lucian Freud and Francis Bacon in the Soho dives.

Not so long ago the BBC broadcast John Hurt performing *Jeffrey Bernard Is Unwell* on Radio 4. I'm sure he was very good in the role, but I had thought the original stage play so thoroughly dreary—just some drunk raving—I wasn't tempted to listen. If you want a comedy drunk I think W. C. Fields was a lot funnier. Indeed in 1972 we published a book on him, *Fields For President*. It did rather well.

47

The Boss from Hell

Dan Franklin, having learnt a great deal from our long-time editors Beatrice Musgrave and Michael Levien, left us in 1982 to join Collins Harvill. He enjoyed a stellar career, and, having worked at Heinemann and Secker & Warburg, joined Jonathan Cape as publishing director in 1993. At Cape (now part of Penguin Random House), he became the admired publisher of Salman Rushdie, Martin Amis, Ian McEwan and other superstar writers. We tried out a couple of copy-editors in place of Dan but neither worked out. Our editorial standards were much higher than most publishers. Beatrice, who worked for the company for twenty-seven years, was particularly demanding, once telling me she needed two editors to work on a manuscript after she'd done her major edit, 'one to style it, another to proofread it'. Michael was easier and could cope with one other editor, but I think they were both overly punctilious. Whenever they worked over an introduction I'd written, it would return as something I no longer recognised as mine. Understandably some of our writers objected to being edited to such a degree.

When I first went into publishing in the late 1940s many companies I worked with seemed to me more like rest homes for upper-class layabouts. So when I started my own company in 1951 I was determined to run a professional outfit where there was no place for pleasant but ineffectual gentlefolk. Professionalism isn't always a matter of education though. We've had many good university-educated members of staff—Dan Franklin was one—but there were others who were unwilling to muck in and pack parcels with the rest of us and saw some jobs as being entirely beneath them. Many of my best editors, Muriel Spark and Elizabeth Berridge included, were non-graduates. They were, however, well educated, hard-working and literary.

Michael Levien was another significant editor who, though he had attended Harrow, had no university degree. Like Elizabeth, he was with us for many years, beginning in the 1950s, and afterwards returning now and then. We had a similar social circle, so, while Wendy and I were living in Earl's Court, we would bump into Michael at parties. Originally he had been working at the Times Bookshop in Wigmore Street and told us he wanted to get into publishing, saying he wasn't too bothered about money (he had a private income from his father) and just wanted something to do. I was very sceptical of his offer to work for us (as one is about people who want to work for nothing) and was going to turn him down, but Wendy motioned me to consider the idea. Eventually we agreed that he could begin a trial period and choose his own hours. He always arrived very punctually and, despite his lack of formal training, soon turned out to be a natural editor.

Michael wrote poetry and had many literary friends. At Harrow his best friend was Julian Fane, the younger son of the Earl of Westmorland, who became a critic and prolific writer. Fane achieved some literary success in the 1950s but was commercially unsuccessful—not that he let that put him off. He was what was known in those days as 'a man of letters', the sort who liked to read and write novels that weren't terrible but were somewhat dull and preferably had lots of French phrases in them. Michael probably liked his books, but taste for that sort of literary fiction had pretty much evaporated by the time Michael came to work for me. Nevertheless he became one of our more outstanding long-time editors.

Eventually Michael had had enough and threw in the towel. He'd been with me thirty years, and the scene had moved on from the cosy world of dowager duchesses writing genteel memoirs about foreign travel. Perhaps the last straw was the book *Defiant Pose* by Stewart Home, which we published in 1991. Gary Pulsifer, my publicist at the time, wanted us to strengthen our contemporary fiction list and pushed for us to publish Home's book, which was a sort of underground novel with lots of rough sex and echoes of William Burroughs. We used Thomi Wroblewski to design the cover as he'd done a few Burroughs books. By the time it came out, Home was on a three year 'art strike' and was refusing to write new books or promote any existing ones. When he did deign to write again he kept writing the same book over and over, and often sent novelist friends to do interviews posing as him. I couldn't understand him at all. For Michael, the themes, language and writing style of books like *Defiant Pose* were so different from most of our fiction list that he felt out of his element. There were, for example, references in Home's novel to extreme sexual practices that neither Michael nor I had heard of, and soon wished we hadn't once we had. The memoir of a classically educated poet, translator and academic like Oliver Bernard was more Michael's cup of tea, but such projects were becoming increasingly unprofitable.

When Gary Pulsifer started as our publicist and rights manager in 1989 he was imaginative and energetic and undoubtedly livened things up. It was Gary's idea, for example, to send out review copies of *The Passionate Penis*, Cocteau's book of homoerotic drawings, with packets of condoms attached. He was particularly good at promoting our list of LGBT authors, something we had already pioneered in a more low key-way decades earlier, and also instigated and edited our tribute to Paul Bowles. I didn't necessarily approve of everything Gary did, but I knew we had to try to remain relevant in our publishing programme.

Eventually Gary became disillusioned. I'd run the business for over forty years by then and was struggling to find someone to take it over. Gary angled for the position, but I felt he simply wasn't up to the job. When I brought in Stephen Stuart-Smith as a possible successor, Gary was hugely resentful. He didn't merely coast from then on, he was actively destructive, taking a kernel of truth and spinning unpleasant stories to sell to the *Evening Standard*'s gossip diary as a stringer. I was furious when I found out. They were often derisive and did neither me nor the company any favours. The gossip stopped only when I threatened to sue the paper.

Things got steadily worse. Our editor at the time, a North American like Gary, would have worked out fine had he not persuaded her to side with him. In her eyes Gary could do no wrong. He told me once that, had he not been gay, he would have married her. Gary used to play all kinds of tricks on our sales manager Richard, a rather old-fashioned individual who was naive and found drink an irresistible temptation. Gary would often get him drunk and tease him. One bizarre thing he did was put nail parings in the drawer of Richard's desk. This happened twice—the second time when Richard was ill and dying of cancer. He had come back just for one day and found this nasty surprise. I was livid. I told Gary I ought to sack him on the spot and would if he ever did anything similar again. I didn't know at the time, but, while I was out, Gary would furtively rake through my personal correspondence looking for anything he could use against me. He even thought my father working as a novelty goods salesman might be something he could utilise.

Soon after this I fell ill. An undiagnosed infection in my foot and ankle had become so bad amputation was mooted. In mid-1996, while I was in the Princess Grace Hospital in Marylebone recovering from serious illness, Gary asked for a two-week holiday at very short notice despite knowing that we were extremely short-staffed. I told him he would have to wait. He never forgave me. His response was to cause a terrible scene, and, in an act of vengeful sabotage, he instituted a walk-out from the offices in Kenway Road. Gary's fellow conspirators included our editor, our new sales manager (who had taken over from Richard after his death) and the production controller who had replaced Beatrice when she retired. The four mutineers gave just one week's notice—an appalling act of treachery considering how ill I was. They almost succeeded in destroying the company. The publishing scene was so difficult in those days and, ironically, only the year before, I had told the *Daily Mail* that my priority was to save jobs. To make matters worse, Gary contacted the *Daily Express* which, having interviewed the gang, published an article under the headline 'Why we had to flee from the boss from hell'! At least the *Express* interviewed me as well. I was able to explain that I was sad to lose my sales manager and my production controller but not sorry that the other two were going. To be frank, I felt I had been too soft on them. I had been informed that they'd been beetling off when I was out of the office to take three-hour lunch breaks on a regular basis. Meanwhile authors had told me the office telephone was never being answered.

As I was stuck in hospital and unable to return to the office during the walk-out, I asked my long-time bookkeeper Tony Lunn to confiscate the office keys from the mutineers. Even so, Tony was suspicious for months afterwards, wondering whether Gary had kept copies and was letting himself in at night to perpetrate more mischief.

Gary went on to set up his own publishing house, Arcadia. He brought out some good books, publishing many writers in translation and continuing to champion LGBT authors. He even took on a few writers I had let go or turned down. Dan Franklin once said that he liked Gary but would not trust him. For myself, after such a terrible betrayal I never spoke to Gary again and blanked him if we ever found ourselves attending the same publishing event.

The whole affair was a terrible hoo-ha, but in the end it didn't matter. I still had a nucleus of loyal staff including my excellent secretary Susan Paine, my loyal bookkeepers Tony Lunn and Trevor Fletcher, who was also my son's godfather, and Stephen Stuart-Smith. Gary and his gang had tried to persuade them to join the mutiny but they remained steadfast. With our editor gone, the most pressing issue was to find someone experienced to replace her. Fortunately I persuaded my daughter Antonia to come aboard as editorial director. She thought long and hard and finally negotiated a tough, business-like contract with me.

Antonia had first worked for Gloria Ferris as a rights assistant at Doubleday and then freelance as an editor for Virago, Faber, Penguin, Hodder and elsewhere. A career at Macmillan Magazines working as an editor on its health publications had followed, and she needed to give three months' notice. During the hiatus Stephen stayed on as part-time editor and, where necessary, we used freelancers. Simon Smith, who became another long-serving staff member, also joined us then. He had been a bookshop manager and had undertaken postgraduate publishing training, but the only thing I could give him at the time was a job in sales. Eventually he moved into our editorial department and became an excellent editor.

I had hoped that Stephen Stuart-Smith might take over from me as managing director at some point, but, having held the fort, he left to devote more time to Enitharmon, the literary press for which he'd already done some editorial work. Founded in 1967 by Alan Clodd, with much encouragement from Kathleen Raine, Enitharmon specialises in poetry, a notoriously difficult field commercially. Stephen took over as director in 1987 and became a very fine publisher, expanding the list to include more prose, fine-art prints and handsome art books.

In the end Gary's departure was a relief. The timing was terrible, but it gave me the opportunity to reorganise and modernise the company. Once Antonia arrived she updated our systems so that we undertake computer typesetting and design in-house, and the company was on a better footing to meet the challenges of the new millennium.

48

The Future of Publishing?

The 1990s wasn't all staff turmoil and avant-garde novels featuring exotic sex acts. We still had space to publish more straightforwardly delightful fare like *Pimporello: A Fable for All Ages* (1991) written and illustrated by Marcel Marceau. I have fond memories of meeting the great mime artist himself at a party thrown by Tambimuttu and was pleased to be able to conduct a conversation in normal speech rather than gestures.

We started the decade with a dual language edition of *Eagle or Sun?*, a collection by the Mexican poet Octavio Paz, but the literary scene was so dire that it didn't get a single review. I first met Paz while he was working in the diplomatic service as an ambassador. We had already published *The Monkey Grammarian* in 1989, and it was sheer luck that he was awarded the Nobel Prize for Literature the following year. Camilo José Cela had won in 1989, and we didn't think the award would go to a Spanish-language writer for a second year in a row. We've published several Nobel winners over the years. While Asturias was the least pleasant, I always felt that Paz was one of our nicest authors.

Another book from that decade was William Donaldson's 1998 memoir *From Winchester to This*. Willie's books were often hilarious. He had been the creator of Henry Root, the writer of extremely funny spoof letters mocking self-important politicians and celebrities. In the 1960s he'd had a hit with his production of *Beyond the Fringe*. He also produced *So Much to Remember: The Life Story of a Great Lady*, a show co-written by and starring my former teenage friend Fenella Fielding. It was a tremendous success at Peter Cook's satirical club the Establishment, but Donaldson managed to sabotage its transfer to the West End. He hired a wine merchant to do the publicity and a director who was too busy with another production to give it the attention it required. One of the actors took disastrous liberties with the text, and Fenella's costume, like the background scenery, was pink so that she tended to disappear as soon as she came on stage.

Having spent years in the black hole of addiction to crack cocaine, Donaldson had written an extraordinarily reflective and unreliable memoir detailing his funny and tragic life. Fearing prosecutions for libel, Hutchinson, who had originally commissioned it, got cold feet so we thought we'd take a look. Antonia was responsible for commissioning the book, and Simon Smith did a tremendous job of editing it, but we needed several cuts. In particular our advice was to delete references to Willie sharing the same cocaine dealer as Princess Margaret. *From Winchester to This* was unusual, funny and entertainingly written, but Donaldson produced what Simon called 'potentially unhelpful publicity' when he gave a pre-publication interview to the *Sunday Times* magazine. Simon wrote to Willie pointing out that much of the interview gave away the entire contents of the book, adding that there was 'no direct reference to the memoirs, however, apart from when you describe them as crap and say that you don't know when they are coming out'.

You probably couldn't find a greater contrast to Willie Donaldson than Sir Rhodes Boyson. I first met the bewhiskered Conservative MP at a Foyles literary lunch. He was very intelligent but could be very nasty and drunken. He'd been a teacher and headmaster before he went into politics and in the early 1970s had written a couple of books on politics and education. He'd also been a junior minister in the Department of Education and Science under Margaret Thatcher. His ideas on education were in vogue with traditionalists, though in my view he was rather too keen on caning children and seemed profoundly homophobic. However, he had a high profile and was very much in the news, so in 1995 we published his autobiography *Speaking My Mind*. It did reasonably well, so I thought *Boyson On Education*, which I published the following year, might sell too. It bombed. He rather lent himself to mockery with his strong Lancashire accent and mutton-chop whiskers. *Spitting Image*, the satirical puppet show, had a field day—and probably sank him.

People ask me why, of the many post-war independents, my firm survived when others didn't. Like Uncle Rudi, many of their founders were brilliant minds and editors but did not handle business well. My father was uninterested in books and publishing, but as a businessman he was probably essential to the successful Vision Press partnership with Rudi. I like to think I combined the best attributes of both relatives—something of my uncle's eye for literature and my father's later business acumen—but really my success was down to luck and hard work. While of course I wanted to make money, I never minded losing some on a good book. We have had to move with the times, publish smaller print runs and find our niche though. For many years I haven't drawn a salary, but I own my home and don't charge the company for the lease of office space. Moreover, my inheritance has helped keep us afloat.

Of my contemporaries I liked Anthony Blond best. We often met at the French House or other watering holes. He was perfectly honest and really was the nicest of them. His sense of humour came across in his books, especially his extraordinarily candid autobiography *Jew Made in England* (2004). Antony was a good publisher and editor but probably not so great at business. His partner told me that the company would have survived had Anthony not lost his nerve. I didn't particularly like the publisher Paul Hamlyn who had worked at Zwemmer's under Uncle Rudi's management, whereas I was friendly with André Deutsch, though we weren't close. André, who was ten years older than me, set up his firm the year after I set up mine. Meanwhile, I thoroughly disliked George Weidenfeld, who founded Weidenfeld & Nicolson in 1949. I thought him extremely rude and a social climber. I was once having lunch at the White Tower with Terence Kilmartin, a distinguished translator who was literary editor of the *Observer*, when Weidenfeld came to our table. He didn't say 'Excuse me' or ask how I was; he just talked to Terence and completely blanked me.

On Publishers Association trips I got to know the Boon family of Mills & Boon fame and liked them a lot, but I never met their star turn Barbara Cartland. I very much liked the poet, novelist and critic D. J. Enright. Dennis had everything—a sense of humour and brilliance as a writer. He wasn't pompous in any way and was a very pleasant man who was extremely supportive of the company. All in all I got on well with most publishers, though I did find the woman who ran Chatto & Windus, where Dennis Enright was a director in the 1970s, rather daunting. She was a tough number like many women in business in those days who probably felt they had to be tougher than the men in order to get on or be respected.

John Calder was an excellent editor and had a very good list, but other aspects of his business were not well handled, and I think he got into debt. I was friendly with both John and Marion Boyars who bought half of Calder and ran it well. I suppose in the end that kind of independent publishing had had its day. The conglomerates came in and bought everything up that was worth having and sent everyone else to the wall. My former solicitor Anthony Rubinstein, who was a specialist in publishing law, said all the senior partners of these independents want to take their investment money and run as soon as the conglomerates come knocking. He advised me that if I wanted to sell, I should do it then, as it would become increasingly difficult. He was right, but I wanted to carry on. Without the business to run I felt I would have gone completely crackers.

I've been working in publishing since the 1940s and can honestly say that the last ten or so years have been the most difficult I have ever encountered in the book trade. I didn't have a lot of money to start with. Apart from a small loan, at the beginning I had to start from scratch. Had I not inherited money latterly from my parents the company would have gone to the wall. There simply isn't enough margin any more. Few books are reviewed these days, and although we have embraced social media it doesn't always repay the effort you put in as far as sales go. In terms of conversion to sales, clicks on a link, I'm told, are about as effective as walking down the street putting flyers in people's letterboxes, though somewhat less bother.

Publishing is no longer parochial, and books are increasingly international. You have to bear in mind the Arab, African and Chinese markets—ones that barely existed before. I once went to a seminar in Amsterdam on the future of books. Afterwards I honestly felt there *was* no future, that it was all going to end. Many factors—including the ending of the Net Book Agreement, competition from other media, increased production costs, underpricing of books, inadequate subsidies, changes in technology and the scandalous lack of support for public lending libraries—make life difficult, especially for smaller publishers.

In pieces I wrote for the *New Statesman* and other publications I talked about the end of the book as we know it. I haven't changed my views with the passage of time—technology has simply made it happen faster. With the advent of digital books, I think eventually perhaps only a small number of physical books will be published. They will be specialist hardbacks, far more expensive and much better designed, much like our special edition of Dalí's *Hidden Faces*. They will be valued like paintings or small works of art, for their own sake or as investments—collectable limited editions for posterity, not cheap and disposable as they tend to be now.

Other countries are much better at supporting literature—the Japanese and Scandinavians are particularly good. Much money and talent now goes into film and television, because literature generally doesn't pay. If the novel is to survive as a form of literature there must be much more money made available to help new writers. Real literature, I feel, should be subsidised in the same way as opera and theatre.

49

Departures

In the course of nearly nine decades I have witnessed rather a lot of comings and goings. I never met my paternal grandfather and knew my maternal one only a little. Both grandfathers were greatly outlived by their troublesome widows whose lives were enlivened by mutual loathing. The feud had worsened greatly after Betty Offenstadt, the black widow, arrived from Germany in 1939 to live in London. Of my two grandmothers, Betty was the first to go, though she took her time about it. She had failed to expire in shock when I announced my engagement to Wendy, a gentile, and survived to carry on feuding with Sophie for some time longer. When Betty became seriously ill with kidney trouble years later my parents were secretly pleased. She was expected to die fairly swiftly, and they couldn't help thinking once she'd gone the inheritance would mean my father would be able to stop working. Sophie, meanwhile, had her own reasons for optimism—outliving her nemesis would mean she had won.

While waiting for news of the progress of Betty's illness from my father, who was at his mother's bedside, the family gathered in La Fourchette, the downstairs lounge of the Cumberland Hotel. It was a short ride away on the number 46 bus, and, though intended primarily for residents, Sophie and Gladys got to know the waitress and went there regularly. Our afternoon tea that day was accompanied by quiet anticipation of Betty's demise. We slurped down numerous cups of tea, and, while the ladies nibbled gloomily on millefeuilles and macaroons, I finally took a telephone call from my father. To my mother's disappointment and Sophie's utter dismay we were informed that Betty had miraculously recovered. Sophie promptly burst into tears, sobbing, 'We'll never get rid of her now!' The exclamation so impressed me that I remember it to this day.

Winnie took the news better than her mother, offering to cook some stewed apples for Arthur to take to hospital to feed Betty. The incident shows the extremes of Sophie's bitterness and bitchiness. Even if you think that sort of thing you don't say it out loud—and definitely not publicly. There were a few raised eyebrows, but fortunately we had the place pretty much to ourselves.

When Betty finally made her exit in 1961, some time later than hoped, there was a certain amount of relief. My mother celebrated by destroying all but a couple of her mother-in-law's photographs. Wendy and I managed to look suitably solemn at Betty's funeral until it came to the eulogy. Unless performed by people who know the deceased, I always find eulogies ridiculous. In this case the rabbi knew nothing of my grandmother, and typically my father had briefed him with all sorts of nonsense—for instance, that Betty, who many people loathed, was much admired and 'the epitome of a Jewish mother'. The eulogy also claimed the family had all loved going round to Betty's for lunch on Saturdays, whereas in fact we had always dreaded it—we went on sufferance because she'd kick up such a fuss if we didn't go. My mother, who was sitting next to Wendy at the funeral, was incensed by all this. She had particularly loathed going to Betty's flat so started grunting and snorting with rage and contempt as the extravagant accolades for her mother-in-law continued, which of course only made it funnier. In the end Wendy burst out laughing and had to pretend she was sobbing with grief. Something similar happened at Sophie's funeral a few years later. In this case her beloved son Rudi had briefed the rabbi with another load of old codswallop about how wonderful his mother was. It really was a torrent of bilge, because most of the time she was another very unpleasant woman. My father wasn't even there because he loathed her so much. When the rabbi ended by saying, 'Let the life of Sophie Friedmann serve as a model for us all!' neither Wendy nor I could restrain our mirth, much to the disapproval of Rudi and his sisters.

My cousin Ivor must have told his rabbi a complete pack of lies when his mother, my Aunt Gladys, died. The resulting eulogy for her was utterly ludicrous. She was actually a very timid lady but it was stated that she had been a spy in the Second World War after achieving degrees in languages at the Sorbonne in Paris. In fact Gladys had only a basic education and, like Winnie, spoke better English than German. Both sisters lent their German passports to the British government during the war—they had dual nationality—but remained British housewives during the entire conflict. This time Antonia and I could barely control our mirth—we were virtually rolling in the aisles it was such rubbish. He made out Gladys had been some sort of Mata Hari and topped it off by claiming that she and Uncle Bobby had later founded a synagogue.

My children will never say that my mother Winnie was anything but a super lady. She was very generous to them, enjoyed being a grandmother and was much better at it than she ever was as a mother. Sadly I don't remember her in quite the same light as my daughters. She was never particularly nasty, but she did have an unpleasant streak. Like her mother and mother-in-law, Winnie seemed to think she was eligible for sainthood. None of them were. However, as a dutiful son I did keep an eye on her, especially after my father died, as she outlived him by twenty years.

Towards the end of her life Winnie got a bit doddery and needed to use crutches. She once went to the cemetery to visit the family plot—her parents and brother Rudi were there—and stumbled and fell on to the grave. She couldn't get up again and was there for around an hour before I came and found her. If I hadn't, she might have been there for days. When she died in 1996 I wasn't inconsolable. She was ninety-three by then and wanted to die—she even tried to commit suicide towards the end. She had been quite ill and in terrible pain with shingles and was being nursed at home. I think she was pretty determined and had worked it all out—though, as it turned out, not as efficiently as had her brother Rudi. I had seen her one Saturday morning, and she was strangely insistent that I take away an umbrella she thought belonged to Antonia. I said, 'Well, why don't you give it to her when you see her?' When the nurse went round the following Monday she found Winnie on the floor. She had taken an overdose of sleeping tablets washed down with whisky. They rushed her to St Mary's in Paddington and quarantined her in a private room on account of the shingles. She got over the overdose but then, in addition to the shingles, contracted a hospital-acquired infection that finished her off ten days later.

Uncle Rudi's death was probably the saddest of the lot. I've already described how his body was found in July 1964 after he had committed a meticulously planned suicide by barbiturate poisoning. His mother had died in February that year at the age of eighty-five, and, having given up working at Zwemmer's Bookshop and fallen out with my father over Vision Press, I think he felt he had nothing to live for. Sophie had forced Rudi to leave his beloved bookshop, saying he was working too hard for too little, when really she just wanted him at home all to herself. Anton Zwemmer actually offered to sell the family the shop when he was retiring, but they were too cautious. It was probably for the best. In the end I would have been lumbered with trying to cope with running it alongside my publishing business.

Other than Rudi, I often had no real sympathy for the senior members of my immediate family. When my father refused to give Rudi a salary for his work at Vision I thought, as I often did, that the lot of them were despicable. Rudi was barely fifty years old but had gone through so much mental turmoil, from his early years of insulin coma treatment, to his strange obsession with matronly women and arrest and incarceration for importuning an undercover policewoman. Rudi was peculiar in all sorts of ways. Even so, I liked him the best of all my relatives—but Sophie, his mother, really ruined his life.

I remember Winnie being pretty upset by Sophie's meanness. On Winnie's sixtieth birthday Sophie deputised Rudi to buy her favourite daughter a present. Instead of the sort of family treasure Mother was expecting—a piece of glamorous and valuable jewellery—Rudi turned up with a pair of cheap slippers! Winnie was outraged. Sophie had given Rudi a very valuable ring she had bought in case she had to do a moonlight flit during the war. Rudi was decent enough to give it to my mother after Sophie's death, which necessitated clearing the flat she and Rudi had shared. Despite it being none of his business, my father made a terrible fuss claiming we could be sued for removing items before it had been assessed for inheritance taxes. I ignored him, and my mother helped me load some heirlooms into the car downstairs. I gave her quite a bit to take home too, including some crystal, but my father made her return it. Gladys managed to whisk away a couple of Dresden statuettes but broke both their heads off on the way home. What was left was sold, much of it for next to nothing. Rather than the thousands it was worth, my grandfather Jacob's huge and valuable stamp collection was sold by the executors for £2.50.

I didn't speak at either of my parents' funerals. There were people who knew my father who spoke at his, which resulted in something reasonable. I certainly wouldn't have found much nice to say about him. Because of the farce at my grandmothers' funerals I told Antonia I didn't want a eulogy for my mother at all. In then end a sensible and appropriate one was given after all because Antonia briefed the rabbi so well. Even in those days the West London Synagogue had a system of helping the bereaved. They asked whether I needed counselling. I told them I didn't. I was feeling more relieved than bereaved.

Other than a few family gatherings, Wendy and I didn't see each other much after the divorce. I believe when a relationship is over, it's over. Wendy had moved to Devizes to be near our daughter Georgie, her husband Bill Trythall, and my grandchildren Louis and Kate. Wendy's doctor had told her she would die if she didn't give up drink, so she had gone to Alcoholics Anonymous but had given up of her own volition by the 1980s. As a result, she lived just long enough to see her grandchildren grow up. Her stepmother Becky returned to Australia after the death of Wendy's father and left her very little when she died in the mid-1980s. Wendy's writing pretty much dried up after she gave up drinking—for years it had been part of her writing process. Her last book was *The Cat Lover*, a collection of short stories I published in 1976.

Wendy died at the end of 2002. Her death was unexpected and something of a shock. She'd had a very inadequate doctor who had failed to tell her she had a weak heart caused by asthma and other issues. He should have been struck off. Wendy, like me, did not believe in organised religion, so she had a humanist funeral which was arranged by Georgie and Bill as Antonia was returning for the ceremony from a trip abroad. I did speak at the funeral, mainly about Wendy's writing and books. Her ashes were scattered by her daughters in the New Forest near where she had grown up.

I understand that humanist funerals are increasingly popular, and so are woodland burials. I wouldn't want one for myself, though—nor for my ashes to be scattered amidst trees. If everyone does it, all the woods and forests will be full of ashes and corpses—something I view as rather unwholesome. The one thing I've stipulated for my own funeral is that it should not be religious and that the wake should be done in style.

50

A Far Cry From Kensington

Over the course of nearly forty years I travelled to Morocco often, but the time came when I had to take my leave of North Africa. My last visit to Marrakesh and Tangier was in 1998, the year before Paul Bowles died. It was a pretty melancholy visit. I was rereading *The Sheltering Sky*, the best of Paul's novels, and asked him to sign it. It's still a riveting read. There seemed little point hanging around with Paul this time—he was busy with interviews with his biographer.

Interviewed for our tribute to Paul Bowles, David Herbert had said to Ira Cohen, 'Come again before I'm dead, will you? It's been such a pleasure.' But, when I arrived in Tangier in 1998, David had died three years earlier and, with no one else to visit, I found myself alone there on Christmas Day. I was staying at El Minzah where the bar had been a model for Humphrey Bogart's café in *Casablanca*. Once the Benedict de France had closed, El Minzah was the best hotel in Tangier, and luckily I had managed to wangle myself a room with a balcony. Thinking it too early to prop up the bar or go back to the terrace and drink all day, I decided to visit David Herbert's grave at the Anglican Church of St Andrew. I hadn't managed to attend his funeral so wanted to pay my respects.

A Christmas Day service was starting as I arrived. I thought I might as well go in, but this proved a mistake. A preacher had come over from Gibraltar to conduct what became a terribly long service. The hymn-singing was atrocious, too. Overcome with boredom, I tried to sneak out but couldn't—they'd locked all the doors. I had hoped I might bump into someone I knew, but there was no one—everyone I knew had either left the city or died. It was a huge relief when wine and refreshments were brought out after the service. After a few slurps I could make my escape. There seemed no point returning to Morocco after that. All the bars I knew, like Dean's and the Parade where Tangerinos would congregate, had gone. Tangier was boring. It was finished.

My health deteriorated throughout the 1990s and 2000s. I've needed hip replacements and lost much of my eyesight to cataracts and optic neuritis—inflammation of the optic nerves. The effects on my mobility and vision increased my sense of loneliness. I know I was drinking too much, especially during periods of personal stress and staff turmoil. On one occasion I'd been boozing in Soho and was stopped by a policeman as I attempted to cross Shaftesbury Avenue to flag down a taxi. It was a tricky business in that condition, and I feared I might fall and end up injured or with grazed anatomy. The policeman, saying he was worried for my safety, locked me in a cell for the afternoon. It was very humiliating, but the police were very kind. They brought me coffee and, after a couple of hours, let me go. They needed the cell for someone more felonious and sent me on my way with a sympathetic warning.

I recently had pneumonia which brought me to death's door. The thought of getting it again terrifies me. Until I caught it, I had no idea how bad it is. At my age it's what kills most people off. I caught it in hospital not long after I'd had a hip replacement. I got all kinds of complications and had to keep going back in. That's the trouble with hospitals these days—they nearly kill off all their patients.

Eventually I realised that I couldn't struggle on my own and put it to Antonia that I could sell my house in Kensington and share a property elsewhere from which we could also run the business. That's how I ended up living in Crouch End where Antonia had put down roots many years back. North London wouldn't have been my first choice of location, but the alternative might have meant struggling on my own or living in a care home, which I dreaded.

There was quite a bit of publicity for the sixtieth anniversary of Peter Owen Publishers in April 2011, including a spread of several pages in the *Sunday Times* magazine. But publishing by this time had become so complex—the technicalities of digital production were way beyond me—that I started thinking of selling the business. When I was awarded the OBE for services to literature in January 2014 it seemed the wrong time to sell.

I was utterly amazed and delighted at getting an OBE. I don't know whether its generally known, but there's a lot that goes on before these awards happen. Jeremy Reed had started the ball rolling decades before. Then my old friend Jenny Botsford had a go at getting me nominated, but didn't get any further. Jenny investigated and eventually talked to the civil servant responsible for putting suggestions before the Honours Committee. They said they hadn't had any information for a couple of years—she hadn't realised she was supposed to keep submitting material in support of a nomination. Luckily Jenny was—by birth, chance and through her PR work—well connected. She had heard the former poet laureate Andrew Motion on the radio, rambling around Stisted in Essex with Clare Balding, and discovered that his grandparents had lived in a house her grandfather had owned in the area. Jenny invited him over to see her collection of old photographs of the village over lunch. He was very touched, so she asked if he'd put in a word with the Honours Committee. She also organised a dinner that Lord Fellowes—the chap who wrote *Downton Abbey*—attended. Julian Fellowes was chairman of an influential literary committee, and she thinks it was the input of Motion and Fellowes that may have finally done the trick. I feared I might have been blacklisted forever because of my criticism of the Arts Council many years back, but by then that was all water under the bridge.

Jenny spent an enormous amount of time writing all the letters that were required to gain support for my OBE. She did make one mistake in writing to D. J. Enright. Dennis had written an introduction to one of our anniversary books and had always been a friend and enthusiastic supporter of the company. Unfortunately he was, by the time she wrote, dead—and had been for some time. Jenny showed me the understandably exasperated and indignant letter his son-in-law Toby Buchan, Lord Tweedsmuir, sent in response. He wrote that it seemed 'fantastically slipshod' for her to have written to a major literary figure seven years after his widely reported death. 'As far as I'm concerned,' he concluded, 'Her Majesty can grant Mr Owen an hereditary dukedom just so long as my wife and I no longer have to write letters pointing out something that a simple Internet check would have revealed at once.' Jenny was mortified.

One never knows who is going to present your award—the Queen delegates quite often these days. This time she was at the races, so it was down to Prince Charles. When you go to collect your gong there are a number of investitures going on, usually several hundred people at a time. Jenny and my daughters Antonia and Georgina accompanied me to the Palace—we were allowed to park nearby as I was, by then, using a walking frame. A footman conducted us to the Queen's Gallery, a long rectangular room where priceless paintings are shown, everything from Rembrandt to Goya plus a sprinkling of moderns. It was very impressive. We were offered a choice of orange juice, coffee, or apple juice from the Prince's Highgrove estate before the ceremony—something of a disappointment as I had expected champagne.

Finally we were arranged in order for the investiture which was to take place in the ballroom. When they told me told me I'd have to walk backwards from the Prince after receiving my medal, I got cold feet and asked for a wheelchair. The Prince chatted with me for two or three minutes. I hadn't known what to expect, he's had such a bad press, but I liked him instinctively. He asked me about the state of independent publishing. 'Bloody awful!' I heard myself reply. He laughed. After being wheeled away from him backwards by footmen, they returned us to the gallery to wait under the Winterhalter portrait of Queen Victoria during the rest of the ceremony. The photographers then took their snaps in the courtyard, we chatted for a while, and that was that.

The ceremony was quite an event, though I felt a bit drained afterwards—there's so much protocol to remember. The extreme efficiency of the Palace staff made it easy though, and nothing was left to chance. Afterwards the four of us enjoyed a celebratory lunch at the Gay Hussar in Soho, for many years my favourite restaurant.

Looking back in detail, as I have needed to in the process of writing this book, some of my life has been so painful that I wouldn't want to live it again. On the other hand, as I write this, I'm eighty-nine and I suppose tiredness and the infirmities of old age tend to darken one's view. On balance, there is much in my life I enjoyed and great success in which to take pride.

My firm celebrates its sixty-fifth anniversary in April 2016. I decided to step down as managing director of the company in July 2015, though I remain chairman. By a stroke of luck my elder daughter Antonia, long-time editorial director of the firm, had embarked on a relationship with Nick Kent, an old flame who had worked for many years as a newspaper journalist and book publisher and who was then living in the South of France. He wanted to spend more time with her, so, as he had years of experience upon which to draw, it was ideal that he return to London and take over as managing director. With him on board, I feel the firm's future is assured.

The enormous multi-national conglomerates are like juggernauts. They cannot act swiftly, and it may be that the more nimble and smaller independents, by being enterprising and seizing on up-and-coming trends, can continue to punch above their weight with smaller print runs and shorter lead-in times to publication. Let us hope that even a more streamlined industry can retain some of its more colourful characters, its championing of new writers and its heart and soul.

I have much to be thankful for: long and valuable friendships, the success of my company, an honour in recognition to services to literature, a chance to travel widely, and, above all, my children and grandchildren. I wish only happiness to them all. I'm grateful to all my long-standing and loyal members of staff. They are too numerous to mention but include my longest-serving editors Beatrice Musgrave and Michael Levien, my sales and marketing directors Daniel McCabe and Elfriede Holden, my bookkeeper Tony Lunn, and, not least, my late wife Wendy Owen who came up with some remarkably good suggestions for books. I am especially proud of our daughter Antonia, and grateful to her for guaranteeing the independent spirit of the firm and ensuring continuity of editorial policy. Publishers tend to be more risk-averse these days, but those who persist tend to be resourceful and enthusiastic. Long may they continue to discover exciting new books from all over the world.

Afterword by James Nye

1 The Story of Owen

> Give company to a lonely man
> and he will talk more than anyone.
> — Cesare Pavese, *This Business of Living* (1938)

> Many people have difficult childhoods.
> Some survive them and some don't.
> — Raymond Marriott, recalling his friend Anna Kavan

Knowing my interest in literary eccentrics, Antonia Owen had often invited me to interview her father, but I had hesitated, deterred by photographs I had seen of him scowling. When I relented and met Peter in November 2014, I found a gentle, friendly and somewhat shy old man who simply didn't like having to pose for photographs. When he and I sifted through his collection, I was surprised by the number of snaps of him, in both childhood and as an adult, looking genuinely happy, belying the often grim account he gave me of his life.

Peter was always keen to launch into tales of his lonely childhood in Nuremberg and London and his long life in international publishing. His memory was prodigious, and, having established a rapport, we decided to set about constructing this memoir for posterity. Peter had made at least three prior attempts at autobiography over the years, all of them abandoned in the early stages. Now frail and with severely impaired vision, it was clear that he needed if not a ghostwriter then an amanuensis. So it was that I ended up playing an ersatz literary equivalent of Eric Fenby to Peter's crumbling Frederick Delius.

Peter would sit in a reproduction Louis XV chair, handmade, like much of Peter's furniture, by his paternal grandfather's company in Bavaria, and ramble on engagingly, surrounded by hundreds of books he had published, all with his adopted name on the spine. Various precious acquisitions and heirlooms furnished his rooms: there were valuable antiques, modernist sculptures and sundry knick-knacks, including a vast collection of pillboxes. His wall decorations included a Picasso print, illustrations by Cocteau and Erté, and the paintings by Francis Souza that Peter had managed not to drunkenly abandon in a telephone box. Peter was somewhat deaf and, a confirmed technophobe, had thrown in the bin the expensive hearing aids Antonia had bought him. Our lengthy conversations thus had to be conducted with me shouting myself hoarse.

By the time Peter died in May 2016 I had recorded over thirty-three hours of interviews with him, all the while mining his enormous and sometimes chaotic archive of books, press clippings, photographs and catalogues. These helped me stimulate and amplify his memories. Transcribing this vast archive of recordings and editing them into their current form was a lengthy task. Correspondence and interviews with many of Peter's friends and colleagues also enriched the project. Peter's memories were naturally associative rather than strictly chronological and, though we have imposed an outwardly chronological shape to it, the memoir still reflects this. Changes in tone reflect Peter's changes of mood. At times he was the gentlemanly elder statesman of independent publishing, at others a scurrilous bohemian gossip.

Early in the process Peter had said that any memoir should be candid, factual and amusing. He had a dry, somewhat dark sense of humour and, though he was sometimes solemn, we often made one another laugh, his spirits often buoyed by alcohol. One morning, while engulfed in an aroma of marzipan, he was particularly cheery: he'd been knocking back glasses of Amaretto. On another day he spent the afternoon finishing off a bottle of cava.

Peter could be very funny though not always advertently. Perhaps he was occasionally pulling my leg but, for example, he genuinely seemed to think that drug enthusiasts like Anna Kavan and Paul Bowles could only ever drink Dubonnet. Did he really go with toothache to a spiritual healer, only to discover that she 'didn't do teeth'?

Peter's candour had limits, and the trustworthiness of his account is occasionally moot. Though he strove to be fair, his memories were partisan, often coloured by his passionate enmities and a need to defend his sense of self. One ex-colleague felt that Peter's memory had, in old age, become 'obligingly selective', while another confessed that he had long ago renounced 'the Peter Owen myth' that the veteran publisher had artfully constructed. Peter focused so much on the negative aspects of his life that it seemed to me that his memory had also become *disobligingly* selective. Hilary Mantel, whose *Wolf Hall* was one of the last novels Peter enjoyed as an audiobook, has commented that 'as soon as we die, we enter into fiction'. With Peter, it seemed, the process happened a lot sooner.

We are all somewhat unreliable narrators of our own and others' lives. Given that none of us can be entirely trusted to give any kind of definitive account, that we reveal as much by omission as inclusion, I thought it useful to set down here the views and memories of some of Peter's friends, family and former colleagues, as well as my own impressions.

2 Myths and Reality

No one would need a doctorate in the psychology of attachment to understand that Peter was permanently damaged by emotional neglect in his early years and was thus dogged by loneliness and problems with relationships, personal and professional, throughout his life. He never forgave his elders, particularly his mother, for their early betrayal. Eighty years after the event he still quaked with rage when recalling the dismissal of his favourite nanny. Forgiveness wasn't Peter's strongest suit—he also fumed about the staff mutiny that had taken place two decades before, and the circumstances of his first divorce. His parents and grandmothers were usually spoken of with contempt but sometimes described as 'not that bad' depending on his mood.

Winnie, Peter's mother, surely did not deserve his continued opprobrium. His friend John Paine recalled remonstrating with Peter over this: 'He was very nasty about his mum. I couldn't understand it. I thought she was a truly lovely lady—a gentle woman. She was marvellous!' Winnie Owen clearly knew her son well, was concerned about him and generous in later years, sending him huge cheques for his birthday while imploring him to be 'careful with the drink'. Prior to his dutiful but regular visits to her, Peter would anxiously fortify himself with scotch. According to one witness, he toasted her death euphorically, quaffing champagne and enthusiastically contemplating his long-awaited inheritance. On the other hand, Peter preserved in a drawer all the birthday and Christmas cards Winnie had sent him along with those signed by Doris Lessing, Jeremy Reed and others he treasured. On his desk Peter kept a photograph of himself, a happy smiling child beside his equally happy mother. Brian Braithwaite, his 1930s schoolmate, remembered Peter with affection and knew nothing of his early trauma, recalling 'a cheerful, healthy boy who was great fun and my particular friend'.

Whatever he felt about Winnie, after her death he virtually recreated her living room, the familiar surroundings of his childhood, in his own, stuffing it full of her furniture. Often unable to pay himself a salary, her significant legacy helped Peter fund his business through lean times. Winnie had provided for Peter in other ways while alive. Though he slimmed down substantially towards the end of his life, earlier he had become quite fat from prodigious boozing and his post-session guzzling of great wodges of the Fortnum & Mason fruitcakes he charged to his mother's account.

As with his mother, when talking of his first wife Wendy, Peter was at first scathing. Still furious she had put her divorce papers in first, he admitted, once he'd vented his spleen, what a joy she had been and even how much he had loved her. Perhaps their marriage was always doomed. In a 1968 profile in *Books and Bookmen*, Michael Bateman noted the contrast between husband and wife with Wendy seeming to him 'as light-hearted' as Peter was 'earnest and serious'.

As for professional relationships, while it's true that 1990s publicity manager Gary Pulsifer behaved vindictively at times, he had some cause for bitterness. Peter had lined him up to succeed him only to renege on the promise. Over the decades Peter often contemplated either selling up or standing down. Stephen Stuart-Smith and Antonia Owen herself were both, like Gary Pulsifer, lured into working for Peter with the promise that they were being lined up as successors. Stuart-Smith told me he was fond of Peter and admired his internationalism, drive, 'courage and chutzpah'. Their dealings, he said, were always amicable, but, never given much say over commissioning or access to the company accounts, he became frustrated. Peter wouldn't trust anyone else with his company and perhaps feared what their scrutiny might reveal. When it became clear Peter was not intending to retire, Stuart-Smith took his leave, having held the fort until Antonia could take over his role. 'I was then and am still', he told me, 'far too idealistic and straightforward to be part of a firm which for all its virtues was run along very eccentric lines.'

Though Peter liked to present himself as a scrupulous businessman of the utmost probity, the reality sometimes fell somewhat short. The estates of Paul and Jane Bowles, as well as those of Shusaku Endo and Salvador Dalí, were not always entirely happy with the way Peter had dealt with their clients, though if Peter, a neurotic man of conscience, did anything seriously wrong one can be sure he suffered for it.

Shusaku Endo, one of the most important of Peter's high profile authors, seems to have been endlessly curious. Besides history and literature, his interests included *suiboku-ga* (ink-brush painting) and *shogi*—a traditional board game something like chess. Keen to show fellow Japanese that Christians need not always be solemn, Endo also studied conjuring and hypnotism and learnt to tango. He viewed Peter Owen with curiosity, amusement and fondness. Regarding Peter's habit of scribbling important notes on scraps of paper which would often scatter to the floor, Endo once asked a friend, 'Don't you think he's crazy? He just randomly pushes those papers into pockets all over his body then drops them all! And why is his face so red? He must drink too much. But I cannot help liking him!' A kindly, philosophical man who was also fond of practical jokes, Endo greatly appreciated Peter's whims and eccentricities. He once paid for Peter to stay in Kyoto at a venerable *ryokan*—one of the traditional Japanese inns—and was amused to hear that Peter had placed the futon on a coffee table to make himself a Western-style bed. During a visit to a magnificent old temple, while Endo carefully explained the landscaping and history of the site, Peter, staring entranced at a fish pond, interrupted him to ask, 'How much is that carp worth?'

For a while Endo seems to have viewed Peter as something like one of the holy innocents, the 'wonderful fools' that often crop up in his fiction. Colleagues often advised him to ditch Peter as an agent, but, instead, he remained determinedly loyal. After all, Peter was the first to discover his work in the Unesco library and bring his novels to an international audience. Unfortunately, in Endo's final few years, their relationship became somewhat strained. Though they were clearly fond of one another, Endo's appreciative letter, the one Peter liked to carry in his wallet, dated from 1985. By 1994, after the disappointment of losing out on the Nobel Prize for Literature, and having become gravely ill, Endo grew impatient with Peter. Letters held in the Harry Ransom Center, University of Texas, reveal that Endo had heard that, while the Nobel committee were deliberating, a rumour had circulated that he had written a pornographic novel early in his career. With a record of awarding peace prizes to warmongers and, more recently, a literature prize to an apologist for genocide, it seems unlikely that the committee would have been swayed in their judgement by a bit of saucy juvenilia, but Endo was certainly dismayed at what he saw as a devious slur. All those who knew Endo assure me that the rumour was baseless but deeply offensive. Endo wrote to Peter pleading with him to defend his honour. It's not clear what Endo expected Peter to do, but, clearly dissatisfied, he wrote again in March 1995 threatening to sack him. There the trail goes cold. If this was Endo's last letter to him it must have hurt Peter almost as badly as posthumous legal action by Endo's estate. Another sadness is that Peter, after decades of anticipation, did not live to see Scorsese's film adaptation of Endo's masterpiece *Silence*, and that, despite its long gestation, it did not achieve the impact hoped.

Peter's dealings with Anaïs Nin were fraught with *faux pas* and misunderstandings, particularly over breaching the anonymity he promised to her first husband and the sale to an archive, without her permission, of letters she had sent him. Writing grovelling apologies after having put his foot in it was something Peter became accustomed to and rather good at. Once Nin was dead, he sold the archive her letters of complaint.

One rumour has it that Peter, infatuated with Nin as many were at the time, had once made a drunken pass at her and been resoundingly rebuffed. Perhaps this is one reason for his later negative assessment of Nin's work.

Though some will view Peter's dismissal of Nin's journals as sacrilege, others will concur. The Australian novelist Helen Garner, discussing a friend's horror that she was to publish her own diaries, recently wrote, 'Did she imagine my diary as a narcissistic spilling of guts, the sort of ghastly self-glorifying mush that women like Anaïs Nin used to spew out?'

Though Peter hated confrontation and, as a result, often put up with a lack of professionalism from colleagues long after he should have sacked them, he was, in the early years, and in spite of his anxiety, quite capable of standing up to bullies. In 1951, the year Peter founded his own company, the corrupt publishing titan Robert Maxwell bought the ailing old wholesaler Simpkin Marshall, making a big show of 'rescuing' the venerable firm. He remaindered their stock—they had taken pride in keeping copies of virtually everything in print—and sold it off cheaply to bookshops. Maxwell refused to honour the company's debts to publishers and left their invoices unpaid. In addition to this loss, publishers found their orders reduced to a trickle until the booksellers sold through the cheap stock at significant profit. In his memoir *Pursuit* (2001), John Calder mentions his admiration for Peter's courage, saying that he was 'the only publisher ... who went to see Maxwell during the period when Maxwell was running and apparently "saving" the company. He ignored Maxwell's threat that anyone who pressed for payment or sued would do no further business with Simpkin Marshall, and he issued a writ. Maxwell paid him to stop an avalanche of further writs, which would have ruined his plan to strip the assets before putting the company into bankruptcy.' Calder admits that, unlike Peter, he and many others were conned by Maxwell and lost the considerable sums they were owed. By 1955 Maxwell had bankrupted the firm.

Understandably Peter liked to gloss over or deny stories that showed him in an unflattering light. One story he vigorously contested concerned news of an outbreak of bubonic plague in India. A stickler for personal hygiene and something of a hypochondriac, Peter warned his staff not to handle parcels or post from the subcontinent without thoroughly disinfecting them first. Modern technology was mostly a mystery to Peter, and contemporaries swear he also extended this injunction to the handling of any faxes that had been transmitted from India.

Working for Peter had its challenges for everyone. 'Of course he could be grumpy at work,' Susan Paine, Peter's loyal secretary and a best friend to Wendy, told me, 'but the world could be falling down around him and Peter would be Peter, beavering away with Radio 2 on all day.' Peter's telephone manner often left a lot to be desired. Antonia told me that she used to cringe when, rather like Basil Fawlty, Peter would pick up the phone and bark, 'Yes, what?!'

Interviewed after the staff mutiny of 1996, Beatrice Musgrave, who retired in 1988 after having worked for Peter for twenty-seven years, told the *Daily*

Express, 'Peter expects a lot from his staff. He's very much his own man, and anyone looking for a team operation would be disappointed. I was happy to fit in to an individual structure … For younger people who want to expand more, it would be difficult. It's very much a one man endeavour there.' 'Call me a masochist if you like,' Susan Paine told me:

> … but I enjoyed working for Peter and being in publishing. I worked for him for two long stints. Mostly we were a happy little gang. It was just Gary who came along and upset the apple cart. He was very bright but could be very nasty. I always thought Peter was a lovely man … though he seemed, when I first met him, rather eccentric. When I got to know him I really thought he was brilliant with books, and thought it madness that people were nasty about him. They should have accepted the fact that he was as he was.

Though naturally shy, emboldened by his success, egged on by Molly Parkin and fortified with Dutch courage, Peter embraced a flamboyant dress sense in the 1960s and 1970s, an echo of the colourful velvet suits and gaudy knitwear he had worn as a dandified child. Antonia, a surprisingly conventional child during the 1960s, was often embarrassed by her parents' attire.

> I went to a posh day school and Wendy would typically turn up at the school gates wearing a vibrant orange coat and a bowler hat or a suit in shocking pink topped off with a 1920s cloche hat.

Peter wore his hair long and wild and sported psychedelic Thai silk shirts, something frilly, or the embroidered variety from Mexico. Both parents contrasted greatly with the conventionally dressed, conservative parents of Antonia's schoolmates. The stylish effect was often undermined, Peter admitted to Molly Parkin, by his shirt-tails hanging out the back of his trousers. 'Peter always kept stain remover handy in the drawer of his desk,' editor Dan Franklin says:

> … and was usually seen dabbing at egg stains on his tie. This went on for years until he bought ties made of snakeskin that he could simply wipe clean. As with his trademark ties, I'm not sure there can have been anyone else in publishing at the time who wore lizard-skin shoes.

Occasionally Peter's sartorial choices got out of hand. Jeremy Reed recalls helping Peter pack his suitcase for a trip to Thailand where, liberally doused in his favourite cheap cologne, he planned to wear a safari jacket complete with epaulettes, knee socks, khaki shorts and even a pith helmet. Jenny Botsford recalled waiting for Peter to appear for dinner dates with some trepidation.

> He'd spend ages getting ready and come down wearing something completely extraordinary, often looking as though his motley ensemble had been fired at him randomly from an elephant gun.

Jenny, who viewed Peter as a good friend, also recalled being relieved when Peter admitted he wasn't intending to propose marriage. 'I told him he was fun to go out with but that, frankly, I'd never envisaged anything more serious.'

When reminded of her teenage dalliance with Peter, *raconteuse par excellence* Fenella Fielding told me 'I do remember Peter O, and Torquay, and all sorts of other details in your letter—things I'd forgotten really till I saw it all, just now, written down.' She sent him her regards. When she and I met up after his death, she struggled to visualise him. 'I have a vague memory of the back of someone's head,' she told me. I put Fenella in touch with Peter's company. In 2017, the year before her own death, Peter Owen Ltd published *Do You Mind If I Smoke?*, the memoir she had written with Simon McKay. Peter would have been tickled pink.

Peter talked on the record of his most significant relationships, but there were many others he mentioned, some of them short-lived encounters on cruise ships or on holiday in Morocco or Thailand. Our interviews quickly became something akin to therapy or the confessional. He could be very indiscreet, but, though he mentioned her often, he never admitted that he had proposed several times to his friend the agent Gloria Ferris in the late 1970s, something Gloria herself told Antonia after Peter's death. Gloria said she regretted turning Peter down. 'I could have tamed him!' she told Antonia. Their only attempt at seeing if they were compatible resulted in failure when, after a boozy night out in the West End, Peter fell out of bed. The experiment ended when both laughed hysterically before passing out until morning. A week later Gloria fell for Rivers Scott, her final partner, with whom she founded the literary agency Scott Ferris Associates. Gloria remained a loyal and supportive friend to Peter, holidaying with him occasionally and helping him through various minor difficulties. She admitted her shock when Peter died—she had thought him indestructible.

3 Eccentrically Mean

'No one in publishing', wrote Michael Bateman in the September 1968 issue of *Books and Bookmen*, 'is as full of contradictions as Peter Owen. He's pretty careful about money. You have to be in publishing. But at the same time his generosity of spirit is bursting at the seams.' As well as being economical when it came to certain issues of truth, Peter had a reputation for thriftiness that frequently crossed the line into outright meanness, something he hypocritically accused many relatives of showing. The only family exceptions he noted were his daughters, especially the ever-generous Antonia, whom Peter decried as a reckless spendthrift, and Winnie, his mother, who 'spoilt' her grandchildren through lavish gifts. 'My mother bought Antonia a fur coat when she was thirteen,' he once said. 'The whole thing was quite ridiculous.'

Peter's meanness was a recurring theme with those I interviewed. It was a trait they mostly regarded with amusement and incredulity rather than animosity. Some saw him as admirably frugal, less so when when it came to the allocation of budgets and salaries. Company editor Dan Franklin recalls that when he joined Peter Owen, 'the firm was run on literally Dickensian lines. I doubt there was any difference between the way Dickens' books were produced in 1850 and the way we were doing it in 1970,' he said. 'Peter had us all saving pieces of string and brown paper for packing books. He also insisted that any unfranked stamps on letters we received be steamed off for reuse. Peter was incredibly mean, but he had to be,' Franklin continued. 'I don't think the company would have survived had he not been. I'm pretty mean myself, and I probably got that from him! Peter was good at splitting costs for launch parties, and we do the same at Jonathan Cape today. In those days Peter was an expert at getting embassies to fund lavish parties to which he'd invite all his friends who would all get completely pissed. There was one awful occasion when some drunken clot had a Norman Wisdom moment and broke a valuable vase. They were great days though,' Franklin recalled, 'and amazing times we had.' John Paine also remembered these boozy launches with fondness.

> I once went to the Brazilian ambassador's party, which was fantastic! Peter was very good on these occasions and gave a brilliant speech. It was perfect—no errors or anything. I was very proud of him. I've never forgotten that.

Though Peter hired public relations firms when he could afford to, in his pomp he saved money by generating publicity himself—something he was particularly good at. He regularly collared journalists to enthuse about his latest literary discovery, and was always ready with a pithy quote. A favourite strategy was to affect the same *hauteur* as his Uncle Rudi and proclaim the rottenness of contemporary fiction, the shallowness of his corporate competitors, and the philistinism of the reading public. 'English homes don't have books,' he once said, 'though they might pick up a particularly disgusting paperback on holiday.' In 1968 he told the *Observer*, 'The first thing you have to learn about publishing in this country is that we are a nation of book borrowers and stealers—but not of book buyers.' 'My firm is unashamedly highbrow,' Peter told the *Kensington Post* in 1967. 'I'd rather read the classics than most of the twaddle called modern literature.' By the 1980s he would readily tell people he'd rather go to bed with a Trollope or an Austen than anything modern he had published himself. In 2011 he explained his company's *raison d'être* to the *Sunday Times* magazine: 'I always wanted to publish good books, not crap. There are still a few people who want good books.'

Peter's reasoning sometimes eluded his colleagues. When Dan Franklin started work in 1970, the Peter Owen offices were at Kendrick Mews in South Kensington; they were then moved to 20 Holland Park Avenue near Notting Hill. 'Using the house as an office was an illegal change of use as far as Kensington Council was concerned, so we had to move offices to his previous home in Earl's Court,' Dan recalls. It was while they were at Kendrick Mews that Francis Bacon lived opposite. 'One story Peter won't tell you', says Franklin, 'is that, rather enterprisingly, he used to go through Francis Bacon's bins to see if he could find any valuable sketches or signatures Bacon had thrown out. Francis, who'd been very supportive and occasionally attended launches, was absolutely livid when he caught Peter at it.'

Franklin also recalls his modest starting pay. The weekly packets enclosed only a few pound notes and coppers. 'It was probably a pittance, but I don't remember feeling hard done by', he says. In the end it was the lack of promotional budgets that persuaded him to leave, not his salary.

> I worked very hard on Shiela Grant Duff's memoir *The Parting of the Ways* (1982). I thought she'd written a masterpiece. Though there were significant features in the *Observer* through Shiela's connections to its trustee David Astor, the rest of the coverage was meagre. There was no publicity budget, and Peter overpriced and underprinted the book. It never stood a chance. He was always sabotaging books like that, and, though I carried of on for a couple of years, eventually I couldn't stand it any more.

Antonia's debut stint working with her father in the late 1980s ended the same way. By then an established freelance book editor, she joined the company only to find Peter was still steaming off stamps and using paper and string for parcels—he couldn't see the virtue of Jiffy Bags, only the price. Realising that Peter trusted none of his staff enough to delegate and would not give her a commissioning budget, she reluctantly decided to quit. 'At the time, I just couldn't see him ever changing,' she said. When Peter lured her back in 1996 as his editorial director after a staff mutiny earlier that year, Antonia, having agreed to give in her notice with the major publisher for whom she was working, made clear her conditions (annual pay increases, her own commissioning budget, consultation on book covers and so on) which both she and Peter signed into an apparently cast-iron contract. In time Peter tore up the contract saying he couldn't afford it. By then committed, Antonia stayed with him for the duration having managed make vital upgrades to the technology by introducing computers, and instigated use of the all-important Jiffy Bags.

Peter had an odd sense of entitlement when it came to people he thought were wealthy, whether it was Paul Bowles, Salvador Dalí, Shusaku Endo, or his editor and contemporary Michael Levien. Though Peter says in his memoir that Michael didn't want to be paid, this is nonsense. 'Peter's blood used to freeze when one mentioned money,' Michael recalled, 'and he didn't exactly lash out with his salaries.' This is an understatement. Peter originally paid him £1 a week to work at Old Brompton Road and 'looked rather sheepish when handing over the meagre envelope'. Muriel Spark was, at this time, paid £5 a week for three days' work.

Michael enjoyed his work despite the frustrations. 'Peter would often torpedo my book suggestions and even turned down unpublished stories by Sylvia Plath, and Jean Rhys's masterpiece *Wide Sargasso Sea* which went instead to André Deutsch.' Both Spark and Levien thought Ithell Colquhoun's hermetic novel *Goose of Hermogenes*, recently republished with material they cut restored, 'unreadable and pretentious'. But, like Spark, he was truly fond of Peter and regarded him as a friend.

> I wouldn't have gone back to work for him so often if there hadn't been a bond. The eccentricity of the company and the offices was part of the charm. We had some good times. Without a doubt Peter did some good publishing and fully deserved his OBE.

Peter was as frugal on holiday as he was in business. He and Wendy often went to Spain and Morocco with John and Susan Paine who both recalled how he would shift hotels, constantly trying to find a cheaper one. 'He once found us an atmospheric boathouse right by the sea for five shillings a night,' John told me. 'We thought it was marvellous, but at night dozens of rats started scampering around in the rafters. Susan and I left sharpish, but Peter insisted he and Wendy stay on because it was so cheap.' Another friend recalled that, while raising funds for charity, the staff at the French House managed to persuade Peter to write out a cheque. The amount, £1.23, was so specifically stingy they had the cheque framed and hung it behind the bar for years. 'Peter could be eccentrically mean', John Paine said of his old friend. 'He could be chary about buying rounds—that was why George Barker and Jeffrey Bernard would threaten to beat him up. I ignored it; they didn't.'

John remained friends with Peter through thick and thin.

> Now and then we had terrible rows. Peter once phoned me up because someone had chucked a brick through his window during the Notting Hill

> Carnival, and, despite having iron bars inside and out, he was in a terrible state—quite berserk with worry. It was a bank holiday, so as a favour I agreed to take a look. No one else would have gone. Getting the glass was a nightmare, and it was a difficult job, but I repaired it all and later gave him the bill for about £30 in the French. He snapped at me that someone else would have done it for £20! He handed back the invoice, so, in front of everyone, I tore it to shreds and told him where to stick it before storming out. Peter picked up all the pieces and glued it back together, then sent it back to me with a cheque for £20. I was disgusted but eventually forgave him. I refused to do any more work for him after that though.

While living in Crouch End with Antonia, Peter grumbled about the utility bills he had agreed to foot. As ever, he would do his ARP warden act, calling for lights to be turned off if anyone left a room unoccupied for so much as a second. When Antonia bought a Christmas tree to put in the front room, Peter objected to paying for the electricity to power decorative lights, an issue Antonia solved by purchasing battery-powered ones.

Peter's first ex-wife was undoubtedly the most significant victim of Peter's meanness. Despite academic difficulties—her maths skills and spelling were poor—before marrying Peter, Wendy Demoulins had shown real talent in her nursing training and had gained top marks in her first-year examinations. Perhaps influenced by his parents' expectations of marriage arrangements in the 1950s, Peter encouraged Wendy to give up her training to become a full-time housewife and mother. This had unforeseen consequences. Once the divorce was finalised in 1976 and the girls had left home, Wendy was left with a meagre settlement which, as it was not index-linked, dwindled in value over the remaining twenty-six years of her life. With no formal qualifications to her name, Wendy found work where she could: long and unsociable hours as a badly paid nursing assistant in the geriatric ward of one of London's worst hospitals, picking mushrooms in a factory and nude modelling at local art schools. She had too little time or energy to continue her writing career, but Peter was unrepentant, still smarting from the fact that she had initiated divorce proceedings rather than him.

Though he would occasionally admit to being 'too parsimonious', Peter's meanness seemed largely instinctive and perhaps inevitable. It surely had its roots in his chronic anxiety and the emotional privations he had experienced in early life. There must have been acute economic tension in a family that had experienced German hyperinflation, who had lost property in the Nazi era, and who knew that their livelihoods could, by precedent, be confiscated without warning. A family that endured experiences like this, then went through the privations of rationing during the war, is not likely to be particularly relaxed about money. No one should be surprised that someone who grew up in the

1930s balked at the way prices inflate during their lifetime. According to the Bank of England's inflation calculator (which averages inflation at 5.2 per cent per year) something that cost £10 in 1930 would set you back over £660 today—a fact hard for anyone to accommodate in daily life. Perhaps we could all have been more understanding, even when Peter's main priority seemed to be keeping his drinks cabinet well stocked with everything from Amarula to Xtabentún via Curaçao and Kahlúa.

Though I, too, witnessed financial grumbling and examples of astonishing parsimoniousness, Peter was often kind and appreciative. As a host, he was certainly generous and thoughtful. Others experienced this little-appreciated side of his character. One was his friend the poet and publisher Peter Ellson with whom Peter liked to stay in rural France, sometimes getting pleasantly lost on solitary walks to distant villages. 'Peter was never mean with me,' Ellson recalls.

> He would insist on taking us to dinner, always bought rounds of drinks, and also paid to fill up the petrol tank if I took him to the airport. When I stayed with him in Crouch End and he was too unwell to make it to a restaurant, Peter ordered a lavish and expensive Chinese takeaway for us. I offered to pay for it, but he wouldn't even accept half the cost, saying he would be insulted if I insisted.

Peter could be generous in other ways, too. As both Jeremy Reed and I can attest, Peter had suffered so much during his periods of breakdown and depression that he was deeply sympathetic to other sufferers. He wasn't the world's greatest gift-giver though. Jeremy recalls Peter returning from foreign adventures and proffering as gifts the complimentary soaps, shampoos and toothpastes he had looted from hotels. He also maintained a wardrobe full of wooden hotel-branded coat-hangers he had swiped.

One of Peter's later friends was financier and artist Kanad Upanishad Chakrabarti who first met Peter at the French in 2001 where they bonded over literature. 'Someone, hearing I liked books, sent me to the other end of the bar where Peter sat in his habitual spot next to the coffee machine. He was very cordial,' Kanad recalls:

> ... and opened up a world of non-English fiction refracted through a specific German-Jewish émigré sensibility—a slightly alien, not fully English but appealing space I could see myself fitting into. Peter always had a hilarious, occasionally cutting manner of summarizing the mores and customs of the countries he had visited. Whenever I called on him at Holland Park or in Haringey, Peter was a wonderful host. He'd procure a platter of sliced meats, pickles and cheese and pull out the all-important bottle of bubbly. I learnt of

his passing with considerable sadness. With him went the days I had spent sharing a few glasses of rotgut at the French with that most pungent yet kindly of raconteurs.

4 Constant Companions and Small Miracles

When we remember we are all mad, the mysteries
disappear and life stands explained.
— Mark Twain, *Notebook*, 1898

Picasso said that everything was a miracle ... that it was a miracle that one did not dissolve in one's bath like a lump of sugar.
— Cocteau, *Opium*, 1957

Though Peter clearly experienced times of conviviality and joy throughout his life he tended to focus on his life's difficulties during our many hours of conversation. The tale he told me was one in which poor health and loneliness were his constant companions from beginning to end. Other than his sight loss, which increased his isolation, his mental health problems surely outweighed all his physical ailments in their impact. For nine decades he endured the systemic poison of unresolved anger, anxiety and resentment, constantly seeking to bury his feelings and anaesthetise himself with generous doses of alcohol or, when needed, prescribed tranquillisers and antidepressants. Alcohol provided welcome moments of euphoria but increased his anxiety and depression and corroded his physical health. A blazing star of publishing in the 1960s and 1970s, Peter had burnt himself out far too quickly. Having heard his story in detail, it's clear to me that many underestimated the amount of courage it took for Peter to carry on and survive at all. It was a miracle he lived so long.

Peter was naturally given to pessimism and would usually focus on life's clouds, rarely its silver linings. He was obdurately insistent on doing the impossible, employed staff yet wanted to do everything himself. He was constantly stressed by what Michael Bateman called the conflict between 'putting out a damn good list or making a decent living'. When he couldn't afford to pay himself a salary he kept the business going anyway. In keeping faith with his insistence on publishing literature of quality, his business became an act of inadvertent philanthropy while still a source of constant worry. He was comfortably well-off later in life but continued to fret about his finances and investments, neurotically listening out for daily reports of share price fluctuations. I couldn't help but feel he would have been better off investing some of his money in a professional psychotherapist rather than stocks and shares.

Naturally sensitive and a patient listener, Jeremy Reed—by calling a poet rather than a psychotherapist—became Peter's unofficial counsellor. When Jeremy first visited his penultimate home in Holland Road it loomed like a locked fortress shrouded in darkness. Peter insisted that any 'unnecessary' lights be turned off and lived mostly by the light of a single lamp. 'It was like the House of Usher,' Jeremy told me. 'Unlike his cleaner and other visitors, Peter never thought the house was haunted. But his desperate loneliness was the real ghost.' Peter would sit at his heavily pixelated television viewing everything through a snowstorm, or listen to Radio 2 at full blast. Long before his deafness encroached, his preference for high volumes evolved as a means of blocking out the intrusive, nagging thoughts he desperately needed to escape. Peter lived overshadowed by the constant spectre of another nervous breakdown and, other than publishing, gossip and booze, had few interests to distract him. Though often touchy and sensitive about his eccentricities, he could sometimes laugh at his absurdities, especially in the euphoria of intoxication. His sense of humour and occasional kindnesses really were his saving graces.

Jeremy undoubtedly played a significant role in Peter's small support network. After their first meeting Peter invited him to dine at a restaurant in Notting Hill. Jeremy, a vegan, nibbled on a salad and watched uncomfortably as Peter consumed vast piles of meat washed down with house red. Peter talked of his chronic loneliness and invited Jeremy to visit regularly. So it was that Jeremy became friend and paid companion, visiting Peter every second Friday for twenty-five years, then, after Peter moved to Crouch End, sitting every weekend beside Peter in his Louis XV throne. Peter could be entertaining but draining, and, to ensure his own psychic survival, Jeremy constructed a firewall of privacy around his own personal life.

Peter was open about the many affairs he had enjoyed with women during and after his first marriage, only a few of which he recorded in his memoir. He was less candid when it came to the subject of his affairs with men, most of them brief, just one long-term. Some of his inner circle were as perturbed by the posthumous revelation of these secret dalliances as they were *blasé* about those he had conducted with women, rather reinforcing his instinct for secrecy. Asked if he might be gay, as he was in at least two published interviews, Peter always denied it; questioned whether he might be bisexual he would hesitate. 'Isn't everyone, a little?' he'd finally say, a fleeting twinkle in his eye. Secrecy in this area, motivated more by shame than a real need for discretion, caused him unnecessary anxiety and distress. To fully empathise with Peter and understand his unhappy brew of loneliness, sadness and regret, knowing this secret is essential. Despite his adventures in sartorial flamboyance, Peter was essentially a shy, private man. It's also worth remembering that he had been born into the era of lethal Nazi homophobia. Paragraph 175 of the German

Criminal Code, the legal statute the Nazis used and enforced to persecute gay people, actually endured from 1871 to 1994. Partial decriminalisation in England and Wales only took place in 1967, when Peter was forty years old, and, in the 1980s, the re-entrenchment of institutionalised homophobia through Section 28 and responses to the AIDS crisis were deeply anxiety-provoking. Peter also feared that 'coming out' would mean disinheritance. By the time his mother died and the threat was over, Peter was nearly seventy and his secrecy was ingrained. He told a beloved friend that, had he met him earlier in life, things would have been different. It was all too late.

At the same time, Peter seemed to make a habit of proposing to beautiful women. Van Gessel, translator of many Shusaku Endo novels, recalls an evening when Peter, somewhat soused, proposed out of the blue to Endo's personal translator Masako 'Mako' Kawashima. She politely declined. After his extremely inconvenient 'marriage of convenience' to 'Ruth', Peter spent much of the rest of his life alone. Susan Paine insists that this second marriage needn't have taken place at all. 'Peter was quite moral in certain ways,' she said.

> The rumours about him and Ruth were quite jokey, but she was old-fashioned and wanted to stop the gossip about them sleeping together, and Peter felt obliged to keep his word, even though he knew it would be a disaster.

Aside from this second marriage, the high-volume radio, recruiting Jeremy Reed's support or propping up the bar at the French, Peter's other attempts to exorcise the ghost of his loneliness stretched to taking in lodgers. The experiment was brief—a predictable failure. Peter kicked out the first of his three lodgers for extreme untidiness and smoking cannabis. The second, a Romanian trainee doctor, fared better for a while, and was even prepared to dress Peter's ulcerated feet. He left to undergo further medical training outside London. The last lodger stayed over a year but, having offended Peter by storing tools in his shed—'He'll take over the whole house!' Peter exclaimed—finally threw in the towel. Rumour has it that Peter had also grumbled about his 'harrowing' body odour.

'Peter was a bit of a perfectionist but would botch things up and make them funny,' Susan Paine recalled. His anxious perfectionism—the neurotic pursuit of an unattainable goal—became increasingly corrosive. It manifested in the precision with which his dozens of ornaments—the pillboxes, figurines and silverware—had to be displayed at Holland Park. Were anything moved even a little, Peter would become desperately agitated until it was restored to its rightful position. By the time Peter moved to Crouch End his eyesight was so poor it took the edge off this obsessive compulsion, though he once fretted wretchedly over an ashtray which someone had casually moved to press into service elsewhere.

Another source of immediate anxiety was the summoning of taxis which involved repeated calls to confirm the driver was coming. On one occasion Peter insisted that I accompany him and his carer to a hospital appointment and asked me call the taxi service so many times I found myself conducting pretend conversations on the telephone in an attempt to placate him. He was so anxious to be punctual that he had risen at 5 a.m. and sat ready by 8 a.m., two hours before the taxi was due to arrive. The visit, made all the more difficult by a wheelchair with flat tyres, was one of great importance to Peter. His specialist wanted to assess whether a recent cataract operation had improved his vision. It hadn't, confirming that operating on his other eye would be pointless. Crestfallen, Peter sat at home for the rest of the day, quietly coming to terms with his disappointment.

Peter lost much of the sight in his right eye to optical neuritis in 1984. The left went the same way in 1987 while he was in Marrakesh. This time, flown back to London as an emergency case, the quick application of steroids saved more of his sight. Peter was devastated by his sight loss—a fact he underplayed, like many of his problems, in his memoir. Peter Ellson helped him through this period. He adjusted eventually but said that he would have committed suicide had not some of his vision returned and, just in case, stockpiled the tranquillisers he had been prescribed. Suicide was a subject Peter often discussed with Jeremy Reed when times were particularly bad. Though never psychotic, a doctor Peter met at the Queen's Elm in Chelsea once prescribed him Stelazine (the antipsychotic trifluoperazine) to help calm his anxiety and obsessiveness, and vitamin B6 to combat the effects of his drinking.

Peter had several falls, some of them major. With a friend from the French he once went to Portugal only to return in plaster having fractured his collar bone after falling from the sea wall. He also once injured his knees after disembarking from a cruise ship and falling into a ditch. One particularly bad fall occurred at a Chinese restaurant in Holland Park. The entrance was at street level and Peter fell down an entire flight of stairs to the restaurant below, ending up in a pool of his own blood and with a broken shoulder. Something of a ragged-trousered misanthropist by then, he was banned from Poon's in Soho because, three times, his trousers fell down when he stood up to pay the bill. On one such occasion he was wearing no underwear and the manager was forced to ask him not to return—it was embarrassing the customers and putting them off their food.

Peter had needed his first hip replacement in the early 1980s while still in his mid-fifties. By June 2011 he had endured another two hip replacements in just over a year and, even when healed, needed to use a walking frame. A bout of pneumonia nearly finished him off. The move to Crouch End to share a house with daughter Antonia followed this unexpected partial resurrection. Exiled from Kensington and familiar Soho waterholes through incapacity, Peter, entrapped in his gilded cage, would use his walking frame to shuffle laboriously about the house, ascending every evening via stairlift to his first-floor bedroom. There the radio would go on at full blast, on one occasion broadcasting the 1987 hit 'Pump Up the Volume' so loudly that the song's command would have been impossible to fulfil. Later Peter might become peckish, descend by stairlift and clank his way to the fridge and raid it for a midnight feast.

In his last years, while Jeremy Reed cared for Peter at weekends, Filomena Estomago looked after him during the week. Peter was fond of Filomena who was endlessly patient with her curmudgeonly charge. For Peter, Filomena was the lowest in the pecking order and sometimes his frustrations would explode in her direction. Carers of her distinction were hard to come by, and, shamefaced, he would later apologise sincerely. The days of semolina and gruel long behind him, he ate heartily, ordering foods from the delicatessen, sometimes gravlax or the finest Belgian pâté which he ate in great slabs with a knife and fork. Peter's granddaughter Kate Wightman (née Trythall), of whom he was particularly fond, would often visit to share free samples from the magazine she worked for. 'It was pot luck really, but we'd always have a wonderful time,' she said.

> I remember bringing Easter eggs and enormous boxes of chocolates, and Peter, having improvised bizarre cocktails with the many obscure spirits and liqueurs in his cabinet, would immediately tuck into the random feast.

Occasionally Peter would order in sushi, another favourite, or takeaway Chinese. He had learnt to cook from one of the books he published and taught Filomena how to make sauerkraut. 'She once told me about Philippine cuisine,' he told me, 'but it sounded so disgusting I didn't pursue the matter. Mind you,' he added, 'it can't have been as bad as her neighbours in the Philippines. She came back one day and was devastated to find they'd barbecued her family dog—the one that had babysat her as a child. Her father never got over it.'

Though Peter grumbled about north London, now that he was unable to live independently, it is difficult to see what Peter could have done had Antonia not agreed to co-habit. On the odd occasion he had recuperated in a care home, the staff found him such a disagreeable client they were reluctant to house him regardless of remuneration. Similarly, when his long-time bookkeeper Tony Lunn and his wife had taken Peter on holiday to Wales, the proprietors of their guest house said they were welcome to come again but on no account should they bring Peter.

Antonia and Peter had their ups and downs. He was a distant figure during her childhood, and it took her time to acknowledge his talents. 'Friends would say they'd seen my father in the paper,' she told the *Sunday Times* magazine, 'and I began to appreciate how clever he was.' She admired his intuitive knack of picking authors and canny buying up of world rights. He let her down badly over the 1996 contract she had wisely insisted upon, but she was unfailingly loyal despite this. Spending so much time with Peter took its toll—her survival depended on regular breaks. Peter once apologised to me for being 'so neurotic' and was similarly appreciative of his daughter's forbearance. 'I don't believe that one necessarily ought to love or even like one's relatives,' he once told the *Sunday Times*.

> I dislike some of mine intensely, but Antonia is actually one of the nicest people I know ... We often laugh at the same things. I went to a funeral the other day and when the hearse turned up it had the name on the side: Bent Undertakers. I saved it up to tell her—I knew she'd like it.

Where others might have thrown in the towel, Peter kept up his regimen of regular tipples. Jeremy called me once to help drag Peter in from the garden where too many potent Sunday cocktails had caused him to keel over. Dan Franklin recalls another dramatic collapse at the company's fiftieth anniversary party. It was hot, and Peter had over-imbibed champagne on an empty stomach. He was conveyed from the party to an ambulance via a stretcher. None of the party-goers felt they could leave Peter's home in Holland Park until he had returned safely from hospital, by which time they had drained the place dry. For Peter, the cardinal sin was not so much alcoholism as not being able to hold one's drink. He was always willing to rise to a challenge. 'One Christmas, long after we'd split up, Wendy bought me a bottle of Grand Marnier,' he told me. 'It's pretty hard to drink a whole bottle unless you're used to it. The only other time I managed it was while watching Princess Diana's funeral.' Peter always denied he was an alcoholic, especially when knocking back liqueurs at ten o'clock in the morning. 'I can stop whenever I like,' he told me, though that time never came while he was alive.

Perhaps no one should condemn Peter—at least, not entirely. However difficult it was to be around his anxiety and obsessiveness at its most extreme, it can't have been much fun for him either. He had his reasons. 'Peter was Peter—unique, that's how I saw him,' said Susan Paine. 'I really liked him as a person. In some ways he was very naive, but that was a kind of niceness about his character.' Her faith in Peter was rewarded when he left her a legacy. Presented with a cheque for a hefty sum, she was thrilled. 'So I was a good judge of character after all!' And what a character it was. 'Such an important part of understanding Peter', his granddaughter Kate pointed out, 'is getting beyond that initial layer. It's only once you scratch the surface you realise the complexity, loyalty, extraordinary kindness and one-of-a-kind eccentricity and humour there. I always wish for one more Sunday afternoon with him.'

Not everyone liked Peter Owen. Though often funny and friendly, he could also be difficult, selfish and demanding. He made enemies. In his memoir there is sometimes a sense that scores are being settled, a strong whiff of hypocrisy in his delineation of the drinking habits, infidelities and sexual peccadilloes of others, and the occasional hint of sexism and even misogyny. Peter was certainly a man of contrasts and puzzles—the libertine bohemian gossip who could be haughty, upright and reserved; the anti-establishment libertarian, fascinated by royalty; the British, yet German-born Jew with an adopted Welsh surname who longed to be recognised by the very establishment of which he was so sceptical and defiant; a man who was liberal in his support for gay rights, euthanasia and other issues, but also a deeply conservative admirer of Margaret Thatcher. Peter was the great countercultural publisher of Tariq Ali and *The Book of Grass* who still found space on his list for Sir Rhodes Boyson; he was the champion of modernists who preferred the comforting familiarity of Jane Austen; a man who was bold yet shy, mean yet generous, canny yet naive, polite yet rude. Whatever his myriad faults, Peter could be funny, thoughtful and kind. That he could inspire so much friendly devotion in spite of his many faults should give even the least of us reason for hope.

The last time I saw Peter I was worried. Over the course of the month I stayed with him while Antonia took a much-needed break he had become surprisingly dependent very quickly. 'I will really miss you', he said fondly as I took my leave. Fortunately his granddaughter Kate arrived and brought joy to his face, thereby lifting a weight from my shoulders.

Peter died aged eighty-nine on 31 May 2016 after a short illness. The humanist funeral he had specified, with 'no religious crap of any kind', was held on 15 June at Golders Green Crematorium, near where his parents are buried. Tributes were paid by Antonia and Ben Owen with music from Ryuichi Sakamoto's soundtrack to Bertolucci's *The Sheltering Sky*, a Satie *Gnossienne*, Kurt Weill's 'September Song' and pieces by Vaughan Williams and the Beatles. As they left, mourners placed sprigs of rosemary on Peter's coffin, for remembrance. Anyone who had encountered such an extraordinary character would surely find him hard to forget.

'Let's do it in style!' Peter had said of his wake. Caterers provided a lavish buffet for mourners back at Crouch End in the house and company offices he had shared with his daughter Antonia, her menagerie of parrots, an elusive cat, a Tibetan mastiff, and her partner Nick Kent, by then managing director and more recently her husband. The following evening a salon was held at the Piccadilly branch of Waterstones in celebration of the company's sixty-fifth anniversary. At Peter Owen Ltd, Antonia and Nick have continued Peter's legacy, keeping in print his strong backlist of contemporary classics and publishing a select list of new books, including Anna Kavan's *Machines in the Head* (2019), stories selected and introduced by Victoria Walker, formerly chair of the Anna Kavan Society, an illustrated and expanded edition of Ithell Colquhoun's *Goose of Hermogenes* (2018), plus new editions of her Ireland and Cornwall travelogues (2016), and her selected shorter writing *Medea's Charms* (2019).

Working with Peter on his memoir was an exhausting but illuminating project. I am glad to have known him and had the privilege of hearing his story and, through him, glimpsed worlds long gone. In some ways his life could be a parable about enjoying the moment versus the dangers of holding on to ancient enmities. An outsider who wanted only to belong, who sometimes felt like an impostor despite all his success, who suffered severe depression despite all that he had to enjoy, Peter remained at heart, for nine decades, a gentle, anxious, lonely little boy who found it hard to forgive. He responded so gratefully to every little kindness that it was hard to say goodbye.

Tributes to Peter Owen

There is no publisher like him for his originality, taste, discrimination and, above all, courage. And at a time when independent publishers have been tumbling into the arms of the big conglomerates, he has remained proudly independent. I admire him so much.

—Doris Lessing

The only publisher in England who produces anything interesting.

—Francis Bacon

Peter Owen—a name to respect! I don't know any house which has taken on so many difficult books to sell and propagate, so many authors whose merit was clouded by bad luck or factors which had nothing to do with their brilliance—Anaïs Nin, Anna Kavan among so many—and all for the pure love of literature. So many good authors—and at least seven of them have gone on to win the Nobel Prize for Literature.

—Laurence Durrell

One of the few remaining publishers who cares about the contents of the books they produce.

—Kathleen Raine

I have always admired his career and his independence. He has steadfastly refused to go the way of all flesh and continues to publish work of high literary if not commercial value.

—Beryl Bainbridge

Peter Owen is an excellent discoverer of the hidden novels around the world and he encourages them to grow.

—Shusaku Endo

You make corporate publishing appear like a graveyard.

—Jeremy Reed

Peter Owen was the only one who would have taken the risk of publishing the first book of an unknown writer in a remote country. I marvelled at my luck in finding this small and highly original publishing house.

—Anita Desai

Hats off to Peter Owen for the remarkable books he has published for so many years. From de Chirico and Dalí to Anna Kavan, he has brought us the best of American and European writing. Never has an investment of £900 produced such riches.

—J. G. Ballard

I admired Peter's courage and chutzpah, as well as the drive that had made a success of Peter Owen Ltd, especially in the 1960s and 1970s. The internationalism displayed on the list was particularly impressive: how we need that now, at a time when it seems unlikely that the British will read their own literature, let alone that of other countries. I enjoyed his humour, cringed at some of his more outlandish attitudes and deplored his meanness. But when it comes down to it, I feel glad to have known and worked with him, and I'll continue to applaud his achievements.

—Stephen Stuart-Smith

Over many years he has published 'difficult' and unknown authors, including foreign novelists when translated fiction was exceptionally hard to sell, before they became famous and were, in some cases, snapped up by the big publishing houses. Peter Owen is, in more ways than one, a unique figure in the literary world of our time.

—D. J. Enright

The last survivor of those great immigrant publishers who fled tyranny in Europe and helped the British defend themselves against their own philistinism. Peter is a wonderful example of a person who thinks books should not be rubbish.

—Duncan Fallowell

I doff my cap to him. His list is full of the esoteric and avant-garde. If it hadn't been for Peter and his one-man band doing it all off a table in SW5 none of it would have happened.

—D. J. Taylor

I've always looked on Peter as a great person, a wonderful credit to his country. He has devoted his life to publishing excellent books, without the advantage of a large commercial organisation. I cannot think of anyone who deserves his OBE more.

—Allan Sillitoe

For many years he has actively, often to his own cost, supported serious literature and dedicated authors. With publishing now dominated by large conglomerates where commercial profit usually outweighs the needs of literature proper, Peter Owen has unflinchingly remained true to his convictions: independence, loyalty to serious books and their authors, awareness of the need to introduce to the British reader as many books as possible from countries in all continents. No publisher in Britain can rival him, and it is a service, cultural and humane, that I feel is worthy of recognition.

—Peter Vansittart

That Peter has survived, indeed thrived, is on the face of it a marvel, but it owes everything to his eye for an opportunity, his thrift, his ability to look for great books beyond these shores. Anyone who loves books owes him an enormous debt.

—Dan Franklin

Peter is part of history, the success story of an independent publisher in a world of corporate goliaths.

—Brian Braithwaite

The books he discovered and published will be voices to speak on behalf of him. And what a great polyphony indeed! Searching, inquisitive voices from all over the world revealing the most inner circles of human nature, the darker places of the soul where the quest for light starts from. I do believe that this profound knowledge and intuition of what true literature consists of will be carried forward by the team at Peter Owen Publishers.

— Alek Popov

Working for Peter was a complete hoot—they don't make them like that any more!

— Lavinia Chamberlain

His name has always been associated, for me, with a love of literature that was never parochial and never anything but literary and adventurous.

—Frederic Raphael

Over the years the list has been consistently a distinguished one.

—Paul Bowles

His commitment to literature and to the reading public over the years and the great contribution his publishing house has made, particularly in broadening our literary horizons to include great writers from Europe and abroad, makes his OBE richly deserved.

—Fay Weldon

Of all the publishing men in my life Peter Owen has been the most constant, the most predictably unpredictable, the most infuriating, the one to whom I always come back.

—Margaret Crosland

Mad of course, but then he *is* one of life's sweeter mysteries.

—Anne Valery

I have always found him lively and willing to take risks.

—Rayner Heppenstall

Peter and I got on, I think, because I never questioned his immense personality or decisions, his drinks cabinet or his directives. I trusted his wisdom as one privileged to see a titan storming through, a publisher who followed and trusted his instincts throughout.

—Patricia Hope Scanlan

Peter Owen discovered me and published my first novel in 1987. Having been courted to descend into corporate publishing since then, I now realise the true value of this remarkable publisher and am returning to the fold. I am honoured and flattered to be alongside some of the most original novelists to have appeared anywhere. I salute you, Mr Owen, and thank you for you courage and for your proven excellence.

—Noel Virtue

So many fond memories of that gentleman propping up his corner at the French, his half-full glass of framboise liqueur held at a precarious angle. With pride I handle the few publications of his in my possession. He was so wide in his concerns, so international in outlook.

—Tom Sroczynski

What a wonderful publisher!

—Erté

Bibliography and Resources

In addition to unpublished letters and manuscripts housed in the Harry Ransom Center and the archives of Peter Owen, Ltd, the following resources were consulted.

1 Books

ARMSTRONG, Neville, *Catching Up with the Future* (Suffolk, 1999)
BAIR, Deirdre, *Anaïs Nin: A Biography* (Bloomsbury, 1996)
BLACKER, Terence, *You Cannot Live As I Have Lived and Not End Up Like This: The Thoroughly Disgraceful Life and Times of William Donaldson* (Ebury Press, 2007)
BLOND, Anthony, *Jew Made in England* (Timewell Press, 2004)
BOSQUET, Alain, *Conversations with Dalí* (E. P. Dutton & Co, 1969)
BOWLES, Jane, and DILLON, Millicent, ed., *Out in the World, Selected Letters of Jane Bowles 1935-1970* (Black Sparrow Press, 1985)
BOWLES, Paul, and MILLER, Jeffrey, ed.), *In Touch: The Letters of Paul Bowles* (Farrar Straus & Giroux, 1994)
BOWLES, Paul, and OWEN, Peter, intro., *The Paul Bowles Reader* (Peter Owen, 2000)
BOWLES, Paul, and HALPERN, Daniel, ed., *Too Far From Home, Selected Writings of Paul Bowles* (The Echo Press, 1993)
BOWLES, Paul, *Up Above the World* (Simon & Schuster, 1966)
BOWLES, Paul, *Without Stopping* (Putnam, 1972)
CALDER, John, *Pursuit: The Memoirs of John Calder* (Alma Books, 2001)
CALLARD, David, *The Case of Anna Kavan* (Peter Owen, 1992)
CARR, Virginia Spencer, *Paul Bowles: A Life* (Peter Owen, 2005)
CLARK, Adrian, and DRONFIELD, Jeremy, *Queer Saint: The Cultured Life of Peter Watson* (John Blake, 2015)
COCTEAU, Jean, *Opium: The Diary of a Cure* (Peter Owen, 1957)
DALÍ, Salvador, *Hidden Faces* (Peter Owen, 1973)
DEXTER, William, *Children of the Void* (Peter Owen, 1955)
DEXTER, William, *World in Eclipse* (Peter Owen, 1954)
DILLON, Millicent, *You Are Not I: A Portrait of Paul Bowles* (University of California Press, 1998)

DONALDSON, William, *From Winchester To This* (Peter Owen, 1998)
ENDO, Shusaku, *Deep River* (Peter Owen, 1994)
ENDO, Shusaku, *The Sea and Poison* (Peter Owen, 1972)
ENDO, Shusaku, *Silence* (Peter Owen, 1976)
ENDO, Shusaku, *Stained Glass Elegies* (Peter Owen, 1984)
ENDO, Shusaku, *When I Whistle* (Peter Owen, 1979)
ENDO, Shusaku, *Wonderful* Fool (Peter Owen, 1973)
FIELDING, Fenella, and MCKAY, Simon, *Do You Mind If I Smoke?* (Peter Owen, 2017)
FORSTER, E. M., *Maurice* (Edward Arnold, 1971)
FRASER, G. S., and FLETCHER, Iain, *Springtime: An Anthology of Young Poets and Writers* (Peter Owen, 1953)
FRIEDMANN, Rudolph, *Kierkegaard: The Analysis of the Psychological Personality* (Peter Nevill, 1949)
GIBSON, Ian, *The Shameful Life of Salvador Dalí* (Faber & Faber, 1997)
HALLIDAY, Nigel Vaux, *More than a Bookshop: Zwemmer's and art in the 20th Century* (Philip Wilson, 1991)
HERBERT, David, *Engaging Eccentrics* (Peter Owen, 1990)
HERBERT, David, *Relations & Revelations: Advice to Jemima* (Peter Owen, 1992)
HERBERT, David, *Second Son: An Autobiography* (Peter Owen, 1972)
HESSE, Hermann, *Siddhartha* (Peter Owen, 1954)
KAVAN, Anna, *A Bright Green Field* (Peter Owen, 1958)
KAVAN, Anna, *Ice* (Peter Owen, 1967)
KAVAN, Anna, *Julia and the Bazooka* (Peter Owen, 1970)
KAVAN, Anna, *Mercury* (Peter Owen, 1994)
KAVAN, Anna, *My Soul in China* (Peter Owen, 1975)
KAWABATA, Yasunari, *The Lake* (Peter Owen, 1977)
LANDESMAN, Jay Irving, *Neurotica 1948-1951* (Jay Landesman Ltd, 1981)
LAUGHLIN, James, *Pound as Wuz* (Peter Owen, 1989)
LAUGHLIN, James, *Some Irreverent Literary History* (Peter Owen, 1989)
MIKES, George, *How To Be an Alien* (André Deutsch, 1946)
MISHIMA, Yukio, *Confessions of a Mask* (Peter Owen, 1960)
NIN, Anaïs, *Fire: From 'A Journal of Love': The Unexpurgated Diary of Anaïs Nin (1934-1937)* (Peter Owen, 1996)
NIN, Anaïs, *Incest: From 'A Journal of Love': The Unexpurgated Diary of Anaïs Nin: 1932-1934* (Peter Owen, 1993)
NIN, Anaïs, *The Journals of Anaïs Nin: Volume 7: 1966-1974* (Peter Owen, 1980)
NIN, Anaïs, *Nearer the Moon: The Unexpurgated Diary of Anaïs Nin: 1937-1939* (Peter Owen, 1996)
ONO, Yoko, *Grapefruit* (Peter Owen, 1970)
ORWELL, George, *Some Thoughts on the Common Toad* (Penguin Books, 2010)
OWEN, Peter, intro., *Everything Is Nice—and Other Fiction: The Peter Owen 50th Anniversary Anthology* (Peter Owen, 2001)
OWEN, Peter, ed., intro., and ENRIGHT, D. J., fwd, *The Peter Owen Anthology* (Peter Owen, 1991)
OWEN, Peter, ed., *Peter Owen: Twenty Years of Independent Publishing* (Peter Owen, 1971)
OWEN, Peter, contributing ed., *Publishing Now: A definitive assessment by key people in the book trade* (Peter Owen, 1993)
OWEN, Peter, contributing ed., *Publishing: The Future* (Peter Owen, 1988)
OWEN, Peter, and OWEN, Wendy, eds, *Springtime Two: An Anthology of Modern Prose and Poetry* (Peter Owen, 1958)

OWEN, Peter, and LEVIEN, Michael, eds, *Springtime Three: An Anthology of Prose and Poetry* (Peter Owen, 1961)
OWEN, Wendy, *There Goes Davey Cohen* (Hutchinson, 1966)
OWEN, Wendy, *Whatever Happened to Ruby?* (Peter Owen, 1968)
PARKIN, Sarah, *The Colony Room Club* (Palm Tree Publishers, 2013)
PULSIFER, Gary, ed., *Paul Bowles by His Friends: A Revealing Portrait* (Peter Owen, 1992)
RAINE, Kathleen, *Autobiographies* (Skoob Books, 1991)
REED, Jeremy, *A Stranger on Earth: The Life and Work of Anna Kavan* (Peter Owen, 2006)
RUSSELL, John, with MIKES, George, and BENTLEY, Nicolas, *The Duke of Bedford's Book of Snobs* (Peter Owen, 1965)
SARTRE, Jean-Paul, and ALEXANDER, Lloyd, translator, *Intimacy and other stories* (Peter Nevill, 1949)
SCOTT STOKES, Henry, *The Life and Death of Yukio Mishima* (Peter Owen, 1975)
SHILLITOE, Richard, *Ithell Colquhoun: Magician Born of Nature* (Lulu, 2009)
SPARK, Muriel, *The Comforters* (Macmillan, 1957)
SPARK, Muriel, *Curriculum Vitae: A Volume of Autobiography* (Constable, 1992)
SPARK, Muriel, *A Far Cry from Kensington* (Constable, 1988)
STANFORD, Derek, *Inside the Forties: Literary Memoirs, 1937-57* (Sidgwick & Jackson, 1977)
STANNARD, Martin, *Muriel Spark: The Biography* (Weidenfeld & Nicolson, 2009)
VIRTUE, Noel, *The Redemption of Elsdon Bird* (Peter Owen, 1987)
WAUGH, Patricia, *Metafiction* (Methuen & Co, 1984)
WILLIAMS, Jane, ed., *Tambimuttu: Bridge Between Two Worlds* (Peter Owen, 1989)
WILKINS, Harold T., *Flying Saucers on the Moon* (Peter Owen, 1954)

2 Newspapers, Journals and Periodicals:

'All happening for Wendy', *London Look* (3 February 1968)
AZIMI, Negar, 'The Madness of Queen Jane', *New Yorker* (12 June 2014)
'B.A.B.', 'Authors & Editors: Peter Owen', *Publishers' Weekly*, Vol. 200, No. 25, pp. 9-10 (20 December 1971)
BAKER, Keiligh, 'Daniel Rosenthal appears in British court charged with murdering his father in France more than three decades ago', *Daily Mail* (16 June 2015)
BAY, André, 'Letter from France: Return of the Prodigal', *Anaïs: An International Journal*, Vol. 3, pp. 45-48, Anaïs Nin Foundation (1985)
BATEMAN, Michael, 'There goes Peter Owen', *Books and Bookmen*, pp. 16-17 (September 1968)
BERGAN, Ronald, 'Me, Paul Bowles and that forgotten night in Tangier', *Guardian* (29 December 2009)
BOND, Anthony, 'Killer dubbed the "mad scientist" after he hacked his own mother and father to death escaped from mental health hospital', *Daily Mail* (11 August 2013)
'Bookman's Diary', 'Young publisher', *John O'London's* (27 April 1951)
'A book of his Owen', *The Hill*, p. 7 (March 1989)
'Bookworm', 'The World's Greatest Publishers: 8. Peter Owen', *Private Eye*, No. 526, p. 4 (1982)
CALDER, John, 'Letter: The shrinking market for literate readers', *Guardian* (17 April 1987)
CHAPMAN, Christine, '"Another Beginning" for Shusaku Endo', *International Herald Tribune* (19 August 1988)

'Daily Echo Reporter', 'The mad scientist who cut up his parents with a hacksaw', *Southern Daily Echo* (17 January 2008)

'A Dalí deal', *Sunday Times* (20 August 1972)

Dix, Carol, 'Books shelved', *Guardian* (31 January 1975)

Edmonds, Richard, 'Cult figure who fought shy of media spotlight', *Birmingham Post, Weekend* (22 August 1992)

Endo, Shusaku, 'I Did Things in Reverse', *The Asiaweek Literary Review*, p. 64 (23 October 1983)

Enright, D. J., 'Dilly-Dali', *The Listener* (13 September 1973)

Fallowell, Duncan, 'Englishman abroad', *Woman's Journal* (October 1990)

Fallowell, Duncan, '"She sat eating caviar and didn't offer me any"', *Telegraph Review* (24 February 2007)

'Fantastic Salvador', *Sunday Express* (12 August 1973)

'Far from the modern crowd', *Evening Standard*, [undated]

'Fortune founded on a pile of paper', *Daily Express* (14 April 1971)

Fergus, T. S., 'What's happening: Won in translation', *Sunday Telegraph* (12 July 1971)

Fowler, Stephen, 'Blazing the Trail: An interview with Peter Owen', *3:AM* (1 December 2009)

Fowler, Stephen, 'Peter Owen', *Vice* (2 December 2009)

Friedmann, Rudolph, 'Kierkegaard: The Analysis of the Psychological Personality', *Horizon*, Vol. VIII, No. 46 (October 1943)

Garner, Helen, 'My early diaries filled me with so much shame I burned them. I'm publishing the rest', *Guardian* (20 October, 2019)

Geare, Michael, 'Ode to a nightingale', [unpublished anniversary interview with Peter Owen, pp. 1-5], (1981)

George, Adrian, 'Tangerine Dreams', *Sunday Times* (11 July 1993)

Gogarty, Paul, 'Goodbye lager—hello Dalí', *Weekend Telegraph* (24 April 1993)

'Good British Writing is so hard to find', *Smith's Trade News*, No. 1804, pp. 20-21 (June 1958)

Hardyment, Pam, 'Homegrown publisher intends to stay put', *Daily Mail*, p. 13 (13 October 1995)

Hempel, Sandra, 'Relative Values: Peter Owen, publisher, and his daughter Antonia, editorial director', *Sunday Times, Magazine* (16 August 1998)

Herbert, David, 'I like it here', *The Spectator* (29 August 1992)

Herman, David, 'Interview: Peter Owen', *Jewish Chronicle* (11 October 2011)

Hickey, William, 'A Pasternak "scoop"', *Daily Express*, p. 3 (7 November 1958)

Hill, Emily, 'Novel Approach', *Dazed & Confused*, Vol. 11, No. 94, pp. 122-125, (February 2011)

Kadri, Z. M., 'From The Editor's Desk: A Conflict of Rights', *Current Book News*, Vol. 1, No. 4, pp. 1-2, Bombay (October 1963)

Kavanagh, P. J., 'Upper-class Con Man', *Guardian* (6 September 1973)

Killen, Mary, 'The classiest of gossips', *Daily Telegraph* (22 August 1992)

Lachman, Gary, 'Jeremy Reed: A supernova in orange and purple ink', *Independent* (30 July 2006)

Lasdun, James, 'Doris Lessing and the Perils of the Pseudonymous Novel', *New Yorker* (23 July 2013)

Lennon, Peter, 'No more hard stuff', *Guardian* (12 December 1994)

Lewis, Roger, 'Join our club and die a horrible death: The Colony Room Club by Sophie Parkin', *Daily Mail* (3 January 2013)

'Londoner's Diary', 'In to lunch', *Evening Standard* (17 February 1994)

'Londoner's Diary', 'Strange encounters', *Evening Standard* (5 November 1992)

'Londoner's Diary', 'These are auspicious times', *Evening Standard* (20 December 1993)

McGlone, Jackie, 'From Muriel Spark to Yoko Ono: Peter Owen relives a life in publishing', *Herald Scotland* (11 July 2011)

Mantel, Hilary, 'Reith Lecture 1: The Day is for the Living', *BBC Radio 4*, Official Transcription, (13 June 2017)

Marshall, Richard, 'Dreaming with his eyes open: Jeremy Reed', *3:AM* (1 December 2005)

Martin, Ruth, 'Behind the imprint: No. 4. Peter Owen', *Smith's Trade News*, pp. 25-27 (24 June 1961)

Meades, Jonathan, 'His place in the sun', *Connoisseur* (April 1996)

'Meet the Publishers: No.2 Peter Nevill, Ltd', *Colophon: The Monthly Magazine for Booklovers*, Vol. 1, No. 2, pp. 33-34 (April 1950)

Melly, George, 'Avida Dollars', *Observer* (9 September 1973)

Melly, George, 'Right over the top with Dalí', *Sunday Telegraph* (15 July 1990)

Morin, Carole, 'Hell in bright colours', *New Statesman & Society* (19 October 1990)

'New Publishing Firm', *W. H. Smith Trade Circular* (21 April 1951)

'New Year's Honours', *Daily Telegraph* (31 December 2013)

'New Year's Honours', *The Times* (31 December 2013)

Nin, Anaïs, 'Two Letters to Anna Kavan', *Anaïs: An International Journal*, Vol. 3, pp. 63-64, Anaïs Nin Foundation (1985)

Nye, Robert, 'Salvador Dalí—*Hidden Faces', Books & Bookmen (October 1973)*

'OBE for Peter Owen', *The Bookseller*, p. 7 (21 March 2014)

'Obituaries: David Herbert', *Daily Telegraph* (5 April 1995)

Owen, Maureen, 'At First Sight', Observer (5 May 1968)

Owen, Peter, '60 years of independence', *Publishers Weekly & Frankfurt Fair Dealer*, pp. 28-29, (14 October 2011)

Owen, Peter, 'Autobiographical book with insights into publishing', [Unpublished book proposal], pp. 1-2 (before 1976)

Owen, Peter, 'Balkan Books', *Books and Bookmen*, p. 98 (December 1966)

Owen, Peter, 'Books lines and sinkers', *Guardian* (13 April 1987)

Owen, Peter, 'Ezra Pound', *Time & Tide*, Vol. 33, No. 52, p. 1553 (27 December 1952)

Owen, Peter, 'How to remain a publisher', *Books and Bookmen*, pp. 29 and 41 (October 1957)

Owen, Peter, 'In my view', *Sunday Times* (11 February 1990)

Owen, Peter, 'I wish I'd published that', *London Standard*, p. 23 (15 January 1985)

Owen, Peter, 'Letters: Hard Stuff', *Observer* (14 December 1994)

Owen, Peter, 'Letters: Muriel Spark', *Times Literary Supplement* (26 March 1971)

Owen, Peter, 'The mechanics of British publishing', *The Bookferret*, Vol. 1, No. 3 (5 October 1972)

Owen, Peter, 'My Visit to India', *Current Book News*, Vol. 1, No. 4, pp. 4-5, Bombay (October 1963)

Owen, Peter, 'No connection', *Bookseller* (21 October 1951)

Owen, Peter, 'One man's week', *Sunday Times* (13 February 1977)

Owen, Peter, 'Opinion', *Town* (January 1967)

Owen, Peter, 'Our big bad books', *Telegraph*, *Weekend* (15 August 1969)

Owen, Peter, 'Peter Owen Visits the USA and Mexico', *The Publisher*, p. 26 (February 1967)

Owen, Peter, 'Publishing 1951-1967', *The Publisher*, p. 10 (April/May 1967)

Owen, Peter, 'Publishing Anna Kavan', *Anaïs: An International Journal*, Vol. 3, pp. 75-76, Anaïs Nin Foundation, (1985)

OWEN, Peter, 'Publishing on a shoe-string', *John O'London's*, Vol. 4, No. 79, p. 381 (6 April 1961)
OWEN, Peter, 'Sayings of the week,' *Observer* (9 June 1968)
OWEN, Peter, 'The Strike Against Fiction, *New Statesman*, p. 331 (8 September 1972)
OWEN, Peter, 'Subsidise or sink', *Guardian* (4 July 1975)
OWEN, Peter, 'Things they said in 1971: "I've got about 50 ties"', *Smith's Trade News*, p. 25 (18 December 1971)
OWEN, Peter, [Untitled column], *Publishing News* (5 January 1990)
OWEN, Peter, [Untitled column], *Publishing* News (3 January 1992)
OWEN, Peter, 'What I Think of Censorship', *London Look*, p. 17 (21 January 1967)
OWEN, Peter, 'What Our Readers Think: Credit where credit is due', *John O'London's*, p. 352 (9 June 1950)
'Peterborough', 'Dalí Bread', *Daily Telegraph* (1 October 1984)
'Peter Owen: Obituary', *The Times* (17 June 2016)
'Peter Owen, publisher: Obituary', *Daily* Telegraph (31 May 2016)
'Points and Prophecies: Another new Publishing House is The Vision Press, Ltd.', *The Bookmart*, Vol. 3, No. 2, p. 32 (7 November 1946)
PEARSON, Kenneth, 'Owen the publisher', *Sunday Times* (28 February 1971)
'Publisher Owen can afford to relax a little', *Kensington Post* (1967)
PULSIFER, Gary, 'Tangerine Dreams: Obituary: David Herbert', *Guardian* (6 April 1995)
RAFFERTY, Kevin, 'The sharpened pencil and acerbic views of Japan's Graham Greene', *Guardian* (22 October 1994)
RANK, Otto, 'House of Incest: A Preface', *Anaïs: An International Journal*, Vol. 3, pp. 49-54, Anaïs Nin Foundation (1985)
'Recipe', *The Evening News & The Star*, p. 6 (19 January 1961)
RIBEIRO, Jorge, 'Of Martyrdom and Apostasy', *The Asiaweek Literary Review*, pp. 63-65 (21 October 1983)
RICKETT, Joel, 'Peter Owen—a family affair', *The Bookseller* (12 May 2001)
SALTER, Jessica, 'Flashback: Peter Owen remembers a book launch party for Anaïs Nin in 1970', *Daily Telegraph*, *Magazine* (2 July 2011)
SEWARDS, Lisa, 'Why we had to flee the boss from hell', *Daily Express* (5 June 1996)
SHAPIRO, Sraya, 'Looking for Hebrew talent', *Jerusalem Post Magazine* (5 July 1968)
'Shusaku Endo Is Dead at 73, Japanese Catholic Novelist', *International Herald Tribune* (1 October 1996)
'Shusaku Endo: Obituary', *Daily Telegraph* (1 October 1996)
'Shusaku Endo: Obituary', *Independent* (1 October 1996)
'Shusaku Endo: Obituary', *The Times* (1 October 1996)
SMITH, Vicky, 'Daniel Rosenthal: How did one of Britain's most brutal murderers walk free from hospital?', *Daily Mirror* (11 August 2013)
SPARK, Muriel, 'Letter: Peter Owen', *Times Literary Supplement* (9 April 1971)
SPENDER, Stephen, and SUSCHITZKY, Wolf, 'Road of Books and Vices', *The Independent Magazine*, pp. 74-78 (18 November 1989)
STANFORD, Derek, 'Tyranny of expectation', *The Scotsman* (8 September 1973)
'Starting New Firm', *Bookseller* (16 April 1951)
STEELE, Ann, 'Chaotic—that's the life for the woman behind Davey Cohen!', *Daily Telegraph* (24 January 1968)
STUHLMANN, Gunther, 'Anna Kavan Revisited', *Anaïs: An International Journal*, Vol. 3, pp. 55–62, Anaïs Nin Foundation (1985)
SULLIVAN, Michael, 'A common heritage', *InPrint*, *Society of Young Publishers* (September 1986)
SYTSMA, Richard E., 'God's Silence in Japan', *The Banner*, pp. 14-15, Grand Rapids, Michigan (5 October 1992)

'The Angry Decade', *Books of the Month*, pp. 10-12 (June 1958)
TAYLOR, D. J., 'Attic offices, skeleton staff', *New Statesman*, pp. 46-47 (9 April 1999)
THOMSON, Liz, 'Born to be a publisher: Liz Thomson talks with Secker's Dan Franklin', *Publishing News* (May 1991)
TURNER, Amy, 'A Legend Between the Sheets', *Sunday Times*, *Magazine*, pp. 50-54 (5 June 2011)
WALKER, John, 'A Catholic View From the Far East', *International Herald Tribune* (18 April 1979)
WALSH, Georgina, 'The cash crisis facing Britain's publishers', *Evening Standard*, p. 10 (16 July 1975)
WALSH, John, 'Half a century of cultural caviar', *Independent*, *Weekend Review* (16 June 2001)
WHITE, Sam, 'The Dalí story, framed with greed', *Evening Standard* (14 September 1984)
WHYMANT, Robert, 'Christians in a hostile land', *Guardian*, p. 5, (23 February 1981)
WOODWARD, Kenneth L., and KIRK, Don, 'Finding Jesus in Japan', *Newsweek* (1 December 1980)

3 Television Broadcast

SEARCH, Jess (producer), 'Arthouse: Spy in the House of Love: Anaïs Nin', *A Soul Purpose Production for Channel Four,* Broadcast 19 July 1998

Index